THE DEMOCRACY FIX

Also by Caroline Fredrickson

Under the Bus: How Working Women Are Being Run Over

THE DEMOCRACY FIX

HOW TO WIN THE FIGHT FOR FAIR RULES, FAIR COURTS, AND FAIR ELECTIONS

CAROLINE FREDRICKSON

THE
NEW
PRESS

NEW YORK
LONDON

Requests for permission to reproduce selections from this book should be mailed to: Permissions Department, The New Press, 120 Wall Street, 31st floor, New York, NY 10005.

Published in the United States by The New Press, New York, 2019
Distributed by Two Rivers Distribution

ISBN 978-1-62097-390-5 (ebook)

LIBRARY OF CONGRESS CATALOGING-IN-PUBLICATION DATA
Names: Fredrickson, Caroline, author.
Title: The democracy fix : how to win the fight for fair rules, fair courts,
    and fair elections / Caroline Fredrickson.
Description: New York : New Press, [2019] | Includes bibliographical
    references.
Identifiers: LCCN 2018042934| ISBN 9781620973899 (hc : alk. paper) | ISBN
    9781620973905 (ebook)
Subjects: LCSH: Democracy—United States. | Right and left (Political
    science)—United States. | Political participation—United States. |
    Elections—United States. | Courts—United States.
Classification: LCC JK1726 .F6664 2019 | DDC 320.973—dc23 LC record available at
    https://lccn.loc.gov/2018042934

The New Press publishes books that promote and enrich public discussion and understanding of the issues vital to our democracy and to a more equitable world. These books are made possible by the enthusiasm of our readers; the support of a committed group of donors, large and small; the collaboration of our many partners in the independent media and the not-for-profit sector; booksellers, who often hand-sell New Press books; librarians; and above all by our authors.

www.thenewpress.com

Book design and composition by Bookbright Media
This book was set in Goudy Oldstyle and Futura

Printed in the United States of America

10 9 8 7 6 5 4 3 2 1

CONTENTS

1

THE FIX

North Carolina tells a story that the Left needs to take seriously. It was supposed to be the future, with progressive forces in ascendance and the imminent collapse of the Far Right. In 2008, Barack Obama defeated John McCain. It was a historic election nationally, but it was particularly so in North Carolina, which seemed to be trending blue after a turbulent, racist past. But the vote was close, and ever since then North Carolina has been a partisan battleground, with Republicans increasingly winning the upper hand. The momentary rise of the Left, buoyed by a charismatic candidate, masked how conservative forces had been plotting to hold power for the long term. In 2010, Republicans recaptured both houses of the state legislature as part of a focused effort led by Karl Rove to flip key statehouses in advance of redistricting. With a 20 percent increase in overall spending on North Carolina races from 2008 to 2010, mostly benefiting Republican campaigns, Rove's efforts were successful. Much of that additional money came from multimillionaire North Carolinian Art Pope and his family, and groups they controlled.[1] In a profile of Pope, *Washington Post* reporter Matea Gold observed that "Pope's family foundation has put more than $55 million into a robust network of conservative think tanks and advocacy groups, building a state version of what his friends Charles and

David Koch have helped create on a national level."[2] Pope was also one of the largest funders behind the efforts in North Carolina to flip enough seats in the statehouse in 2010 to allow the Republican Party to control the redistricting that would follow the 2010 census.[3]

In 2012, when Republicans captured the governorship as well, conservatives in North Carolina took full advantage of one-party control of government, going on a drunken bender of right-wing legislating to implement the policy ideas generated by Art Pope's empire. They went wild on social issues, restricting abortion and attacking gay rights. For their corporate partners, they allowed fracking, curbed lawsuits against hog farms, and—despite their claim to support local control—preempted local jurisdictions' right to pass ordinances affecting their own residents, from raising the minimum wage to anti-discrimination measures. Pope, whose wealth supported the groups driving the anti-gay and pro-corporate agenda, was put in charge of the state budget by GOP governor Pat McCrory.

Most significantly, Republicans focused on locking in their power. They started by reversing years of expanding the franchise, rigging election rules in their favor in one piece of legislation, dubbed the "monster law," that changed the board of elections; redrew district lines to benefit the GOP; and made it harder to vote by limiting early voting, requiring photo IDs, and adding hurdles to the registration process, all with an eye to limiting access to the polls for people of color, who tend to vote Democratic.[4] The Republicans even altered historically nonpartisan judicial elections to add party affiliation and gerrymandered those districts as well. Other states rig districts, acknowledged House Minority Leader Darren Jackson, a Democrat who saw his party locked out of power. But, he bemoaned, "we remain the top dog in gerrymandering. Nobody does it like North Carolina, we're No. 1."[5]

Federal courts have put a stop, for the moment, to North Carolina's restrictions on the franchise. In her ruling in *NAACP
v. McCrory*, Judge Diana Gribbon Motz of the Fourth Circuit
described the disproportionate impact the bill had on minority
voters; the provisions, she wrote, seemed to "target African Americans with almost surgical precision."[6] Lawsuits also derailed the
legislature's 2011 partisan gerrymander, which was found unconstitutional. A couple of court decisions, however, should not lead
us to believe that the Right's plan has failed. Conservatives have
a plan—control the infrastructure of government and control
the state for a long, long time. North Carolina is just a snapshot
of what has been happening nationwide for decades.

Voter suppression and gerrymandering have given the Right
the upper hand across the country. After the 2016 elections,
Democrats hit a low in state legislatures they haven't seen since
Warren Harding was president in 1921. Republicans control
56 percent of state legislative seats, having made significant
gains during the presidency of Barack Obama. Over the course
of Obama's two terms, the Republicans added almost 1,000 state
legislative seats, gaining control of 67 of the 98 partisan legislative chambers. In addition, in 24 states, in 2017 Republicans
had the governorship in addition to both legislative chambers,
while Democrats held total control in only five states—Hawaii,
California, Oregon, Connecticut, and Rhode Island. While the
2017 and 2018 off-year and special elections offered a glimmer of
hope that the one-party nation has not yet arrived, a visceral and
possibly transient anti–Donald Trump reaction is not going to fix
our problems.

The GOP takeover of state governments was no accident. In
2010, Republicans dumped $30 million into state races—triple
the amount invested by Democrats—to wrest control of the
once-in-a-decade process of congressional redistricting and,
with their new statehouse majorities, to draw maps that favored

Republicans and pass laws that disenfranchised Democrats and people of color. In 2012, Democrats received 1.4 million more votes nationwide for House races, yet Republicans won control of the House by a 234 to 201 margin. And the GOP's state successes played a key role in defeating Hillary Clinton in 2016. Those same states that had been transformed from purple to crimson red in 2010 and 2012 adopted voter suppression laws that helped put crucial battleground states on Donald Trump's tally. This combination of dark money, voter suppression, and gerrymandering makes future gains in either state or federal elections a challenge for progressives and moderates.

But rigging elections was only one part of the plan. Just as it developed strategies to flip statehouses, the Right also had a plan to take over the courts. Dubbed "the least dangerous branch" by Alexander Hamilton because they have neither purse nor sword, the courts are nonetheless key players in policy decisions, and right-leaning oligarchs know that the courts are a necessary piece of the infrastructure to protect and augment their enormous wealth. The Chamber of Commerce, the Judicial Crisis Network, the Republican State Leadership Committee, and others spent millions campaigning against President Obama's Supreme Court nominee Merrick Garland and for Trump's right-wing nominees Neil Gorsuch and Brett Kavanaugh, as well as toward electing judges in the states, including, in 2016, a new state chief justice in Arkansas who rules by "prayer, not politics." The Left invested almost nothing to support Garland and shudders at the impropriety of taking part in judicial elections. The result: far-right dominance of the judiciary with all that entails—rulings against campaign finance reform, voting rights, unions, and transparent government. Anthony Kennedy's retirement from the Supreme Court gave the Republican Party an even more right-wing five-person majority, with four of those five justices nominated by presidents who lost the popular vote.

With the help of the Chamber of Commerce and right-wing think tanks, conservative judges and legislatures have adopted rules that keep defrauded consumers, victims of sexual harassment, misclassified workers, and children harmed by lead out of the courtroom, while the U.S. Supreme Court has given a broad understanding to arbitration clauses, allowing corporations to move cases from the public and precedent-setting court system to a private, company-funded arbitration system. And corporate interests have worked to control the courts' secretive rulemaking committees to push further restrictions, including to the discovery process that was designed to help plaintiffs get the necessary documents and other materials to be able to succeed in meritorious lawsuits. Senator Sheldon Whitehouse dubbed this "May it please the corp."[7] Dry and boring as it seems, these back rooms are where decisions get made that can thwart enforcement of fundamental rights and progressive policies.

The Right has learned that *power precedes policy* and not the other way around. Chief Justice John Roberts in his nomination hearing solemnly stated that "judges are like umpires. Umpires don't make the rules; they apply them."[8] He was given great credit for claiming for judges a position of complete neutrality, but in fact—just like in baseball—"calling balls and strikes" depends on where the judge sets the strike zone. Republicans have long understood the fact that when one team helps draft and apply the rules of the game, it is more likely to win. Thus, in elections, rather than just presenting platforms to win votes, they stack the deck by stripping certain voters of access to the ballot box, watering down election laws so they can fill the airwaves with dark-money-funded attack ads, and shaping congressional and state legislative districts to give their party an unfair advantage. They cut down on access to the courts, closing the courthouse doors to deny victims remedies for violations of core rights without having to go to the trouble to repeal statutes. And they go after control of the court system itself by investing huge sums in efforts to promote or oppose judicial nominees at the federal and state levels. Conveniently, the resulting judiciary is much more amenable to pro-corporate and anti–civil rights arguments.

This book does not claim to be a comprehensive overview of each of these topics. There are fine books by experts far better versed in each topic than I—on voting rights, gerrymandering, procedural justice, court packing, constitutional interpretation, and fake news—but I aim to show how these elements fit together as part of a plan for permanent ascendancy by the Right, as a sort of ecosystem where each element reinforces the others, strengthening the grip on power. More importantly, I will address what the Left must do to unrig this system. Scholars Jacob Hacker and Paul Pierson recognize the challenge, saying, "As hard as it may be to direct public attention and enthusiasm toward procedural and institutional reforms, fixing the playing field of American politics remains the essential task."[9] Like the Right, we must learn that the process requires two steps: first, we need to capture power, and second, we must craft fair and equitable rules that will endure beyond the next election cycle.

Some key provisions on our unrigging to-do list include fighting for the right to vote for all citizens, fair districts, and limits on money in politics. In the short term, making progress will require a tactical partnership with Democrats by getting them elected and funding their campaigns. But once we have legislatures that are amenable to major reform, we will have to pressure the elected officials to make changes that endure and aren't subject to easy repeal with a change in party in the statehouse. Dependent on the votes of people of color, Democrats are less likely to engage in voter suppression, but we need rules that enshrine the right to vote for when the GOP comes back into power. And certainly, with respect to partisan gerrymandering, Democrats do not have clean hands and will need to be pushed and prodded to adopt a system they can't manipulate—if they were strategic, partisans would realize that nonpartisan redistricting actually provides more protections for democrats *and* Democrats because it is harder for the Right to undo. For that same reason, activists also need to push for clean-money campaigns; progressives want to attack wealth inequality, but we won't be successful if we have to depend on plutocrats to fund our work. Similarly, progressives need to advance strong anti-corruption laws and a revitalized government ethics system to ensure that lobbyists and wealthy donors aren't pulling the strings behind our lawmakers. Those who believe that government exists to help people must fight against conservative efforts to drive cynicism and distrust of public sector solutions. And we need to revitalize our First Amendment jurisprudence so it reflects an understanding that the Constitution is meant to support democracy, not inhibit it. Money and votes are not equivalent.

Our courts must be fair and representative, with evenhanded rules. This goal too, though idealistic, supports progressive outcomes—to have judges who are not biased against victims of corporate or government wrongdoing, we need judges who are not picked and coached by conservative interests. While many rightly favor doing away with election of judges, until that happens, we cannot cede the battlefield. So step one is to fight like hell to advance, *elect*, and support good judges, including by engaging progressive donors to lobby senators (and using pressure tactics if necessary), building a pipeline of talented lawyers for the bench, and providing judges and nominees with well-crafted legal policy to guide them.

To accomplish these goals, the Left needs a strong media hub to generate the content to engage and mobilize the progressive base. The Russians and the Right have outplayed us on Facebook, Twitter, and other social media, not to mention Fox News and *Breitbart*, affecting votes and mobilizing mobs. We need a response that offers viral content to attack the Right and rebut their charges as well as to goose our base to vote. Unlike the Right, however, the Left should not use lies and distortions; just as we defend government, we need to defend truth and accurate reporting. Our strength is that we have artists and entertainers on our side who can create engaging tools that will empower and unify the diverse progressive constituency. Because the Left benefits more from an independent media and "truthiness," we also must support good journalism. Ultimately, through technological solutions and education, Americans must be given the tools to identify fake news.

While progressives may not want to sink to the depths of Karl Rove or Steve Bannon (or Ann Coulter or Roger Ailes . . .) that doesn't mean we can't fight fiercely for what matters and understand that the fight for the policies we want has to *follow*, not *precede*, the fight to obtain power. To unrig the system, we need power—then we can write our own playbook, with rules that advance and protect a vibrant democracy. This book aims to distill the rigged strategies that have allowed the Right to get a stranglehold on American politics and to offer a progressive playbook for taking power back.

I have been a Capitol Hill staffer, from junior legislative aide to Senate chief of staff, and worked in the White House and as a lobbyist for progressive causes, all of which has allowed me to observe just how much more the Right understands that power's main use is . . . to lock in power. Unless the Left grasps that truth, our mantra as Americans will remain "Power to the plutocrats" rather than "Power to the people."

2

THE WILL TO POWER

It was 1971 and Lewis Powell, a corporate lawyer in Richmond, Virginia, who had been president of the American Bar Association, a member of the board of the giant tobacco company Philip Morris, and represented the Tobacco Institute and several tobacco companies, had come to believe that American capitalism was facing a dire threat. Americans were angry about corporate pollution; President Richard M. Nixon had responded by signing the National Environmental Policy Act, which established the White House Council on Environmental Quality, and by creating the Environmental Protection Agency through executive order. Across the country, activists marched for Earth Day and Congress passed the first air pollution standards.[1] Ralph Nader and other consumer advocates had successfully fought for safer cars and other products. It was a transitional moment, according to historian Kim Phillips-Fein, as "the environmental movement charged industry with poisoning the land, air, and water of the country, while the consumer movement accused business of manipulating consumers into buying dangerous products."[2]

Business leaders saw the new government agencies as a direct, and ominous, result of the activists' grassroots and legislative actions that were pushing corporate America off its pedestal.

Americans no longer reflexively believed the statement of Charles Erwin Wilson, CEO of General Motors, that "what's good for GM is good for America."[3] Powell's concern was reflected in the files he kept on Nader and others, including a long article about the consumer activist that appeared in *Fortune*, calling Nader a "passionate man" who sought to "smash . . . corporate power."[4]

Powell believed that corporate America needed a decisive response to the perceived threat to the free enterprise system. In a lengthy memo, the soon-to-be Supreme Court justice laid out his concerns and proposed responses to the Chamber of Commerce, where he served as chairman of the education committee. Powell argued that business needed to protect itself over the long term with an aggressive strategy to rebut the left-wing criticism of capitalism coming "from the college campus, the pulpit, the media, the intellectual and literary journals," and particularly from Ralph Nader and his ilk, who had made effective use of public interest litigation combined with savvy communications strategies.[5]

The document he penned, now known as the Powell Memo, has been described as the road map for conservative dominance of public policymaking. For any such plan to be successful, Powell understood, conservatives would have to fund a broad array of institutions that would exert control over the instrumentalities of power, including the courts, the legislature, and the media. Importantly, the tobacco lawyer insisted, it would require "careful long-range planning and implementation, in consistency of action over an indefinite period of years, in the scale of financing available only through joint effort, and in the political power available only through united action and national organizations."[6] What Powell grasped is that policy victories come *after* gaining control of the levers of power—and not before.

The Powell Memo found a receptive audience in the business world and with libertarian and pro-business donors, help-ing to shape the coordination among corporate and founda-tion money, legal strategists, and campaign operatives to build long-term victories. Moneyed individuals and entities invested heavily in building infrastructure—think tanks to develop pro-posals, media outlets to disseminate them, legislative strategies to equip their side with bills and talking points, electoral schemes to secure political advantage, and legal efforts to stack the courts with ideological judges armed with pro-corporate and anti–civil rights views and assisted by rules limiting courtroom access that would skew the odds further in favor of the plutocrats and right-wing donors.

The impact has been devastating.

Right away, Powell's memo reverberated with corporate Amer-ica. Eugene Sydnor, the Chamber of Commerce's education director, wrote to Powell that he had made a "vitally important case for American Business to go on the offensive after such a long period of inaction and indecision in telling the American people the facts of life as they unhappily exist today."[7] Soon after receiving the memorandum, the chamber organized a task force of forty business leaders to review its contents and make plans for implementation.[8] Powell separately sent a personal note to Ross Malone, vice president and general counsel at General Motors, to see if the "top management of GM might be interested in encouraging the chamber to become a vital force to defend the enterprise system and the freedoms which it sustains."[9] Corpo-rate executives circulated the memo, including a member of the legal staff of DuPont who sent it to the CEO, calling it "useful."[10] The ideas gained currency among corporate leaders such as Donald Kendall, the CEO of PepsiCo; were discussed in corpo-rate reports from GE, H.J. Heinz, and Standard Oil; and were embraced by conservative scholars and intellectuals, including Robert Bork and Irving Kristol, writing for the *Wall Street Journal*.[11] Business groups quickly founded the Business Roundtable to provide coordinated lobbying power on Capitol Hill. Founded in 1972, within five years, it brought together over half of the Fortune 200 corporations, together valued at 50 percent of the entire American economy.[12] And the chamber invested in professionalizing its staff, making the CEO a permanent position, bulking up its lobbying operation to become the biggest player in Washington, which it remains, and becoming one of the leading conduits for independent expenditures in political campaigns.[13]

In the early 1970s, corporate America was eager to find a way to thwart the progressive tide, says historian Kim Phillips-Fine: "Strident, melodramatic, and alarmist, Powell's memorandum . . . struck a nerve in the tense political world of the early 1970s, giving voice to sentiments that, no matter how extreme they might have seemed, were coming to sound like common sense in the business world during those anxious years."[14] The New Deal had initiated a long period of restraints on corporate power—companies had to pay minimum wage and overtime, bargain with unions, cease to discriminate, stop polluting—all anathema to the ethos of the "free market," which they believed meant that the corporation existed solely to benefit its shareholders and executives and not workers or communities.

But what really put action behind Powell's words was Watergate. Soon after Powell sent his memo to the chamber, the business community began to see storm clouds on the horizon, despite President Nixon's landslide 1972 election win. Nixon's criminal conduct was leading to impeachment hearings and allowed Democrats to ride a wave of anti-Republican fervor, winning a significant majority in Congress in 1974. "The danger had suddenly escalated," recalled Bryce Harlow, a lobbyist for Procter &

Gamble, who had been instrumental in organizing the business community to get involved in politics and right-wing infrastructure building.[15] Powell's warnings seemed even more on point, and conservatives began serious efforts to create a set of institutions that would support their interests over the long term, during Republican and Democratic administrations, but also lead to structural changes that would embed Republicans and pro-business policies in government permanently.

Perhaps the most important readers of the memo were people with a great deal of wealth. John M. Olin, who made his fortune in chemicals and founded the Olin Foundation, wrote William Baroody Sr., the president of the American Enterprise Institute, that "the Powell Memorandum gives a reason for a well organized effort to re-establish the validity and importance of the American free enterprise system."[16] As an activist business movement came into being, new conservative family and corporate philanthropies emerged to partner in funding a plan to ensure long-term control of power—Coors, Olin, Bradley, Scaife, and Koch, to name a few funders. Presenting to the conservative Philanthropy Roundtable, Koch operative Richard Fink urged funders to think about Friedrich Hayek's description of the production process as a model for their giving, arguing that transformation necessitated the "development of intellectual raw materials, their conversion into specific policy products, and the marketing and distribution of these products to citizen consumers."[17] It was a vertical monopoly model, driven by wealthy donors who would put money into an infrastructure for producing ideas and then marketing them.

Funders quickly aligned to identify a set of groups, occupying different but complementary roles at the state and national levels, that they would invest in for the long term, understanding that generating intellectual capital was a necessary precondition of successful litigation and public policy efforts. In her book on the conservative legal movement, law professor Ann Southworth observes that "conservative foundations focused on organizations they expected to succeed, rather than distributing grants more broadly, and they coordinated their philanthropy to maximize its impact."[18] These funders nurtured groups focused on power and long-term change rather than simply funding their pet issues. A report for the National Committee for Responsive Philanthropy found that "conservative grantmaking has focused on building strong institutions by providing general operating support, rather than project-specific grants. . . . The foundations funded their grantees for the long term—in some cases for two decades or more."[19] They provided space for the organizations to grow and to cultivate scholarship, knowing that the groundwork for meaningful and lasting change requires patience.

And thus the plan was adopted, with a concentrated effort to gain power by developing ideas through think tanks and academic "fellowships"; disseminating viewpoints and publications via a new right-wing media, along with an arm to attack mainstream media as fatally biased; filling judgeships with movement conservatives; and creating a pipeline of elected and appointed leaders through electoral strategies and mentoring. Where Lewis Powell's memo was most potent was in its recognition that public policy victories depend on political power, power that must be, Powell underscored, "assiduously cultivated; and that when necessary, it must be used aggressively and with determination—without embarrassment and without the reluctance which has been so characteristic of American business."[20]

WINNER-TAKE-ALL THOUGHT LEADERSHIP

One of the founders of the Heritage Foundation, beer magnate Joseph Coors, was deeply affected by the Powell Memo, recalling many years later how reading it had "stirred him."[21] Powell had been insistent that corporate America needed to fund a stable of scholars who would promote a pro-capitalist message in scholarly journals as well as in the popular press, where their academic status would give weight to their arguments.[22] Coors, along with hard-right leader Paul Weyrich, heeded Powell's call that the Right needed to counter liberal academia with thought leadership, founding the Heritage Foundation as an affirmatively hard-edged political and partisan organization.[23] The Heritage Foundation quickly gained "iconic" status—its prodigious publication of policy papers causing Senator Daniel Patrick Moynihan to remark that the "GOP has become a party of ideas."[24]

The goal of the Heritage Foundation and like-minded think tanks was and remains to influence public opinion in policy debates and build support for conservative initiatives. The media relations component, which Powell called a "war room," included a speakers' bureau to provide rapid response and to counter the perceived liberalism of the press. With a mission of persuasion, the think tanks did not operate under the evidence-based strictures of academe. Instead, their publications were structured to drive a political narrative, providing rhetorical and "scholarly" support for conservative goals, and their personnel were groomed to march through the revolving door to provide a steady pipeline of trustworthy policy experts to serve in government.[25] Mark Schmitt, a director at the New America foundation, argues that this approach sets conservative think tanks apart from those on the left, finding that "one side plays it as winner-take-all competition, the other mildly seeks consensus, ultimately winning the other side's agreement not to reverse the most uncontroversial bit of the status quo, after which both sides and their funders congratulate themselves on having found common ground."[26] The Heritage Foundation's budget, in contrast to the more liberal Brookings Institution, for example, devotes far more resources to the dissemination of its viewpoints, or marketing, to make the ideas more accessible for members of Congress, local leaders, and other Republican officials. Scholars Jacob Hacker and Paul Pierson comment that Brookings's mission statement "reads like a university brochure ('an independent, nonpartisan organization devoted to research and public education'); the Heritage Foundation's, a manifesto ('a think tank . . . whose mission is to formulate and promote conservative public policies based on the principles of free enterprise, limited government, individual freedom, traditional American values, and a strong national defense')."[27]

The American Enterprise Institute's Baroody shared Powell's view that the corporate world needed to compete in the "marketplace of ideas," challenging what he saw as the dominance of left-wing perspectives in the "intellectual mainstream."[28] The American Enterprise Institute had been a studiously nonpartisan although quite conservative think tank, founded in the 1930s to protect free enterprise from the perceived socialism of the New Deal. Baroody thought that the Right had been outmaneuvered by the Left "through systematic employment of techniques and devices designed to establish what might loosely be referred to as an intellectual reservoir of leftist ideology" in universities that gave an "aura of respectability" unmatched by "existing resources on the conservative side of the fence."[29] Establishing a new Center for the Study of Government Regulation, Baroody hired a young legal scholar—Antonin Scalia—to edit its journal, which set out to attack regulation through scholarly analysis rather than by simply disagreeing with it. Backing up the antiregulatory position with studies that showed an alleged harm to the economy or productivity was more likely to win converts and influence the American public, Baroody believed.[30] Like the other leaders influenced by the Powell Memo, he saw the need for a varied set of organizations to provide support for business-friendly policies. He was instrumental in founding several other think tanks to fill out the areas of necessary thought leadership, including the Center for Strategic and International Studies at Georgetown, to provide a hawkish perspective on foreign policy, and the Hoover Institution at Stanford. Baroody even built relationships overseas, with the goal of creating an international alliance of conservative organizations generating and cultivating public opinion.[31]

Appearing on Fox News in 2015 to denounce President Obama's comments about ISIS, John Bolton, a Bush-era ambassador to the United Nations, sported a Heritage Foundation tie. Heritage proudly later pitched the necktie on its website with a photo of Bolton, asking, "What can you wear to reinforce your conservative *bona fides*?"[32] And conservative bona fides are exactly what Fox and other right-wing "news" outlets are looking for—the close ties between the think tanks designed to spout talking points and policy reports in service of conservative political objectives and their allied cable and web news outlets could not be more obvious. These news organizations rely on the reports and talking heads from the right-wing think tanks to disseminate and give traction to an extremist agenda. The news companies need content—and the think tanks supply it.

(UN)FAIR AND (UN)BALANCED

The campaign of 2016 may have seemed unique, with the aggressive role played by Fox News on cable and *Breitbart* online in supporting Donald Trump, but the architecture of right-wing media was first imagined in the 1950s. In 1954, Clarence Manion, an early prototype of Steve Bannon, began to build the echo chamber for conservative candidates through his radio program, which created a template for the inflammatory talk radio later practiced by Rush Limbaugh. Manion's show became a platform for emerging leaders on the far right and began to push the Republican Party in that direction, even supporting a third-party challenger to President Dwight D. Eisenhower. Like many current purveyors of "alternative facts," Manion chose an anti-establishment and anti-elite frame to shake up the mainstream party. *National Review*, also founded around this time, aligned with Manion in attacking Eisenhower, giving off more than a whiff of anti-Semitism in the process. According to its first issue, in 1955, "a small band of Eastern financiers, international bankers and industrialists organized the Eisenhower boom and entrusted its inflation to a New York advertising firm. The rest is history."[33] The conservative magazine *Human Events* shared the mission of presenting overtly biased reporting. The magazine stated that "in reporting the news, *Human Events* is objective; it aims for accurate representation of the facts. But it is not impartial. It looks at events through eyes that are biased in favor of limited constitutional government, local self-government, private enterprise, and individual freedom."[34] Bias, these publications posited, is a valid approach to journalism. The leaders of each publication and program worked closely with one another, sharing an overlap in donors and leadership, with Manion sitting on the board of the *National Weekly*, the parent of *National Review*, and editors and writers for *Human Events* and *National Review* appearing on his radio program.[35]

But these efforts still existed on the political fringes, with limited impact on the majority of Americans. Conservatives, Powell among them, realized that they could not simply talk to each other. To protect the free enterprise system they saw as under threat, they needed to move public opinion, and ultimately public policy, and this required capturing some of the audience from the networks and newspapers that provided news to the majority of Americans. William J. Gill, who pioneered an early effort to bring conservative voices into the mainstream media, agreed with Powell that the Right needed to "shape the public's opinion on issues, to further develop conservative media organizations and to bring the right's point of view to the public."[36] Powell's memo reflected his agreement with Gill that the major news agencies were not providing adequate coverage of conservative points of view and that without "a truly national vehicle for dissemination of the news on a day-in-day-out basis, we could never hope to correct some of the grave problems afflicting our country."[37]

Nicole Hemmer, who has studied the rise of the conservative media, said that leaders on the right recognized that "they had to do more than sell Americans on conservative ideas. They had to discredit the established media. That's because in mid-century, most Americans believed that the news they heard on networks and read in newspapers was objective. . . . [The conservatives] argued that objectivity was a mask covering entrenched liberal bias, and they saw their new media ventures as an answer to that bias."[38] Debunking the dominant frame was an essential part of advancing the counternarrative these conservatives preferred. Powell himself was quite taken with *The News Twisters*, a book by Edith Efron, a writer for *TV Guide* who had reviewed TV news coverage during several weeks of the 1968 election, counting one hundred thousand words she had picked describing Hubert Humphrey and Richard Nixon, the Democratic and Republican presidential candidates. Verdict: the news organizations toed "the elitist-liberal-left line in all controversies."[39] Writing to Gene Sydnor of the Chamber of Commerce, Powell commented that "Miss Efron's technique is precisely in accord with one of the suggestions in my memorandum of September 23, namely, the monitoring of television programs to determine factually and in detail the extent of biased and unfair treatment of business and the enterprise system." He then suggested to Sydnor that the chamber fund a serious effort for continuous monitoring of media.[40] He also advised the chamber in another letter to help support organizations that would monitor both media and textbooks for what he considered to be anti-capitalist rhetoric and teaching, saying that both should be "kept under constant surveillance."[41]

With the election of Richard Nixon, the conservative media had an ally with an even bigger bully pulpit. The administration joined the critique of the networks and large newspapers, marking the beginning of a significant shift in the media on the national stage. In a concerted effort to assert "liberal bias," the Right won a victory in making the corporate news organizations begin to question their approach to reporting and forcing them to feature voices that were explicitly conservative as opposed to allegedly neutral. Hemmer writes that by 1971, "CBS Radio had launched *Spectrum*, a debate show featuring conservatives like Stan Evans, James Kilpatrick, and Phyllis Schlafly. That same year *60 Minutes* pitted conservative Kilpatrick against liberal Nicholas von Hoffman in a regular segment called 'Point/Counterpoint.' By then, even the publisher of *Human Events*, in the midst of selling his paper as an alternative to liberal media, had to admit that conservatives were popping up all over established media—even on the editorial pages of 'that holy house organ of Liberalism—the *New York Times*.'"[42]

With a growing opportunity to advance its own views on the news, the Right invested even more in building the counternarrative, and this required reports, talking heads, and other content to flow both to these mainstream channels and to the growing set of alternative outlets that catered to conservative readers and viewers. The Media Research Center was founded in 1987 specifically to "document, expose and neutralize the liberal media bias." Internally, it consists of divisions to monitor the news on all outlets, to call out alleged anti-capitalist reporting, and to disseminate right-wing ideas to the broader public; today it also has an online news service for the Right.[43] In line with their long-term view, the funders also provided significant backing to college newspapers and radio stations to train and nurture future reporters. Their interest was not simply in having an immediate counter to what they perceived as a hostile media environment, but in building a pipeline of journalists who could go from the *Dartmouth Review* to Fox News and the *Wall Street Journal*, like the *Journal*'s Hugo Restall or Fox's Laura Ingraham.

It is hard to overestimate the impact of this effort. From attacks on the allegedly liberal media to the vast array of voices on the right establishing a counternarrative of "alternative facts," Fox News and *Breitbart* now command an enormous audience and exert a tremendous influence on what is considered news.

ED MEESE'S REVENGE

Corporate America was not going to protect itself solely through thought leadership and PR, however, it also needed an activist legal counterpart to engage in litigation and control the courts. "This is a vast area of opportunity for the Chamber," Powell wrote, "if it is willing to undertake the role of spokesman for American business and if, in turn, business is willing to provide the funds."[44] Being a lawyer, he knew the importance of strategic litigation to advance the interests of corporate America as well as having courtroom rules tilted toward business litigants. The Right quickly lined up funding and fervent advocacy behind new litigating groups—or "public interest law firms"—to fight affirmative action, environmental rules, reproductive rights, and the labor movement, as well as efforts to influence the rules by which the courts consider cases. The Chamber of Commerce's Litigation Center, created in 1977, has enjoyed an incredibly successful run in the current conservative and pro-business Supreme Court, estimated to have an almost 70 percent win record since Chief Justice Roberts took the court's helm in 2005. Legal observers calculate that the chamber's advocacy has helped make the Roberts Court the "most pro-business high tribunal since the 1930s."[45] As scholar Erwin Chemerinsky points out, pro-business means anti-worker, anti-consumer, anti–civil rights, and anti-environment.[46]

Other legal groups fight to expand the role of churches in public life and to attack women's reproductive rights; to challenge affirmative action and other civil rights protections, including in the voting sphere; and to undermine environmental and land-use regulations.[47] For example, the National Right to Work Legal Defense Foundation has brought cases with novel legal theories to challenge the laws that allow unions to bargain collectively and represent workers effectively—which harms and demoralizes workers and also strikes at the heart of financial support for the Democratic Party. The Center for Individual Rights attacks the separation of church and state as an avenue to undermine women's reproductive rights and LGBT job protections and access to public services (like ordering a wedding cake or hiring a videographer to cover gay nuptials). In the public spotlight for its efforts to acquire Secretary of State Hillary Clinton's emails through Freedom of Information Act ligation, Judicial Watch was established in 1994 to sue the Clintons and has not stopped since.[48]

Powell argued, however, not just for an affirmative strategy but also for defensive mechanisms to keep Naderites and other corporate foes out of the courtroom altogether and thus to make sure the rules governing litigation would favor business and not consumers or workers. Civil justice "reform" was the sine qua non for protecting the private enterprise system Powell so revered. Senator Sheldon Whitehouse, in his book *Captured*, documents how corporations have swung the rules in their favor. In 1998, Whitehouse writes, the chamber followed Powell's advice and launched its Institute for Legal Reform, a "national legal reform advocate . . . working to change the laws, [and] also changing the legal climate."[49] Its stated goal is curbing lawsuit abuse by lobbying governments at all levels—even international bodies—to make it hard for victims of corporate wrongdoing to have any legal recourse.[50] Aided and abetted by the chamber and conservative think tanks, judges and legislatures have adopted rules to keep defrauded consumers, victims of sexual harassment, misclassified workers, and children harmed by lead out of the courtroom.

Once Ronald Reagan was in the White House, Powell would see his memo's recommendations on legal reform gain momentum. Elected on an agenda of rolling back regulations, Reagan and his political appointees saw private rights of action as an impediment to reining in so-called big government. In particular, they believed that provisions providing lawyers' fees encouraged lawsuits against companies and government agencies and that the litigation itself was engineered by liberal activists to shape agency policy and the interpretation of federal statutes. Similarly, they faulted the use of class actions that enabled activists to influence corporate behavior through large damage awards, with lawyers like Ralph Nader coercing carmakers to build safer vehicles through threats of further lawsuits. Reagan called these liberal groups "a bunch of ideological ambulance chasers doing their own thing at the expense of the . . . poor who actually need help" and as "working for left-wing special interest groups at the expense of the public."[51] While this period did not spell the end of progressive litigation groups, it certainly did portend a strong and effective counterforce from corporate America. Some argue that corporations simply pushing back hobbled the left-wing advocates. Others point to an America that was fatigued with an anti-corporate agenda—undoubtedly, Reagan's election demonstrated a country that was out of sync with attacks on the "free enterprise system" and susceptible to anti-regulatory arguments. Defensive work is less exciting than aggressive challenges to government and private sector abuses—and Nader and his allies fell out of the news cycle.[52]

Reagan hired many lawyers from the nascent anti-regulatory legal organizations to fill positions in Washington where they could continue, from the inside, to dismantle federal statutory protections. Enraged by what they saw as anti-corporate litigation that had spiraled out of control between Nixon's presidency and Reagan's election—much of it in the environmental and consumer areas—they were eager to reassert the importance of private property and assumption of risk by consumers, workers, and victims of pollution. Pushing legislation to cut fees for any lawsuit against the federal government in his first year, President Reagan also directed his Office of Legal Policy in the Department of Justice to look at how to cut back on damage suits brought against state government officials accused of violations of federally protected rights.[53]

With Democrats still wielding power on the Hill, Reagan and his allies had little success with legislation. Deputy Attorney General Edward Schmults recognized that the Supreme Court, with Lewis Powell serving as one of the nine justices, would be a more hospitable environment to craft restrictive policies to block lawsuits. In a letter to then counselor to the president Edwin Meese about the legislation to limit fees, Schmults wrote, "From a political standpoint, . . . it is probable that a serious fee reform bill would sharply divide Congress . . . [and] like other controversial legislation, it is unlikely that the bill would be enacted into law. . . . As in the past, real progress in curtailing abuses in the award of attorneys' fees is likely to be gained through the Supreme Court, where we have enjoyed considerable success in recent years. . . . An administration fee reform bill will bring to the public eye many of the policies we have been espousing before the courts."[54] In other words, keep this out of the press and achieve the same goal through the courts. Indeed, these efforts bore fruit as the Supreme Court went on to issue sweeping decisions protecting corporate America.

That's why the Federalist Society, which works to ensure that judges will be favorable to these cases, has long been a priority of right-wing funders—Powell himself, sitting on the Supreme Court when the group was founded, embodied how important courts were to fulfillment of his plan. From its beginnings in 1982, the Federalist Society benefited from the methodical and thoughtful support of the philanthropists influenced by, or in alignment with, the goals of the Powell Memo, receiving funding from its beginnings as a small law student group to its current powerhouse status.[55] James Piereson, former president of the Olin Foundation, describes the patient approach these funders took to their grantees. According to Piereson, "they know that the world is going to be changed in increments, by and large."[56] With its inordinate influence on the selection of judges and promotion of "originalist" legal theory, the group has been described—by former vice president Dick Cheney—as "one of the most influential in the world of law and public policy." Olin's dollars, and those of other conservative foundations, made this possible through the steady and unquestioning support they gave the Federalist Society over decades.[57] The funders allowed the organization room to both grow and make decisions independently and did not flinch when it adopted strong ideological positions—indeed, that was the goal.

The Federalist Society quickly made an outsize imprint on the development of the law and legal policy. Scholars Michael Avery and Danielle McLaughlin provide a good thumbnail sketch.

> Four Supreme Court justices—Antonin Scalia, Clarence Thomas, John Roberts, and Samuel Alito—are current or former members of the Federalist Society. [New justices Neil Gorsuch and Brett Kavanaugh are also members; Scalia died in 2016.] Every single federal judge appointed by President George H.W. Bush or President George W. Bush was either a member or approved by members of the society. During the Bush years, young Federalist Society lawyers dominated the legal staffs of the Justice Department and other important government agencies. The dockets of the federal courts are brimming with test cases brought or defended by Federalist Society members in the government and in conservative public interest firms to challenge government regulation of the economy; roll back affirmative action; invalidate laws providing access to the courts by aggrieved workers, consumers, and environmentalists; expand state support for religious institutions and programs; oppose marriage equality; increase statutory impediments to women's ability to obtain an abortion; defend state's rights; increase presidential power; and otherwise advance a broad conservative agenda.[58]

The society was founded at a propitious moment. With Ronald Reagan's election, the Justice Department took on the role of incubator for right-wing legal theories and became a proving ground for young idealistic and ideological attorneys coming out of the Federalist Society chapters. Society membership became a "tell" for conservatives, signaling a clear ideological identity and willingness to fight on the front lines of policy battles. Moreover, for nonmembers, it was clear how joining could advance one's career. Writes scholar Steven Teles, it was a "a very powerful message that the terms of advancement associated with political ambition were being set on their head; clear ideological position-ing, not cautiousness, was now an affirmative qualification for appointed office."[59] Federalist Society members quickly vaulted into the most prestigious clerkships. Judge Robert Bork and Judge Antonin Scalia, who as faculty had helped with the founding of the society, hired law clerks from society chapters when they joined the Court of Appeals for the DC Circuit, as did other Reagan judges.

The young conservatives were particularly emboldened to fight against liberal understandings of the Constitution, devel-oping and honing a theory of interpretation that would lead to more conservative victories. Reagan's attorney general Ed Meese himself saw the utility of originalism and used the vast resources of the Justice Department to elaborate on the theory and mar-ket it; in 1987, the department's Office of Legal Policy published *Original Meaning Jurisprudence: A Sourcebook*, a manual on how to reach preferred constitutional outcomes in critical areas such as reproductive rights and property protections as well as a broad theory of constitutional interpretation.[60] Journalist Charlie Savage writes that Meese turned the Justice Department into "a giant think tank where these passionate young conservative legal activists developed new legal theories to advance the Rea-gan agenda."[61]

With chapters at law schools and in major cities, the member-ship of the Federalist Society is not that large, but it is powerful. It holds events that reach a much broader number than the thir-teen thousand dues-paying members it claimed in 2013.[62] The network has become more and more powerful over time, with certain judges hiring only Federalist Society law clerks, creating a pipeline for the next generation of jurists. Witness the elevation of Justice Neil Gorsuch, a regular participant in the society's activities, a former law clerk to Justice Anthony Kennedy, and someone who made the organization's short list for the Supreme Court, President Donald Trump's only source for candidates. President Trump inherited a record number of vacancies on the federal bench to fill, due to the very effective Senate Republican obstruction of President Obama's nominees. Not just the Supreme Court, but also the courts of appeal and the federal trial courts will bear the imprint of Donald Trump—and the Federalist Society—for decades. Lifetime appointments mean that the courts can become out of sync with the American public, and there's little recourse.

Leonard Leo, a high-ranking Federalist Society official, suggests that any criticism of the organization's role in selecting judges for the Trump administration is misplaced. "The institution is not embarrassed by the fact that we want a judiciary that will say what the law is and not what it should be, so this idea that somehow we are in the dark shadows of Washington trying to pack the courts is really utter nonsense," Mr. Leo said. "Some senators just don't really understand who we are and what we do."[63] But Leo himself refuted his own statement, crowing in May 2017 that "I would love to see the courts unrecognizable."[64] And all we need to do is review the most devastating legal decisions in recent years to see the impact of the organization and its members. From *Citizens United v. Federal Election Commission*, which allowed dark money to flood into political campaigns, to *National Federation of Independent Business v. Sebelius*, which challenged the constitutionality of the Affordable Care Act and resulted in major harm to the Medicaid provisions of the law, Federalist Society members have driven the litigation, and the organization has served as an incubator of the theories and as a cheerleader for the efforts, with allied judges providing a friendly audience.[65]

In 2006, the *Wall Street Journal* applauded the ascendency of Federalist Society members into the judiciary, including the Supreme Court, writing that "they are now poised to influence the law and culture for 20 years or more. *All those Federalist Society seminars may have finally paid off. Call it Ed Meese's revenge.*"[66]

The legal table had now been set to please the palate of American business and conservative interests. The Right had a strong network to nurture and promote right-wing lawyers to the bench, an academic cohort to supply ideas and strategies for litigation, a bevy of legal groups to bring the cases, and a court system hostile to claims against corporations.

BLOCKING THE BOX—THE BALLOT BOX, THAT IS

The courts, think tanks, and media operations were all designed to promote and defend policy preferences—but for preferences to become law, conservative funders and corporations recognized that they needed a strategy to win legislative and electoral battles. Networking conservative legislators with corporate lobbyists and equipping them with legislative ideas was a piece of that plan. In 1973, Paul Weyrich, the co-founder of the Heritage Foundation, helped create the American Legislative Exchange Council, or ALEC.[67] Also credited with co-founding the Moral Majority with Jerry Falwell,[68] Weyrich's "articulate fervor and organization-building skills were instrumental in propelling the right wing of the Republican Party to power and prominence in the 1980s and '90s," said the *New York Times* in his obituary.[69] Weyrich saw ALEC as a vital pillar of the conservative landscape, advancing both free enterprise and fundamentalist religious values through legislation. ALEC's birth was witnessed by many godfathers. According to ALEC's website, a rogues' gallery of current and future conservative leaders came together to support the organization.

> At [a] meeting, in September 1973, state legislators, including then Illinois State Rep. Henry Hyde, conservative activist Paul Weyrich, and Lou Barnett, a veteran of then Gov. Ronald Reagan's 1968 presidential campaign, together with a handful of others, launched the American Legislative Exchange Council. Among those who were involved with ALEC in its formative years were: Robert Kasten and Tommy Thompson of Wisconsin; John Engler of Michigan; Terry Branstad of Iowa, and John Kasich of Ohio, all of whom moved on to become governors or members of Congress. Congressional members who were active during this same period included Senators John Buckley of New York and Jesse Helms of North Carolina, and Congressmen Phil Crane of Illinois and Jack Kemp of New York.[70]

ALEC's focus is on recruiting and supporting conservative legislators by providing them with model legislation drafted by its task forces helmed by corporate lobbyists. Seeing the value of advancing identical bills in state legislatures across the country, ALEC's founders recognized that state and local victories could translate ultimately into national policy. Though ALEC describes itself as "the nation's largest, non-partisan, individual public-private membership association of state legislators," its orientation is decidedly right-wing, anti-worker, anti-environment, and anti–civil rights. Its legislative agenda makes that abundantly clear. Former head of Trump's Environmental Protection Agency Scott Pruitt was an ALEC task force chairman as an Oklahoma state legislator, and he found nothing wrong with putting corporate lobbyists and elected officials together to draft bills. In 2003, he spoke to *Governing* magazine about ALEC, saying, "ALEC is unique in the sense that it puts legislators and companies together and they create policy collectively." That's the right approach, Pruitt argued, because "the actual stakeholders who are affected by policy aren't at the table as much as they should be. Serving with them is very beneficial, in my opinion."[71]

In addition to the Koch brothers, who have given in excess of $1 million to ALEC, other key funders have included the Olin and Bradley Foundations, as well as Richard Scaife and Peter Coors's Castle Rock Foundation.[72] And corporate America has had very self-interested reasons for supporting ALEC; in addition to the tax write-off they get for giving to a "charity," corporations can write the laws that benefit them the most, out of public view. Brendan Fischer, former general counsel with the Center for Media and Democracy, says ALEC's game plan is to move law-making into the shadows. Unlike typical lobbying in the statehouse, where a corporate executive might grab a few minutes of a legislator's time, "with ALEC, legislators fly to ALEC meetings, usually on the corporate dime. Meetings are held in places like Amelia Island, Florida, or New Orleans, or [in 2013] in Chicago, usually at the nicest hotel in town. The corporate members that benefit from ALEC model legislation are footing the bill for legislators' travel expenses." Wined and dined, the legislators spend quality time with a range of corporate lobbyists who feed them ideas and talking points so that "by the time legislators get back to the state, they are the ones who are already convinced that a particular bill or policy idea is right for the state."[73]

The impact has been dramatic. With its task forces pumping out legislation, ALEC has its fingerprints on over 1,500 bills introduced in statehouses per year. A Brookings report documents a very high success rate for ALEC legislation. The researcher, Molly Jackman, makes three major findings: "First, ALEC model bills are, word-for-word, introduced in our state legislatures at a non-trivial rate. Second, they have a good chance—better than most legislation—of being enacted into law. Finally, the bills that pass are most often linked to contro-versial social and economic issues."[74] While ALEC's initial focus, in keeping with Weyrich's hard-right social agenda, was fighting women's reproductive rights and the Equal Rights Amendment, the task forces now place more emphasis on regulatory and eco-nomic issues[75]—although ALEC has also been a big player on "stand your ground" legislation and anti–gun control efforts, as well as devastating attacks on unions.

ALEC's funding from the Kochs, Scaife, et al. has enabled it to build a strong advantage over its liberal competitors. In 2011, the investigative organization ProPublica provided a public service by creating an online database of ALEC bills that allows users to connect the organization, corporate donors, and legislative out-comes. ProPublica created the database in part to provide a bit of help to a vastly underfunded progressive infrastructure, noting that "ALEC has no real counterpart on the left."[76] Founded in 2014, the State Innovation Exchange, or SIX, hopes to provide a counterpart to ALEC on the left by supporting and network-ing progressive state legislators. It is a necessary addition to the landscape and we must hope—and work to ensure that—it suc-ceeds. SIX has had an impressive beginning and is benefiting from a greater focus by progressive funders on the states. But the Left must remain engaged in the states to have any hope of the impact long wielded by ALEC, and not just for the next two years but for the next twenty, thirty, and beyond. ALEC has been a potent enemy of democracy, systematically undermining prin-ciples many thought were rock solid, and it has worked to erect barriers to voting and to destroy a major funding mechanism for progressive candidates, organizations, and issue campaigns as well as protector of workers—the labor movement.[77] And of course, its effort to strip the courts of jurisdiction has gone hand in glove with its substantive work; the beauty of it, from conservatives' perspective, is that few pay attention to changes to court rules and thus they happen more or less in the dark. Statutory rights are still on the books, but no one can exercise them because the courthouse doors are now closed.

The private prison industry provides a good window into how ALEC operates—and wins. Teaming up with ALEC, the Corrections Corporation of America (now known as CoreCivic) lavishly funded the campaigns of Arizona officials and worked with the ALEC-affiliated members of the state legislature on SB 1070, an infamous bill that allowed local law enforcement to arrest and imprison undocumented immigrants. More state funding for private prisons, ALEC and the company argued, was a necessary companion to the detention bill they had fought for because there would be so many new inmates. The joining of proposals to detain immigrants in private prisons was a gold mine for Corrections Corporation's executives and ALEC politicians.[78]

Along with the pro-corporate and anti-regulatory policies pushed by ALEC, it has also embraced an agenda of vote suppression and gerrymandering, designed to keep statehouses and congressional seats in Republican hands. For a decade ALEC has pushed voter ID laws to make it harder for younger and older people, poorer communities and people of color to participate in the franchise. Similarly, ALEC has advanced a legislative agenda to curb early voting, make registration more complicated and expensive, require proof of citizenship, and limit ballot initiatives.[79] In a similar vein, conservative leaders understood that having a well-financed bill-drafting operation was not enough.

To really cement their wins, they needed the right legislators. But how to get them? As a corollary to ALEC's legislative work to limit access to the ballot box for Democrats and minority voters, conservative activists saw that they could exert even more control over electoral outcomes by drafting district maps to maximize their partisan advantage. Drawing district lines to favor one political party over another has a long history. The practice of gerrymandering is named after Elbridge Gerry, who as governor of Massachusetts in 1812 created a very favorable state map for his Democratic-Republican party. The shape of one district, drawn to limit the ability of the Federalist Party to elect representatives, looked rather like a salamander, allowing a clever cartoonist to draw it and dub it a "gerrymander," after its amphibious doppelganger.[80] The results demonstrate why partisans have used the gerrymander ever since: in the 1812 election, Gerry's party received 50,164 votes and won 29 seats; the opposing Federalists' vote total exceeded that by over 1,500 votes, but they won only 11 seats because of how the districts were drawn.[81] Now with algorithms, stronger voter alignment with a political party—more voters who vote the straight party ticket—and more data about people's voting history, it has become easier and easier to create electoral maps that provide almost 100 percent certainty of which party will win. Karl Rove could not have said it any more clearly: "He who controls the pen draws the line, and he who draws the line decides the outcome of most contests."[82]

In the late 2000s, the Republican Party was in a position to take full advantage of new data-analysis tools and its already dominant position in statehouses. In 2009, Karl Rove proposed a diabolical plan, called REDMAP, to ensure more GOP districts, even if they had fewer voters. His vision, announced in a *Wall Street Journal* opinion piece, was to focus on a small number of state legislative seats that would determine which party would be able to control the pen after the 2010 census.[83] In 2010, Republicans dumped $30 million into state races—triple the amount of Democrats—to wrest control of the once-in-a-decade process of congressional redistricting and then, with their new statehouse majorities, draw maps that favored Republicans and pass laws that disenfranchised Democrats and people of color. According to ProPublica, the Republican State Leadership Committee, which implemented REDMAP, "is organized as a type of political group that can take in unlimited corporate donations. It must disclose its contributors. But that doesn't mean it's always possible to trace the origins of the money."[84] In 2012, Democrats received 1.4 million more votes, yet Republicans won control of the U.S. House by a 234 to 201 margin. This combination of dark money, voter suppression, and gerrymandering makes gains in either state or federal elections a challenge for Democrats. REDMAP continues to play an outsize role in who wins state and congressional races across the United States.

Many look back to the election of Ronald Reagan as a watershed for conservatives in their efforts to rescind the New Deal and much of the civil rights and women's rights movements, but in reality that effort began earlier, with the synergies created by corporate power, right-wing zealotry, and electoral maneuvering memorialized in the Powell Memo.[85] With coordination and funding, conservatives upended the political landscape over the course of decades. What Powell grasped is that in order to win and stay on top, it is enormously valuable—no, essential—to write the rules in one's own favor. Conservatives directed money to legal groups that could influence who the judges were, supplied legal theories that were heavily tilted toward business for judges to apply, and brought cases before those same judges, whose rulings have continued to move the law rightward. The funders also played heavily in the legislative arena, supporting groups that generated policy ideas for state and federal legislators, with an emphasis on changes that created unfair advantages for conservatives in the courts and in elections, including rigging districts through gerrymandering. And these conservative leaders also ensured favorable news coverage by coordinating with right-wing media outlets and funding groups to attack mainstream reporting.

Do we ever learn our lesson? Years go by and we see the impact of the "vast right-wing conspiracy"[86] (Hillary Clinton, by the way, was right on this one) on policy and politics, and yet we continue to quibble about issue details, and moderate and liberal funders focus on microprograms with short time spans that allow them to pursue pet projects but fail to build institutions.[87]

3

ELECTIONS HAVE CONSEQUENCES

White supremacists, racists, and Ku Klux Klan members descended on Charlottesville, Virginia, in August 2017. Their tiki-torch-lit rally, reminiscent of both Klan and Nazi marches, was met by protesters. After fights broke out and one of the white supremacists murdered a peaceful protester, President Donald Trump sided with the racists, to no one's surprise, stating that there were "very fine people on both sides" and that the violence was in fact perpetrated by the so-called alt-left. Just hours after the Trump press conference, a judge issued a decision finding Texas guilty of intentionally discriminating against minority voters for the seventh time since 2011. This time, the finding was based on the drawing of electoral district lines meant to limit the political power of African Americans and Latinos. In the previous rulings, the courts had blocked voter ID laws and election maps adopted by the Republican-controlled state legislature, finding them explicitly racist.[1] The legislators who enacted these laws were not "fine people."

With a mix of voter suppression laws, gerrymandered districts, and floods of campaign cash from plutocratic donors, the Right has sought to make elections a fait accompli for its candidates. Rather than contesting the issues in elections, Republican operatives have worked to change the rules to make it easier for their side to win. They limit access to the polls by requiring photo IDs, by shortening early voting periods, by making it harder to register and imposing criminal penalties on those who do it wrong, and by purging voter rolls—all in the name of protecting elections against voter fraud, which is virtually nonexistent. To make it even more difficult for progressives to win, Republicans have engaged in flagrant racial gerrymandering, minimizing the ability of African Americans to elect their favored candidates, as well as partisan gerrymandering, using computer algorithms to hone districts that will elect as few Democrats as possible. And the Right has worked through the courts to unleash dark-money campaign spending, cloaking their efforts to buy elections in the language of the First Amendment. While they attack unions because unions help workers, that's not the only reason—the Right understands that labor organizations are a key funding and volunteer source for the Democratic Party and progressive candidates. Barriers to voting for certain Americans, rigged districts, unconstrained spending by billionaires in elections, and attacks on unions have made elections an afterthought, turning democracy on its head.

Voter suppression lived on in America well after the Civil War ended, slaves were liberated, and the Fifteenth Amendment guaranteed black men the right to vote. The Fifteenth Amendment was essentially written out of the Constitution in Jim Crow America by white supremacists, including the White Citizens' Councils and the Ku Klux Klan. Racist whites prevented African Americans from voting through violence and intimidation and, throughout the twentieth century and particularly in the South, election officials devised numerous methods to keep African Americans from exercising the franchise. Literacy tests, poll taxes, and other devices were used as barriers to voting for non-whites. Mississippi changed its constitution in 1890 explicitly to strip blacks of the franchise, and other southern states soon followed suit.[2] In 1965, Congress passed the Voting Rights Act (VRA) to provide a federal backstop and enforcement powers designed to give the Fifteenth Amendment teeth. The VRA was part of a suite of federal laws that sought to dismantle the racist laws and practices that barred African Americans from employment, housing, access to restaurants and hotels, and, most significantly, limited their ability to participate in elections.

Lyndon Johnson said that the VRA was meant to right "a clear and simple wrong. Millions of Americans are denied the right to vote because of their color. This law will ensure them the right to vote."[3] John Lewis, elected to Congress with the help of newly enfranchised African American voters, said that "when Lyndon Johnson signed the Voting Rights Act, he helped free and liberate all of us."[4] The law barred any use of literacy tests or other devices dreamed up by the Jim Crow architects and gave the Department of Justice the power to stop covered jurisdictions—those states and localities with a history of denying voting rights to minorities—from making changes to their rules governing elections. This provision, called Section 5, meant that seven states would have to submit every electoral change in advance for analysis by a team of civil rights lawyers at the Department of Justice before the changes could be adopted. Moving polling places, altering voting hours and days, and redrawing voting jurisdictions would all need the blessing of Department of Justice lawyers before being implemented. In subsequent reauthorizations of the VRA, Congress added provisions to help groups with limited English proficiency vote in their native languages, allowed eighteen-year-olds to vote, and barred literacy tests not just in the South but across the country.[5]

The Voting Rights Act bore immediate fruit, as African Americans were able to register and vote in significantly higher numbers. In Mississippi, for example, voter registration among African Americans soared from 7 percent to 54 percent within just three years of the VRA's enactment. And in the South overall, in the decades that followed, blacks went from a 31 percent registration rate to 71 percent, as people began to see their votes count. The number of black elected officials went from a scant five hundred in 1965 to over ten thousand in the next several decades, with over forty African Americans serving in Congress by 2017.[6]

Voting rights advocates pressed for more mechanisms to ease the voting process, arguing that voting is a right, not a privilege, and that significant barriers to the franchise still existed. Over time, they were successful in getting Congress to pass the National Voter Registration Act in 1993—otherwise known as the "Motor Voter Act" because voters could register while getting or renewing a driver's license—as well as adding early voting and same-day voter registration in numerous states. In the five years after passage of Motor Voter, African American registration went up by 10 percent.[7] With every advance, more African Americans were able to participate, culminating in the election of President Barack Obama in 2008, when black voters turned out at nearly the same rate as white voters for the first time.[8]

While Republicans were originally the "party of Lincoln," by the 1960s, Democrats had become the party working to expand the franchise, at least at the national level. Even though southern white Democrats had instigated and perpetuated Jim Crow, President Johnson saw the VRA as the most important element of the civil rights legislative agenda that was now a major platform of the Democratic party. He also acknowledged that the new law would accelerate the hemorrhaging of southern whites from the party. Today, racism is still a powerful force, but the Republican Party now also has a pragmatic reason to suppress black votes: African Americans overwhelmingly vote Democratic.

The adoption of the VRA forced conservative leaders to change their tactics. Overtly racist arguments for voter suppression laws mostly disappeared as conservatives learned new tropes to disguise the intent behind their policy proposals. In his book *Give Us the Ballot*, journalist Ari Berman characterizes the post-VRA provisions as "subtler than those of the 1890s or 1960s, camouflaging efforts to deter voting with laws that rarely invoked race, introduced with equal fervor in North and South alike."[9] Paul Weyrich, co-founder of the Heritage Foundation, ALEC, and the Moral Majority, helped lead the charge against broad access to the voting booth. Speaking at a Religious Roundtable rally in August 1980 featuring presidential candidate Ronald Reagan, Weyrich spelled out the plan for vote suppression that was to characterize the approach of the Right going forward. "Now many of our Christians have what I call the 'goo goo' syndrome—good government," Weyrich said. "They want everybody to vote. I don't want everybody to vote. Elections are not won by a majority of people. They never have been from the beginning of our country, and they are not now. As a matter of fact, our leverage in the elections quite candidly goes up as the voting populace goes down."[10] Weyrich did not need to explain to his audience who he didn't want to vote. ALEC, one of the groups Weyrich started, became the source of many of the voter suppression proposals that soon followed.

These anti-voting provisions followed two main approaches. The first was to change the debate around voting from increasing access to the ballot box to combating voter fraud—a fabricated bogeyman unsupported by any actual evidence. Elevating a nearly nonexistent problem offered a seemingly race-neutral rhetorical tool to undermine voting rights. The second approach was to attack the fundamental voting rights protections of the VRA as outdated and no longer necessary. President George W. Bush's Supreme Court appointees, including Chief Justice John Roberts—a longtime opponent of the Voting Rights Act—undermined the core purpose of the VRA in *Shelby County v. Holder* by making Section 5 unenforceable, calling the idea of requiring states to get approval for changing their election laws a relic of a former, benighted era and no longer relevant in an age when discrimination had been vanquished. The weakening of federal protections resulted in even more state laws limiting access to the ballot box, along with voting districts crafted to strongly favor Republicans. In the immediate aftermath of the *Shelby County* decision, indeed within hours, states that had been blocked from adopting laws designed to limit the rights of minorities to vote, pulled those laws off the shelf and rushed them to votes.

IT'S STILL RAINING: CRIPPLING THE VOTING RIGHTS ACT

Serving in the Justice Department under Attorney General Ed Meese, John Roberts found the Voting Rights Act—indeed any racially targeted remedies—to be an affront to his vision of the Constitution. Not a southerner, the Indiana native nonetheless believed that it was anathema to deny states the ability to make decisions about their own voting laws. He had come to Washington to work as a law clerk to Justice William Rehnquist, who shared Roberts's dislike of race-conscious legislation. Consistent with that view, Rehnquist joined an opinion, *City of Mobile v. Bolden* (1980), that made enforcement of the Voting Rights

Act much more difficult by requiring *proof of intent* to disenfranchise African Americans rather than simply showing that the law had the effect of doing so. Ari Berman explains that "Rehnquist's opposition to civil rights laws on federalism grounds and the rebranding of that opposition as principled color blindness became a staple of the Reagan administration position on civil rights." Or as Harvard law professor Randall Kennedy put it, "Color blindness became a mechanism for maintaining the old regime in a respectable way."[11] This hypocrisy was recognized even by some conservative commentators. Writing in the *New Republic*, Charles Krauthammer and Owen Fiss suggested that Rehnquist had erased the post–Civil War amendments from the Constitution, describing the justice's vision as "a return to the antebellum Constitution," when slavery was still the law.[12]

Rehnquist and Roberts had the intellectual support of conservative law professors, including Antonin Scalia, who had begun to attack any policy or legislation that sought to address the vestiges of slavery or racism. Cynically claiming Martin Luther King Jr.'s "I Have a Dream" speech as their inspiration, their goal was the exact opposite of King's. Scalia, who called affirmative action "disease as cure," wrote that he found it "an embarrassment" to teach equal protection law. According to Scalia, there was no justification for having a different standard for blacks than that applied to whites. Even with a history of discrimination and voter suppression, in Scalia's view, a race-based remedy such as the VRA was "based upon concepts of racial indebtedness and racial entitlement rather than individual worth and individual need; that is to say . . . it is racist."[13]

By the time Roberts had moved from his clerkship to the Justice Department during the Reagan administration, Congress had taken up the Voting Rights Act reauthorization with an interest in fixing what VRA supporters saw as an error made by

the Supreme Court in *Mobile v. Bolden* in requiring a finding of
intent to discriminate rather than just the effect of doing so. At
the Justice Department, Judge Roberts fought hard for the intent
standard, saying it should be a heavy burden to establish voting
discrimination because these cases are "the most intrusive inter-
ference imaginable by the federal courts into state and local processes." According to Roberts, looking at actual discrimination,
rather than at the intent to discriminate, would "establish essentially a quota system for electoral politics." Just as he argued that
quotas are bad in other contexts—education, employment—he
argued they are bad in elections.[14] His argument that an effects
test would require proportional representation was vigorously
disputed even by other lawyers in the Reagan Justice Department.[15] Nonetheless, Roberts worked to persuade his higher-ups
at Justice that the Constitution should be "color blind" and that
the Voting Rights Act reauthorization was not constitutional.[16]
As Gerry Hebert, a longtime voting rights lawyer, told the *New
York Times*, "In their zest for the colorblind society they professed
to see, they didn't recognize that the long couple hundred years
of segregation and discrimination continued to have present-day
effects. I would say they had a fundamental lack of understanding of the 14th and 15th Amendments, and what Congress could
do under those amendments—I still don't think Roberts understands it."[17] Roberts did not get his way in 1982, but he finally
won the day once he became chief justice in 2005.

In *Shelby*, Roberts wrote for the majority, holding that Section
5 of the VRA had been a "drastic departure from basic principles
of federalism" and was in any case no longer necessary. "History did not end in 1965," he wrote. "Largely because of the Voting Rights Act, voting tests were abolished, disparities in voter
registration and turnout due to race were erased, and African-
Americans attained political office in record numbers."[18] Justice

Ruth Bader Ginsburg, in a fiery dissent, chastised Roberts for the opinion's "hubris," noting that in fact the Justice Department had cataloged more problematic voting changes between 1982 and 2004 than it had between 1965 and the 1982 reauthorization, including cases of Republican legislators calling African Americans "aborigines" and saying that black turnout needed to be suppressed before they were delivered to the polls via "HUD-financed buses."[19] Ginsburg challenged the fiction that black voters no longer faced discrimination because more of them were voting and getting elected to office. She wrote prophetically in her dissent that "throwing out preclearance when it has worked and is continuing to work to stop discriminatory changes is like throwing away your umbrella in a rainstorm because you are not getting wet."[20] The Shelby County decision let loose a flood of new voter suppression legislation, now blessed by a Supreme Court that saw a color-blind society purged of racism.

SHARK ATTACKS: VOTER FRAUD IS A FRAUD

Even before Shelby County put wind in their sails, leaders on the right had been devising a range of new and nefarious mechanisms to make it harder for likely Democratic voters to influence election outcomes. In contrast to civil rights advocates' campaign for the right to vote, these conservative activists espouse "voter integrity," arguing that fraud in voting is the more important concern. Despite the fact that in-person voter fraud is about as common as a four-leaf clover or a billion-dollar lottery ticket—Florida has more shark attacks than fraudulent voters,[21] and Justin Levitt of Loyola Law School in a study found only thirty-one "credible incidents" of fraud out of a billion votes cast[22]—the Right has turned voter fraud into a rallying cry to advance its most pernicious anti-voter policies.

Karl Rove was an early and expert practitioner of using "voter fraud" as a bludgeon to swing an election to his side. It was in 1994 when Rove first learned the art of making baseless allegations of misconduct to flip an election. His candidate for chief justice of the Alabama Supreme Court had lost by a little over three hundred votes, but Rove was not content to accept the results. A member of Rove's campaign team recalled to reporter Joshua Green that "our role was to try to keep people motivated about Perry Hooper's election and then to undermine the other side's support by casting them as liars, cheaters, stealers, immoral—all of that."[23] Rove sent operatives and investigators across the state to watch the recount process and find evidence of fraud. Turning false accusations into a weapon, Rove helped "spread tales of poll watchers threatened with arrest; probate judges locking themselves in their offices and refusing to admit campaign workers; votes being cast in absentia for comatose nursing-home patients; and Democrats caught in a cemetery writing down the names of the dead in order to put them on absentee ballots."[24] After a year-long battle that ended up in the Supreme Court, Rove won, and allegations of voter fraud became a key play in the sleazy campaign playbook.

The 2000 election moved these tactics to a bigger stage. In the closely fought Florida battle, George Bush's campaign worked with the state's secretary of state, Katherine Harris, to dump thousands of eligible African American voters from the voter rolls. Employing aggressive legal tactics, the campaign also used intimidation, summoning a horde of GOP Hill aides from Washington to swarm the Miami-Dade County canvassing board, screaming and yelling and thumping their fists on the glass doors. We should keep that picture in our head—a bunch of thick-necked goons, fresh from drinking pitchers of beer at Bullfeathers on Capitol Hill, airlifted to Florida. The horde bore down on the office that was supposed to be neutral in assessing the validity of the ballots—the intimidation factor was high. Republicans fought to have military ballots counted from the counties where Bush did well but to exclude those from counties won by Gore, yet they denounced Democrats for disrespecting people in uniform. Despite Republicans' stranglehold on the Florida government, the Bush campaign still accused Democrats of trying to steal the election.[25] It's no surprise that Gore ended up conceding. Nor is it a surprise that the conservative-dominated Supreme Court decided to pick George Bush as the next president. Sandra Day O'Connor later came to regret her vote.[26] Alas, it was too late.

Bush's Justice Department under Attorney General John Ashcroft flipped the mission of its Civil Rights Division on its head, turning the division's focus from enforcing voting rights to stopping voters from voting. The attorney general championed "a new ethic of enforcement of our voting rights" and focused the resources of the Justice Department on investigating alleged voter fraud. Ashcroft lamented that "votes have been bought, voters intimidated and ballot boxes stuffed," and he added that dead people had voted and people had signed up for absentee ballots "believing they were applications for public relief."[27] The racial signaling could not have been clearer. The year 2002 was a banner one for vote suppression, with Karl Rove in the White House and Ashcroft at the Justice Department. Across the country, Republicans targeted minority voters to swing the United States Senate to the GOP. Investing in brigades of poll watchers and challenging efforts by Democrats to get people to the polls, the Republicans were successful in their efforts to tip the balance. The lead-up to Election Day was a whack-a-mole for Democrats, as voter suppression efforts multiplied through smear tactics in mailers, challenges to voter registrations, and intimidation. "Take

Arkansas, home of the tight Senate race between Republican Sen. Tim Hutchinson and Democrat Mark Pryor," wrote *Washington Post* columnist E.J. Dionne. "On the first day of early voting in Pine Bluff last week, a group of Republican 'poll watchers' showed up with cameras and charged that election officials were not properly checking voter identifications."[28]

In some cases, the Right used intimidation and outright lies to suppress the vote. In Maryland, where Republican Bob Ehrlich was running against Democrat Kathleen Kennedy Townsend, GOP campaign staff distributed flyers in Maryland's black residential areas that read, "URGENT NOTICE. Come out to Vote November 6. Before you Come out to vote—Pay your parking tickets, motor vehicle tickets, your rent, and most important, ANY WARRANTS." The election took place November 5.[29] Not content to lie just about the date to ensure fewer African American voters, the GOP operatives also insinuated that those who voted who were behind on their bills or had a police record should stay away. Of course, the intent was also to deter people afraid they would be hassled by cops who might assume they owed money or had done time.

African American leaders in Maryland were outraged. Not only did Republicans work to suppress the black vote by lying about the date of the election and using scare tactics, but they also attempted to convince those African Americans who did show up on the right date that GOP gubernatorial candidate Ehrlich had been endorsed by a diverse group of Democrats. Congressman Elijah Cummings was handed a leaflet when he went to vote at his polling place in the Baltimore district he represents. "They handed me this big, beautiful piece of literature. It was better than any of the literature I have ever produced," recounted Cummings. "I said, 'Boy this is a wonderful photo.' There's my pastor, and [then Housing and Urban Development secretary] Mel Martinez, and [former Baltimore delegate] Tony Fulton and myself. Then I saw Ehrlich in the picture, and I saw the words and I said, 'Uh oh.'" Cummings tried to counter the effect of the fake leaflet, entitled "Democrats for Ehrlich." He had been working to get Kathleen Kennedy Townsend elected and denounced the fraud committed by her opponent on radio, television, and in a recorded call for voters. But the damage was done: Ehrlich won.[30]

"It worked once," Ehrlich must have thought, "why not try again?" In 2006, just before Election Day, his campaign distributed a brochure in the majority African American Prince George's County. A *Washington Post* story describes how Ehrlich's campaign mailed "a glossy red, black and green flier—the colors that represent African American power—sporting pictures of County Executive Jack B. Johnson, his predecessor, Wayne K. Curry and past NAACP president and former U.S. Senate candidate Kweisi Mfume. Above the pictures of the three Democrats the flier read, 'Ehrlich-Steele Democrats,' and underneath it announced: 'These are OUR Choices.'"[31] Slight problem—not one of these individuals had come out for Ehrlich, and Curry alone had indicated his support for Senate candidate Michael S. Steele. When the Democratic Party tried to get the fliers removed from polling sites, the Ehrlich campaign convinced a judge that there wasn't enough time and, in any case, there were First Amendment concerns. The courtroom hearing ended close to 6 p.m., near the time for polls to close, prompting the judge to say, "I'm not going to do it. It's too late." The only silver lining: Ehrlich lost anyway.

Where minority voters couldn't be manipulated by lies into voting for Republicans or scared away altogether by threats of jail time, the Right used voter fraud allegations to upend Democratic victories. Rove was so fixated on using charges of voter fraud to rig elections for Republicans that he tasked several United States attorneys in 2006 with investigating trumped-up charges of illegal voting in races where a Democrat had won in a close election. Finding nothing to support charges, a number of the prosecutors refused to go along and Rove had them all fired. In Washington State, U.S. Attorney John McKay was expected to find that the Democrat in the governor's race had gotten illegal votes. McKay, who was being considered as a candidate for a federal judgeship, arrived at the White House prepared to discuss his qualifications and instead was railed at for having failed to bring the charges. So, no judgeship for McKay; instead he was kicked to the curb. "There was no evidence," McKay stated later, "and I am not going to drag innocent people in front of a grand jury." After several other U.S. attorneys were similarly cashiered for refusing to pursue spurious allegations, Congress and the public were enraged (Congress was in Democratic hands at the time). Attorney General Alberto Gonzales was summoned to the Hill and in one hearing said, "I don't recall" or a like phrase sixty-four times. By August 2007, most of his senior team had been pushed out or had left and Gonzales himself quit.[32]

Taking the standard voter fraud trope and mixing in overt racism, Donald Trump concocted an even more toxic brew during the 2016 election. Rick Hasen, a law professor and expert on voting rights, comments that "both before and after the election, Trump made wild and unsubstantiated claims about voter fraud and the system being 'rigged.' Before the election, many of the claims were about voters voting five, 10, or 15 times by impersonating other voters. The ridiculous and unproven charges of voter fraud had a racial tinge, with suggestions the fraud would happen in majority minority communities." Trump blew this dog whistle when addressing an audience in Wilkes-Barre, Pennsylvania, shortly before the election: "I just hear such reports about Philadelphia. . . . I hear these horror shows, and we have to make sure that this election is not stolen from us and is not taken away from us." He added, "Everybody knows what I'm talking about."[33]

To his lies about fraudulent voting, Trump added an old twist: a call to action by white supremacists to stop voters of color from getting to the polls. He insinuated at rally after rally that the election could be stolen by illegal voters coming out to swamp the votes of his supporters and summoned his base to form poll-watch groups to ensure that those voters did not vote. "Voter fraud is all too common, and then they criticize us for saying that," he said at a rally in Colorado Springs. "But take a look at Philadelphia, what's been going on, take a look at Chicago, take a look at St. Louis. Take a look at some of these cities, where you see things happening that are horrendous."[34]

Roger Stone, a senior Trump campaign operative, organized what he called "exit polling" to see who was voting at "targeted" precincts, in essence placing thugs at certain voting sites to intimidate voters. White supremacists responded energetically, committing to turn out at minority polling places. Neo-Nazi leader Andrew Anglin bragged to *Politico* about his intention to deploy thousands of white nationalists around the country. Working with the racist website the Right Stuff, the Trump allies described planning to hide cameras at polls in Philadelphia and to pass out alcohol and pot in the "ghetto" to keep Philadelphia's minority residents from voting.

A Right Stuff organizer explained the plan as follows:

> Many polling locations are in schools, and black schools are so disorderly that pretty much any official-looking white person with a clipboard can gain access to them ahead of time and set up a hidden camera. You don't really ever even have to speak with an adult. Simply walk in like you belong there and no one even asks you why you are

there. So we usually go in teams of two, one person driving and one person dressed as a blue collar worker with a
clipboard, and we set up a hidden camera in the school
cafeteria. Go during lunchtime and the teachers are all so
busy trying to contain the kids that no one says anything.
We already have a few set up.[35]

Among the groups that planned to send members to the polls
were the neo-Nazi National Socialist Movement, the Ku Klux
Klan, and the American Freedom Party, in some cases working
directly with the Trump campaign. Another group, the Oath
Keepers, made up mostly of retired military and police officers,
called on its members to show up under cover, like regular voters
(Oath Keepers are known for appearing in public settings bear-
ing weapons).

I AM SOMEBODY—I JUST CAN'T PROVE IT

Chartez Tucker lost his wallet with his ID in it, and with it, his
right to vote. Now he doesn't have many documents to prove his
identity; an out-of-date copy of a Michigan ID and some old and
rumpled pieces of mail are really his only proof that he exists.
"I am somebody," he said to a reporter with *Bridge Magazine*, a
publication of the Center for Michigan. "I just can't prove it."
The forty-five-year-old was making the rounds of agencies to get
a state ID to allow him to rent a place to live, a process that can
take over half a year, with many bureaucratic hurdles. Spending money on transportation to government offices and replacing lost copies of birth certificates and other documents is often
beyond the means of low-income people. "They make it so hard,"
Tucker said, after repeated unsuccessful trips to the Social Security office.[36]

Project Vote estimates that those likely to lack IDs are over-whelmingly poor people, particularly people of color: 13 percent of blacks, 10 percent of Latinos, and 12 percent of those living in households with incomes under $25,000 lack an ID.[37] And to get an ID in Michigan people need four types of paperwork: one with their Social Security number; a birth certificate or pass-port; documents that provide further identity verification, such as school records or marriage or divorce records; and two pieces to show domicile, such as a phone bill, bank statement, or lease.[38]

False claims of voter fraud were not just rhetorical. They were aimed at justifying policies that would keep non-Republican voters from voting, and at the top of the list was requiring pho-to ID to vote. The effort was also a priority initiative for ALEC, the group co-founded by Paul Weyrich to bring corporate lob-byists and conservative legislators together to generate policy ideas and provide financing for right-wing state leaders. Jour-nalist John Nichols describes ALEC's plan to hype voter fraud as a major problem and promote voter ID laws as the answer.[39] Right after Barack Obama was elected president, the maga-zine *Inside ALEC* made "Preventing Election Fraud" its cover article, and three legislators signed on to helm the process to create and sell a draft bill. One of the three, Russell Pearce, the state senator who penned Arizona's unconstitutional anti-immigrant law, made sure ALEC members saw the connection not only to suppressing black votes but also to keeping Latinos from participating in elections. Kansas Republican Kris Kobach encouraged anti-immigrant legislators to sign on, warning that "illegally registered aliens" were voting. They had no trouble working the bill through the ALEC process, gaining the sup-port of legislative, corporate, and advocacy group members, including the NRA. Legislators returned home with a draft photo ID bill to introduce.[40]

In 2010, Republicans made significant gains in statehouses around the country and the photo ID push began in earnest. Those elections gave Republicans control of both chambers of the legislature in twenty-five states, an increase of eleven.[41] Alabama, Kansas, Mississippi, Rhode Island, South Carolina, Tennessee, Texas, and Wisconsin adopted the ALEC-model bill in 2011.[42] With further statehouse gains in 2012, ALEC and its allies put much of their energy into pushing the bill in the presidential battleground states. While legal challenges blocked some of these bills from taking effect, the *Shelby County* decision allowed legislators to revive them. According to the National Conference of State Legislatures, thirty-four states have some form of ID requirement as of June 2018.[43] More photo ID laws mean fewer voters of color, fewer younger voters, and fewer voters from other traditionally Democratic constituencies.

In Wisconsin, voting rights advocates sued the state, arguing that its ID law was nothing but an effort to suppress votes. After a thorough trial, Judge Lynn Adelman agreed. With stiff penalties and little partisan advantage to be gained, Adelman wrote, "a person would have to be insane to commit voter impersonation fraud." The punishment in Wisconsin included three years of jail time and a $10,000 fine, all to change one vote.[44] Some conservative leaders, in their honest moments, have admitted to the solely partisan benefit of claiming in-person voter fraud. Speaking to the *Houston Chronicle* in 2007, Royal Masset, then political director of the Texas Republican Party, conceded that while most Republicans assert that fraud is denying them victories, the facts don't bear that out; however, he continued, the ID requirement was helpful because it could lower Democratic turnout by 3 percent.[45] Similarly, Pennsylvania majority leader Mike Turzai urged support for the voter ID law in 2012 because it would "allow Governor Romney to win the state of Pennsylvania."[46]

Studies conclusively demonstrate that the photo ID laws have had a disproportionate impact on eligible minority voters. In a 2017 report, researchers at the University of Wisconsin found that the new ID law blocked seventeen thousand or more registered voters from voting in Wisconsin in November 2016. Its impact was far greater on low-income and minority Wisconsin voters. According to the *New York Times*, "21.1 percent of registrants earning less than $25,000 a year were estimated to have been deterred from voting, compared with 2.7 percent of registrants making $100,000 a year or more. More than 27 percent of blacks reported being deterred, compared with about 8 percent of whites." The *Times* went on to note that "the Wisconsin study broadly confirms the results of another survey of nonvoters conducted by Rice University scholars after the 2014 congressional election. That study concluded that 9 percent of nonvoters in Texas's 23rd Congressional District were discouraged from voting by Texas's voter ID law—often, as in Wisconsin, because they mistakenly believed they lacked a valid ID."[47]

But photo IDs are not the only tactic used to change the composition of the electorate. The Right has also worked to roll back efforts that increased early voting; to impose restrictions on "souls to the polls," when churches organize group trips to vote; to limit the use of student IDs; to purge voter rolls; to require proof of citizenship to register; to disenfranchise former felons; and to make voter registration more difficult overall—including imposing criminal penalties for errors in registration documents.

In North Carolina, in the hours after *Shelby* was issued, Republicans pulled back from the floor a voter ID bill that would have allowed multiple IDs to be used to vote and helped voters obtain free IDs if they did not have one. Instead, the Rules Committee chair quickly swapped in a new bill—"the full bill"—happy that the "headache" would no longer block their efforts. The full bill halved early voting, removing one of the Sundays that was a popular day for African American churches to get worshippers to polling places, undid same-day registration, and barred student IDs from being used to vote, even when the IDs were state-issued.[48] Absent the *Shelby* decision, the bill never would have become law, because it would not have passed muster under Section 5. But it did pass, just two days after being introduced, on a party-line vote. Trumped-up allegations of voter fraud by voting "expert" Hans von Spakovsky, a Heritage Foundation fellow and former Justice Department lawyer under John Ashcroft, consultant Dick Morris, and Republican state legislators dominated the Fox News coverage during the debate, and the bill's supporters aggressively pitched their fallacious argument that voter fraud is widespread in America.[49]

Donald Trump sought to house a high-profile attack on voting rights in the White House in his cynically named Presidential Advisory Commission on Election Integrity. Helmed by a long-standing foe of access to the ballot, former Kansas secretary of state Kris Kobach, the commission (now shuttered) sought to wage war on the franchise, promoting bogus allegations of voter fraud, encouraging voter purges, and demanding sensitive voter data from the states as a way to intimidate eligible voters from participating in elections. Kobach had lobbied Trump during the campaign to pursue these measures based on his work in Kansas, where he had successfully pushed the state to require proof of citizenship to register. That measure alone blocked one out of seven Kansans from registering after it was adopted in 2013, with a heavy impact on younger voters. In 2016, the law was enjoined by a federal appellate court, which found that "there was an almost certain risk that thousands of otherwise qualified Kansans would be unable to vote in November."[50] As that case got underway, Kobach broadened his focus to try to apply that rule to the entire United States by amending the National Voter Registration Act—the so-called Motor Voter Act—to require all voters to produce citizenship documents. Kobach is also a booster of the Interstate Crosscheck System, which, according to the *Washington Post*, "is supposed to detect possible cases of people voting in multiple locations." In reality, the program is riddled with errors, finding many false positives. Researchers from Stanford, Harvard, and Microsoft calculated that Crosscheck "would eliminate about 200 registrations used to cast legitimate votes for every one registration used to cast a double vote."[51]

But even without new amendments proposed by Kobach, the Motor Voter Act, passed to simplify voter registration and ultimately increase voting, is already being used by Trump's Justice Department as an excuse to do the opposite. The Justice Department had, until Trump, consistently interpreted the Motor Voter Act to forbid removing people from voter rolls just because they failed to vote and don't reply to a state mailing confirming their residency. After Ohio passed a law to purge voters who don't vote in three elections, the Obama Justice Department joined the ACLU in challenging the law. Hundreds of thousands of voters were at risk of losing their right to vote in the 2016 election. A federal appellate court blocked the law, but in the subsequent appeal to the Supreme Court, the Justice Department changed its position, joining Ohio in defending the law. No one on the career staff at the Justice Department would sign the brief, leaving only the Trump political appointees to sign on. Instead, many former department lawyers, including former attorney general Eric Holder, filed a brief contesting the switch in position. "A lot of folks who had worked at the Department on the Motor Voter Act were very upset by the change of course," says Samuel

Bagenstos, a University of Michigan law professor who served as the number two official in the Civil Rights Division for two years during the Obama administration. "And it seemed very notable that there were no career attorneys signed on the brief." Justin Levitt, an election law expert, underscores how extraordinary it is for the office of the Justice Department's solicitor general to jump sides midcase. "This is not merely a policy change. It is a change by the office that has the role in the courts of deciding what the law says on behalf of the federal government," says Levitt. "Every time the office of the solicitor general changes position without an intervening change in the law, it damages its credibility a little bit." On the other side, George Mason University's Antonin Scalia Law School Supreme Court Clinic filed a brief entitled "Brief of Former Attorneys of the Civil Rights Division of the United States Department of Justice." One of its six signatories was Hans von Spakovsky.[52] Not surprisingly, the Supreme Court, with new member Neil Gorsuch, found that Ohio could move forward with its voter purge. We can expect this to happen now in many other states.[53]

Considered together, the photo ID push, the purges, the changes to early voting, and other constraints on the right to vote have represented "the greatest attacks on voting rights since segregation," according to Ben Jealous, former NAACP president.[54] Bill Clinton lamented, in an address to students in 2011, "There has never been in my lifetime, since we got rid of the poll tax and all the Jim Crow burdens on voting, the determined effort to limit the franchise that we see today."[55] Over 5 million voters lost their ability to vote because of the new anti-voter laws adopted in the years after President Obama was first elected and accelerated by the *Shelby County* decision—numbers greater than the vote difference between the two presidential candidates in 2000 and 2004 nationwide.[56]

VOTING SHOULD BE EASY

Our goal should be to encourage all Americans to vote. This is the premise of an elected democracy—not intentionally suppressing the vote of any individual or group. To that end, Americans should be able to

- register on Election Day,
- be registered automatically when they get a driver's license, and
- vote from home by mail.

All of these reforms would help increase participation among groups that traditionally have had a harder time because of family obligations, work restrictions, and geography, not to mention intimidation at the polls—and whose votes are essential for the Left.

Same-day registration eliminates the need to register in advance of an election. Instead, those who are eligible to vote can both register and vote on the same day. Some states allow this process on Election Day, during early voting, or both. Demos, a nonprofit think tank focused on protecting and expanding democracy, argues that same-day registration has multiple benefits. It lowers costs and helps voters who face more barriers to the ballot box, such as those who are less mobile or elderly or are new to voting in that jurisdiction. Same-day registration would also eliminate the ability of right-wing operatives to purge voter rolls in advance of an election. The rolls would be updated every election when people show up to vote. And it would limit the need for provisional ballots, which are given to voters whose names are not on the rolls but who believe they have registered. Twenty-five percent of provisional ballots in the 2008 election were rejected, in each case denying the franchise to someone who believed themselves eligible to vote and who had shown up at the polls to do so.[57] As Brenda Wright, senior adviser for legal strategies at Demos, told me, "Many citizens become most interested and engaged with elections in the last few weeks before Election Day, when candidate debates and campaigns reach their peak. But registration deadlines may already have passed at that point. Same-day registration remedies that problem and gives people a fail-safe if they missed the registration deadline." Most important for progressives, it increases voter turnout, with those states that have implemented it seeing the highest voter participation in the nation. Wright says that "four of the top five states for voter turnout in both the 2012 and 2016 presidential elections offered same-day registration." Young people and people of color see particular benefits. Again from Wright: "In North Carolina, for example, 41 percent of those using same-day registration were African American, though African Americans represent only 20 percent of the voting-age population. Young people, who tend to be geographically mobile and need to update their registration addresses more frequently, also benefit from same-day registration. Research indicates that allowing young people to register to vote on Election Day could increase youth turnout in presidential elections by as much as 14 percentage points."

So far, fifteen states (California, Colorado, Connecticut, Hawaii, Idaho, Illinois, Iowa, Maine, Maryland, Minnesota, Montana, New Hampshire, North Carolina, Wisconsin, and Wyoming) and the District of Columbia have some form of same-day registration. Maine, Minnesota, and Wisconsin led the way by enacting their same-day registration laws in the early to mid-1970s. The ACLU's People Power campaign includes same-day registration among its goals and is putting activists on the ground to move this forward in several more states.

Another way to improve election participation is to make

voter registration automatic, allowing people to opt out of voter registration rather than opting in when they get a license. Nine states and the District of Columbia have implemented this program as of August 2018.[58] Election experts believe it would significantly increase registration. According to the Brennan Center for Justice, "It would add up to 50 million eligible voters to the rolls, save money, and increase accuracy—while protecting the integrity of elections."[59] The Brennan Center's Wendy Weiser has her eye on New Jersey, Washington State, Massachusetts, and Maryland as well as Nevada, where a ballot initiative goes to the voters in fall of 2018. Recognizing the appeal to average voters of this commonsensical reform, conservative activists have woken up to the danger of automatic voter registration expanding the electorate. Weiser, while worried about the resources on the right, believes automatic voter registration will be hard to slow down.

Even as we fight in the states to expand registration, a particularly exciting approach is to expand voting rights in counties and municipalities. Some of the approaches are quite easy—just registering young people in schools and government agencies might put millions of additional voters on the rolls, and other policies such as adding new voters to the permanent early voting list so they would automatically get a ballot by mail would add to those numbers.[60] With more young people and people of color living in urban areas, these types of reforms could have a palpable impact, especially where state officials are hostile to voting rights.

Voting by mail—or a more appealing name, "voting at home"—is another way to allow more voters to participate at a lower cost. A proponent of this policy, former Oregon secretary of state Phil Keisling, told me that he believes it would go a long way toward increasing voter turnout. And it would obviate the need to keep fighting voter ID laws and targeted poll closings,

long lines, and shorter early voting periods. With evidence from
three states already—Colorado, Oregon, and Washington—the
proposal has been demonstrated to get more young people and
minorities to participate.[61] "Here's how it works," said Keisling.
"Instead of requiring voters to cast ballots at official polling
places or apply in advance for absentee ballots, these states mail
ballots to all registered voters at their homes. Voters then have
about two weeks to fill out their ballots and either mail them
back or deliver them personally to any one of hundreds of official ballot drop sites located strategically across their states—in,
for example, schools, libraries, police and fire stations, and post
offices, and at secure, freestanding metal boxes that are available
twenty-four hours a day. For security, election officials match the
signature on every ballot with the one on the voter's registration
card." It takes a variety of vote suppression tactics off the table.
And there's no evidence of fraud.

The only catch: Some Republicans don't like it for these very
same reasons. But in twenty-one states, voters could go around
the legislature by using the ballot-initiative process. These states,
especially Florida, Michigan, Missouri, and Ohio, could really
move the needle in national elections.[62] Other states with Democratic legislatures, such as California and Hawaii, could pass a
bill, and California is already moving in this direction. Launched
in 2017, the National Vote at Home Institute is supporting efforts
to advance this initiative around the country, with backing from
unions and other partners. One reason this idea is important
is because we all know that voter registration isn't enough—we
have to get people to vote. Universal vote by mail would get more
registered voters to participate and have an extra-strong impact
in midterm elections, when minority and lower-income voters
are less likely to participate. And sometime soon, hopefully, we
will have online voting, the ultimate democratization of democ-

racy, once we can be assured of a system that the Russians or the Right can't easily hack and manipulate.[63]

While the rhetoric about the importance of "fair democracy" may induce yawns at a time when the Right is increasingly expressing a vile and racist vision for America, ensuring that more voters can exercise their right to vote is one of the most powerful things we can do right now to move the country in a more progressive direction in the future as the electorate becomes more black and brown.

HALLEY'S COMET: THE REDISTRICTING GAME

During the debates over ratification of the Constitution, Alexander Hamilton explained that "the true principle of a republic is, that the people should choose whom they please to govern them."[64] At that time, Hamilton's argument was enfeebled by the fact that so many Americans did not get to choose who governed them. The politicians chose their class of voters: white, male property owners. But even now, after having expanded our electorate to include more people—African Americans and women as well as Native Americans and younger people—forces on the right have developed new ways to make sure that politicians still choose their voters, rather than the other way around. Although more American voters supported Hillary Clinton and Democratic candidates for the U.S. Senate and House of Representatives than their opponents in the 2016 election, aggressive Republican redrawing of congressional district lines—gerrymandering—has denied this majority its ability to elect the president or control Congress.

In the apportionment clause of Article I of the Constitution, the framers detailed how seats in the House of Representatives would be allocated as the nation grew. It has been understood by the Supreme Court to require that election districts for congressional, state, and local offices be drawn to include an equal number of people, or as near as "practicable" (for congressional districts), or "substantially" equal (for state and local districts). It means that districts must be close in population size to others in each state. The Constitution also sets a time frame for this process by requiring a count of the population every ten years—the census—which then provides the numbers for the apportionment of congressional districts among the states.[65] Applied in tandem with the Voting Rights Act, which was passed to ensure that minority voters would have an "effective" vote, the apportionment clause helps establish a fair way of distributing electoral power among the people.[66] While the reality of this promise has required much litigation and debate, few should disagree that "one person, one vote" should be the goal of our system.[67]

With the advent of complex algorithms and computer-driven models for drawing maps of congressional districts, partisans, especially those on the right, have used increasingly devious methods to gain more seats even without more votes. In recent years, operatives on the right have been able to manipulate district lines to deny the opposing Democratic Party, and minority voters, the right to an "effective" vote by drawing districts that enhanced the GOP electoral advantage. With the census and subsequent redistricting happening only every ten years, many political players on the left pay little attention because there's always something else that is more urgent. But the Right plays the long game: its funders and advocates have digested the message of the Powell Memo that consistent investment in infrastructure leads to control of power. For them, patience is a virtue that pays off generously in lasting legislative and policy victories. Jeff Timmer, a Michigan Republican who has worked to craft district lines in that state, likens redistricting to Halley's comet.

"It comes around on a recurring, predicable basis. It's great to be a Halley's comet expert when it comes around. But in between times, no one really has any use for it. You know, one of the inside secrets of politics is how critical redistricting is."[68]

In 1969, during the Vietnam War and the civil rights movement, when racial tensions were especially high in the South, Republican strategist Kevin Phillips had a Machiavellian insight: the Voting Rights Act could actually serve as a forceful weapon for Republicans in breaking the Democratic stronghold in the South. His theory was that black leaders would want districts that were primarily black, ensuring more blacks were elected as Democrats. Subsequently, racist white Democrats, seeing their party go from electing a phalanx of white Dixiecrats to electing African Americans, would shift their allegiance to the white Republican Party. Louis Menand of the *New Yorker* captured the strategy, writing, "The key to exploiting this shift in party alignment . . . was not to oppose the civil-rights movement but to force the Democratic Party to take ownership of it."[69] With white voters making up a larger share of the electorate, Republicans would consistently win most elections, along with a handful of African American Democrats. Twenty years later, Ben Ginsberg, serving as the lawyer for the Republican National Committee during the late 1980s, based his plan on what Phillips had proposed to the RNC in 1969: to draw maps in the South that would create a primarily African American Democratic Party and allow the Republicans to dominate the region by creating a few densely majority-minority districts that would in effect segregate the black vote into fewer districts, leaving the remainder open to Republicans.[70]

Ginsberg had a partner in Lee Atwater, George H.W. Bush's master strategist. Atwater had infamously developed racially charged advertising in favor of Bush, attacking his opponent

Michael Dukakis because a black convict, Willie Horton, had raped and killed a white woman while on furlough from a Massachusetts state prison when Dukakis was governor. The ad used racial imagery to make Horton as terrifying as possible for bigoted white voters, amplifying his dark skin color and his somewhat tenuous connection with Dukakis.[71] Nonetheless, Atwater was flexible and recognized that a tactical alliance with some African American political leaders might be very good for the Republicans. The black leaders got districts that would reliably elect black politicians, but Atwater knew Republicans would claim more districts overall. Anita Earls, a North Carolina civil rights lawyer and former executive director of the Southern Coalition for Social Justice in Durham, North Carolina, described the impact: "What's uniform across the South is that Republicans are using race as a central basis in drawing districts for partisan advantage. The bigger picture is to ultimately make the Democratic Party in the South be represented only by people of color."[72]

After the 1986 Supreme Court case *Thornburg v. Gingles*, Ginsberg and Atwater knew that the time was ripe to seize on Phillips's ideas. The case held that the Voting Rights Act required that minority voters be able to elect representatives of their choice in states with a history of racial-bloc voting.[73] Ginsberg explains the rationale: "We began looking at the data, and we saw that white Southern Democrats had dominated the redistricting process literally since the Civil War, and that had created underrepresentation for two groups, Republicans and minority voters. It was evident, especially to blacks and Republicans, that there was an alliance to build in the state legislatures that were going to be handling redistrictings."[74]

Ginsberg made a trek to the Congressional Black Caucus Foundation in 1990 to make a pitch for collaboration. "The fact is that minorities remain grossly underrepresented in Congress, state legislatures and local boards and commissions," he said to the assembled members. "The culprit is the gerrymander. . . . It has been done to Republicans . . . and to racial minority groups."[75] The Justice Department lawyers in charge of protecting minority voting rights jumped on board enthusiastically to help create majority-minority districts, doing outreach to community organizations and civil rights groups, and certainly, many more African Americans were able to win elections in the new districts. But in the process, the South as a whole became much more solid for Republicans. Some black leaders in the South were worried about just this outcome.

Two black North Carolina state legislators, Dan Blue and Toby Fitch, came to Washington to argue against a new redistricting plan for the state in 1991. "If blacks go too far they will find themselves confined to 'political reservations' with less political influence than they have today," said Fitch.[76] The new maps pushed as many blacks as possible into a few voting districts, making the suburbs and rural areas even whiter and safer for the GOP. Representation was segregated, with southern white Republicans and African American Democrats gaining more seats in Congress.

Today, it is impossible to disentangle the partisan advantage from the racist impulse that originally drove the gerrymandering; as African Americans overwhelmingly vote Democratic, the Republican Party and the Right have yet another reason to create districts that limit black voting strength. Journalist David Daley says that "the strategy became known as the unholy alliance. . . . Ginsberg had another name for it . . . Project Ratfuck."[77]

DRAW THE LINES, MAKE THE RULES

Michigan Chamber of Commerce president Bob LaBrant saw redistricting as a neglected arena for partisan gains long before many others. In the 1970s he had been working at the Chamber of Commerce in Appleton, Wisconsin, when he read the Powell Memo. He immediately agreed with Powell's arguments but saw the need to add a focus on elections, which was, surprisingly, something of a lacuna in Powell's memo. Although the chamber and other wealthy players quickly jumped into funding think tanks and litigation groups, it took a little longer for them to engage in direct political efforts despite LaBrant's forceful arguments. Once Tom Donahue took over the U.S. Chamber of Commerce in 1997, however, he was persuaded by LaBrant, and the chamber began to funnel large contributions to the Republican State Leadership Committee (RSLC), the organization leading the charge for Republican dominance of state legislatures.[78] Revealingly, LaBrant's memoir was titled PAC Man. Redistricting expert and journalist David Daley commented that "LaBrant recognized Karl Rove's dictum early on—you draw the lines, you make the rules—and figured out how to use the chamber's PAC to not just grab a seat at the table, but to help pay to rent the room."[79] LaBrant's philosophy was very direct: once a party has power, "you exercise it." If the other side has it, you try to take it away "under the cloak of good government."[80] LaBrant is right, and Democrats and the Left need to learn this lesson. Winning control of redistricting doesn't completely predetermine the outcome, but it certainly helps make sure you are in the game.

Karl Rove and his associate Chris Jankowski saw the advantage for Republicans—and an even better ratfuck—in tactically focusing the Right's fire hose of money to swing certain statehouses, which would then be able to gerrymander at will. In 2010, Rove laid out the REDMAP plan for all to see in an editorial in the Wall Street Journal. "Some of the most important contests this fall will be way down the ballot in communities like Portsmouth, Ohio, and West Lafayette, Ind., and neighborhoods like Brushy Creek in Round Rock, Texas, and Murrysville Township in Westmoreland County, Pa.," Rove wrote. "These are the state legislative races that will determine who redraws congressional district lines after this year's census, a process that could determine which party controls upwards of 20 seats and whether many other seats will be competitive."[81]

While Democrats contested these seats, their candidates did not get the equivalent support from donors or the party that their opponents got, even though these were, by Rove's design and public announcement, races in states where the statehouse could switch parties with only a few seats changing hands. The resulting maps would determine who controlled Congress for many years to come; by substituting Republican control for Democratic, the state legislatures would also be fertile ground for advancing voter suppression laws, locking in Republican dominance even more firmly. Rove noted, "Republican strategists are focused on 107 seats in 16 states. Winning these seats would give them control of drawing district lines for nearly 190 congressional seats."[82] Rove and Jankowski picked states where legislators, not independent commissions, drew the maps, where the party divide was nearly even, and where a Republican governor would sign a new plan, and they reached out to donors to fund the initiative. The RSLC, Rove's organizational partner, proudly promoted the REDMAP on its website, noting where a state was facing a loss of seats because of the census, and thus a heightened redistricting process.

To fund the initiative, the RSLC raised more than $30 million in 2009–10, and invested $18 million after Labor Day 2010 alone. Specifically, the RSLC did the following:

- Spent $1.4 million targeting four New York state senate seats, winning two and control of the New York state senate. (–2 congressional seats—because of census)

- Spent nearly $1 million in Pennsylvania House races, targeting and winning three of the toughest races in the state. (−1 congressional seat)
- Spent nearly $1 million in Ohio House races, targeting six seats, five of which were won by Republicans. Notably, President Obama carried five of these six legislative districts in 2008. (−2 congressional seats)
- Spent $1 million in Michigan working with the Michigan House Republican Campaign Committee and Michigan Republican Party to pick up twenty seats. (−1 congressional seat)
- Spent $750,000 in Texas as part of an effort that resulted in twenty-two House pickups. (+4 congressional seats)
- Spent $1.1 million in Wisconsin to take control of the state senate and assembly.
- Committed resources in Colorado (more than $550,000) and North Carolina (more than $1.2 million).
- Invested more than $3 million across a number of other states, including Illinois, Indiana, Iowa, Kentucky, Maine, Nevada, New Hampshire, New Jersey, Oregon, Tennessee, and Washington.[83]

Rove and Jankowski were extraordinarily successful. With a fairly small amount of money in the world of campaigns, they helped win enough seats to change the control of several key state legislatures, including Michigan, Ohio, Pennsylvania, and Wisconsin.[84] In 2012, the first test of the new maps, President Obama cruised to reelection over Mitt Romney and Democrats won twenty-three out of thirty-three Senate contests, but despite Democrats winning 1.4 million more votes nationwide, Republicans held thirty-three more seats in the House.[85]

The RSLC gloated, "President Obama won reelection in 2012

by nearly 3 points nationally, and banked 126 more electoral votes than Governor Mitt Romney. Democratic candidates for the U.S. House won 1.1 million more votes than their Republican opponents. But the Speaker of the U.S. House of Representatives is a Republican and presides over a 33-seat House Republican majority during the 113th Congress. How? One needs to look no farther than four states that voted Democratic on a statewide level in 2012, yet elected a strong Republican delegation to represent them in Congress: Michigan, Ohio, Pennsylvania and Wisconsin." As the RSLC report noted, while good candidate recruitment and funding were important, everything depended on the "district lines, and this was an area where Republicans had an unquestioned advantage." They felt confident about future elections after building a Republican "firewall."[86] And they were right to feel so confident.

Ryan Lizza and David Wasserman of the *New Yorker* studied the demographics of the House districts post-REDMAP. Reviewing their reporting, Daley noted

> Republican districts in 2012, after redistricting, had been drawn more white, even as national trends marched toward greater diversity. The average district won by a Republican in 2012 was 2 percent more white than it had been in 2010. Those 80 conservatives [who called for Boehner to link defunding Obamacare to a government shutdown] were elected from districts, on average, that were 75 percent white, compared to the national average of 63. In the 2012 presidential election, Obama defeated Romney by 4 percentage points. In the 80 districts held by the insurgent conservatives, Romney won by an average of 23 points. The congressmen—and 76 of the 80 were men—managed even larger victory margins, an average of 34 points.[87]

What was particularly depressing was the fact that in 2008, the electorate was more black and brown than ever before. President Obama won this constituency decisively, carrying 75 percent of the black, Latino, and Asian vote, which was 4 percent higher than in 2004.[88] These numbers had given added impetus to Rove's ratfuck, as he was determined to ensure these voters would not take the South from the Republican column.

Drawing maps is not that complicated. Computer programs do all the heavy lifting and can be used to shape fair and nonpartisan districts or to engineer rock-solid districts for a particular party. It's not a surprise that the latter approach has mostly won out. Voters have stronger identification with a party than before; that fact, combined with data about consumer preferences, social media use, race, and other census information makes it easy to shape districts to favor one party or the other, with district lines making sharp turns and cutting off areas as necessary: when district lines draw cartoon characters, lizards, or a drunken sailor, the picture is not accidental.[89] With maps drawn cleverly enough, even a bluish state can turn red. And the gerrymanders require Democrats to win supermajorities to overcome them. Nationwide, Democrats need an extra eight points to win a majority of House seats, and in individual states it is even greater. Sam Wang and Brian Remlinger of the Princeton Gerrymandering Project calculate that "in individual gerrymandered states such as North Carolina or Pennsylvania, Democrats need to win by 15 percentage points or more to have a shot at taking a majority."[90]

Former president Obama is now focused on redistricting, having founded a new group with former attorney general Eric Holder in 2017—the National Democratic Redistricting Committee (NDRC). That was not the focus of the president or the Democratic National Committee (DNC) in 2010, when Rove announced his REDMAP plan. (The party's resources were directed toward the 2012 presidential election, not the midterms, and the DNC was in a turf war with Obama's own organization, Organizing for America. Critics attribute Obama's apathy to his primary interest in building his own legacy and securing his own reelection rather than building the party.[91]) In any case the DNC was consumed with its own internal crises, including the leadership of Congresswoman Debbie Wasserman Schultz, who was a controversial leader within the party.[92]

Democrats basically ceded the ground in races that were going to determine control of state governments and therefore the apportionment of state and congressional districts. The progressive media was on outrage-overdrive about the *Citizens United* decision, a Supreme Court ruling that had unleashed corporate funding of campaigns, and paid scant attention to the fact that the Right had laid the groundwork to seize the redistricting process. Steve Israel, a Democratic congressman from New York who ran the Democratic Congressional Campaign Committee (DCCC) post-2010 midterms, accused Democrats of committing political malpractice in that cycle. Despite big congressional pickups in 2006 and 2008, Democrats "started losing state legislatures and governors across America—and that's what destroyed us in 2010 and 2012," said Israel. "Had we devoted resources to protecting Democrats in state Houses across America, the Republicans still would have won the majority in 2010. But we would have had a seat at the table in redistricting and we might have been able to take it away from them in 2012. The DNC, they just whistled past the graveyard."[93] Tom Reynolds, a Republican who represented New York in Congress and was the chairman of RED-MAP, commented, "The Obama team has done some amazing things, those guys are really something, but the Democrats plain got skunked on the state houses."[94]

Unlike many other Democrats, Israel also understands the

synergies Republicans have created by focusing on judges as well as legislators. Israel calls Republican plans to control the courts, statehouses, congressional districts, and Supreme Court a "quadruple gerrymander."[95] Partisan judges ensure that the gerrymandered districts survive court review. In North Carolina, for example, the Republican State Leadership Committee poured money into saving sitting justice Paul Newby, who was way behind Democrat Sam Ervin thirty days out from the election in 2012. The RSLC funds allowed Newby, who went on to eke out a win, to spend ten times as much on the race as Ervin, with much of that largesse concentrated in the final weeks. Newby promptly turned around and joined his colleagues in a 4–3 vote to uphold the maps Republicans had helped to create.[96]

In a truly vicious cycle, each round of redistricting under gerrymandered rules leads to greater gains for Republicans. With more safe districts and more members, the legislature can adopt even more advantageous maps and more onerous voting restrictions. In 2015, after its gerrymander, the Wisconsin state legislature adopted a string of voter suppression laws and unleashed even more dark money for campaigns.[97] Long a Democratic stronghold, Pennsylvania looked to be a lock for Democrats in 2010 with a seemingly invincible advantage of almost 1.2 million more registered Democrats than Republicans. The state had not gone for the Republican presidential candidate since 1988. In 2008, Democrats had won twelve of the nineteen seats in the state. But with Rove and Jankowski's REDMAP at work in 2010, the numbers were reversed, with twelve seats going to Republicans and only seven to Democrats. Once in control, the GOP made the district lines even better for themselves, packing Democrats into even fewer districts and garnering a thirteen-to-five advantage in the House in 2012, despite Obama winning the state and Democratic candidates getting more votes than Republicans.[98]

The media outlet RealClearPolitics called Pennsylvania's maps the "gerrymander of the decade." Republican mapmakers sliced and diced and spliced, breaking up districts and adding pieces to others in order to ensure a long-term hold on the seats.[99] David Daley describes how Democratic votes were "packed" into urban districts giving Democrats fewer seats and making sure there were many wasted votes. The amazing maps made one constituent describe her district as "Donald Duck kicking Goofy."[100] The new legislature, dominated by the Republicans, pushed for further restrictions on the right to vote. Ultimately, between the gerrymander, voter suppression, and a flood of campaign dollars, the state went to Donald Trump in 2016, toppling a major portion of what Hillary Clinton considered to be her "blue wall."

While some might say that this is simply politics and that "everyone does it," Republicans have used this strategy far more ruthlessly than ever before. Sam Wang of the Princeton Gerrymandering Project analyzed the election returns of 2012, coming to the now not startling conclusion that "both sides may do it, but one side does it more often." He looked at what would happen if votes cast actually resulted in winning elections. "In North Carolina, where the two-party House vote was 51 percent Democratic, 49 percent Republican, the average simulated delegation was seven Democrats and six Republicans. The actual outcome? Four Democrats, nine Republicans—a split that occurred in less than 1 percent of simulations. If districts were drawn fairly, this lopsided discrepancy would hardly ever occur."[101] Wang is a data guy, but what concerned him was that "gerrymandering is a major form of disenfranchisement. In the seven states where Republicans redrew the districts, 16.7 million votes were cast for Republicans and 16.4 million votes were cast for Democrats. This elected 73 Republicans and 34 Democrats." This meant that almost 2 million voters did not have their votes count.[102] Most of those voters were Democrats. "The outcome was already cooked in, if you will, because of the way the districts were drawn," according to John McGlennon, who teaches government and public policy at William & Mary.[103]

THROWING THE RING IN THE VOLCANO

Activists on the left and in the Democratic Party have begun to wake up after sleeping through sustained losses that undercut representation and progressive policymaking. From what was a fraught relationship between party leaders and voting rights advocates because of their historically divergent goals for districts and the "unholy alliance" crafted by Ben Ginsberg and Karl Rove in the South, there is now much more agreement over strategy around redistricting. Recognizing how much ground the Left has to make up, Obama's attorney general Eric Holder has set up a group to focus solely on redistricting in favor of Democrats. Holder's group, the National Democratic Redistricting Committee, sees victory in the next election cycle as preventing or ending "trifectas," where Republicans control both houses of the state legislature and the governorship. The organization is targeting presidential battleground states where Republicans have had complete control, including Ohio and Florida, as well as key states with some Democratic power, such as Minnesota and Colorado, which need to be defended against Republican efforts to block a Democratic role in mapmaking.[104]

On the legal front, several challenges to racial and partisan gerrymandering have led to court victories and others are in the pipeline. In 2016 and 2017, litigants sued to block the maps in North Carolina, Virginia, and Alabama, resulting in decisions that the Republican-controlled legislatures had unconstitutionally used race to draw congressional and state legislative maps. It may not herald the end of the original ratfuck, but the trend of legal decisions has certainly reduced its bite.[105]

In 2018 the Supreme Court considered a direct attack on the partisan gerrymander. In *Gill v. Whitford*, the plaintiffs argued that the Wisconsin plan adopted after the 2010 census was so extreme in skewing electoral maps in favor of Republicans that it violates equal protection. While the Supreme Court has recognized that extreme gerrymandering could amount to a constitutional violation, the court has not been able to articulate a standard to measure when a map goes too far. Advocates of redistricting reform believe that the data makes it clear that the courts can and must address the problem—as technology continues to improve, the courts can exacerbate partisan gerrymandering or fix it. They believe that the Supreme Court could choose among "several simple standards to examine the fairness of maps," allowing lower courts to refine its application.[106] In the *Gill* case, the plaintiffs for the first time presented the justices with a way to evaluate when one side goes too far, suggesting a formula to test when too many votes have been wasted. Law professor Nicholas Stephanopoulos, who devised the formula, described it this way:

> To grasp the efficiency gap, you have to realize that partisan gerrymandering is always carried out in one of two ways. Either a party *cracks* (that is, splits) the other party's voters among many districts in which their preferred candidates lose by relatively narrow margins. Or a party *packs* the other side's voters into a few districts in which their preferred candidates win by overwhelming margins. Both cracking and packing produce *wasted votes* that don't contribute to a candidate's election. In the case of cracking, these are all of the votes cast for a losing candidate. In the case of packing, they're all of the votes cast for a winning

candidate in excess of the 50 percent (plus one) needed
for victory. The efficiency gap is simply one party's total
wasted votes, minus the other party's total wasted votes,
divided by all of the votes cast in the election.[107]

The Supreme Court punted on the substantive issue for the
moment, sending the case back to the lower court to address
whether the plaintiffs have standing. In his opinion, Chief Justice John Roberts found that the plaintiffs had not proven that,
in addition to harm to the Democratic Party, they had suffered
harm as individual voters. He wrote that "not a single plaintiff
sought to prove that he or she lives in a [gerrymandered] district." With Justice Anthony Kennedy's departure, the road forward may be more difficult. Nonetheless, lawmakers and voting
rights advocates were left with some hope that they might prevail in their next appearance before the Supreme Court—Justice
Elena Kagan helpfully laid out a road map for advocates in how
to structure the next lawsuit based on violations of the plaintiffs'
First Amendment rights.[108]

Even if the U.S. Supreme Court doesn't ultimately invalidate
gerrymandered districts, state constitutions present another
route to eliminate the practice. Pennsylvania's highest court,
after gaining a Democratic majority, found the Republican map
unconstitutional based on the state charter.[109] Professor Josh
Douglas, an election law expert at the University of Kentucky,
explains that almost every state constitution provides protection
for the right to vote, unlike the federal one. Where courts are
friendly or at least impartial, this route is being explored by litigators as another way to bring an end to red maps.[110] Where good-
government interests and Democratic operatives come together
is a shared belief in fair maps. Political strategist Tom Bonier says,
"It's hard to argue against transparency and public input. But

[the operatives] also know that fair maps would produce a much better landscape for Democrats."[111]

And if legal challenges aren't successful, we need to support legislative and ballot-initiative campaigns by investing financial and grassroots resources. In twenty-six states, citizens can force a nonpartisan process for drawing district lines on reluctant legislators by moving ballot initiatives. Twelve of those states already use a commission system, and in several others reformers have a real opportunity to push the change forward. In California, the voters demanded an independent commission; similarly in Iowa, Florida, and Arizona, fed-up constituents moved the issue via ballot initiative when they recognized that the state legislators would never make the necessary changes. In May 2018, Ohio voters circumvented the recalcitrant state legislature to approve a ballot measure.[112] Despite the NDRC's focus on helping Democrats, Eric Holder recognizes that a nonpartisan commission won by ballot initiative is likely the best and longest-lasting fix, saying "In some ways, that's the best way to do it, but state constitutions don't allow that to happen in all 50 states."[113] In the states without an initiative option, it may well prove more difficult. But there is growing bipartisan support for restrictions on gerrymandering from some Republicans, including John McCain, John Kasich, Arnold Schwarzenegger, and others, as well as from a group of current and former members of Congress and state legislators who signed an amicus brief in the *Gill* case.[114]

Why should the Left want to join with good-government groups in this effort rather than simply pushing Democrats to gerrymander in response? There are several reasons: First, if we are as cynical as the Right, we will turn off voters who will think that both sides are equally corrupt. Republicans want to deconstruct government, so their behavior is consistent with their ideology;

we believe government should work for people, so we can't be as shameless. In any case, this approach is popular with our base, which is pushing it forward. Allegra Kirkland of *Talking Points Memo* observes that "these grassroots activists appear motivated as much by a commitment to small 'd' democratic principles as by a partisan desire to maximize Democratic gains."[115]

Gerrymandering helps *incumbents*, not progressives, so we have to remember that the Democrats gerrymander to keep themselves in power, not necessarily to serve the people—and just like Republicans, they have engaged in map drawing that eliminates the political power of certain groups who might vote for a primary challenger. In the short term, getting more Democrats elected will help us get better districts, but then we need to push for a nonpartisan process. We need to keep the Democrats honest and challenge them if they are not. And, as a tactical matter, it would be harder for a new Republican majority in a state to undo nonpartisan redistricting than to rewrite a partisan plan in their own favor. Kathay Feng, national redistricting director at good-government group Common Cause says, "I analogize this to *The Lord of the Rings*. You gotta take this ring away from them and throw it in the volcano. The power to draw lines for the next ten years to benefit yourself, your party and your buddies is very tempting to hold onto. And it brings out ugly monsters in both parties." Throwing the ring away, Feng says, "is the only way we can move beyond this tug-of-war."[116]

But redistricting happens only after the census, and if the census is flawed, all the efforts to create fair districts after the fact will be wasted. High on the list of dirty tricks by the Right is the attempt to add a question about citizenship to the 2020 census, which, as Michael Scherer wrote in the *Washington Post*, "could shift the nation's balance of political power from cities to more rural communities over the next decade and give Republicans a new advantage in drawing electoral boundaries."[117] The question, likely to make Latinos more reluctant to participate, would ensure an undercount, leading to a loss of political representation as well as federal benefits. In addition to the new question, the Trump administration has severely underfunded and understaffed the Census Bureau.[118] Unlike in 2010, however, there is already a group of advocates and funders focused on both political and legal responses to the Right's shenanigans, including lawsuits to expose government wrongdoing (or maybe more accurately "nondoing") and mobilization by groups like MoveOn. Nonetheless, the challenge is daunting.

A reform that would address wasted votes nationally is the national popular vote. Using the Constitution's compact clause, which allows states to enter into agreements, the National Popular Vote bill, introduced in many states, would award the presidency to the candidate with the highest popular vote total. In this way, a group of states could in effect render the Electoral College obsolete. New York, California, and Illinois might once again matter to politicians when making policy—not just for raising money. Under the Constitution, states determine how to allocate their own electoral votes and can choose to assign their votes to the national popular vote winner. So far, the popular vote bill has passed in eleven states, accounting for a total of 165 electoral votes. Once the popular vote gains 270 or more electoral votes, the compact will take effect. No longer could the presidency go to the loser of the popular vote as it did for Bush and Trump. Candidates would thus be forced to campaign everywhere, not just in battleground states, making it less attractive to try to rig elections in those heretofore key states. By giving the views of small and rural states much more weight than those of larger, more urban and more diverse ones, the Electoral College—like the U.S. Senate—is anti-democratic and anti-Democratic, not to mention a holdover from slavery, designed to ensure slave-holding states could count their slaves toward their share of electors (the infamous "three-fifths compromise"). "It's embarrassing," said Paul Finkelman, visiting law professor at the University of Saskatchewan in Canada. "I think if most Americans knew what the origins of the Electoral College is, they would be disgusted."[119]

So it will take a mix of approaches to slay the gerrymander—continued legal battles, a push for nonpartisan commissions, and adopting various reforms including multimember districts and the National Popular Vote. But what we need most of all is for Americans to care that they are being manipulated and pandered to by politicians, and to vote in all elections and make their voices heard.

THE DARK-MONEY SWAMP

In the 1970s, the business community began to get aggressive about building its political influence through campaign contributions. Justin Dart was an early evangelist. As chairman of the board of Dart Industries, a conglomerate of drug companies as well as Tupperware, Dart worked to get corporate America to bulk up its campaign spending. Addressing a conference of corporate executives in 1978, he urged his fellow business leaders to create political action committees (PACs) to develop lobbying capacity and to leverage the voices of their workers and shareholders to take political action in line with the company's interests. Dart told the group that a "company that doesn't have a PAC is either apathetic, unintelligent, or you've got a death wish."[120] Dart was far to the right—a staunch opponent of the New Deal and the regulatory state—and recognized that his voice would ring louder in Washington if accompanied by a check.[121] George H.W. Bush also spoke to the business executives, exhorting them to use their resources to support candidates who were pro-deregulation.[122] The Chamber of Commerce, along with other business associations on the far right, had organized a series of such meetings to build the political strength of corporate America. For those business leaders inculcated to believe in absolute free marketism, as pushed by economist Milton Friedman, the Heritage Foundation, and other mouthpieces for dismantling government, this was a clarion call. Justin Fox, a columnist for Bloomberg Opinion and author of business books, explains why business leaders tend to be so pro-deregulation, even if it might be bad for American business in the long term: "I don't think anyone has come up with an argument for or description of better business behavior that has anything like the elegance and power of the economists' 'incentives matter.' As long as it remains possible to get rich via less-than-upstanding behavior, and enjoy those riches, a lot of people in business will choose that path."[123] Corporate America did indeed choose that path, with Justin Dart as their pied piper to the bottom of the swamp.

After a ruling by the Federal Election Commission in 1975 that corporations could solicit their workers for political contributions to a company PAC, business leaders saw an opening to make a real impact on government. Prior to the decision, the companies could spend only corporate treasury money to solicit PAC donations from shareholders and top leadership; now they were free to go beyond that to all employees. Historian Kim Phillips-Fein describes Dart's methods as follows:

> Every year Dart Industries' corporate headquarters would bombard the company's eight hundred executives with letters, pamphlets, reports, and copies of political speeches delivered by Dart, while also organizing "economic

education" meetings to give employees information on political issues. Dart informed his managers and executives that he personally gave the legal maximum of $5,000 a year and recommended that anyone earning over $100,000 contribute at least 1 percent of his salary. If his executives did not take out their checkbooks after receiving the mailings, Dart would follow up with a telephone call. "If they don't give, they get a sell," he told the *Wall Street Journal*, meaning that if they turned down the initial requests, he gave them his personal pitch.[124]

Dart and the chamber had a significant impact. At the beginning of the 1970s, big businesses and business trade associations did not have many public affairs offices, lobbyists, or PACs, but by the end of the decade that had changed. In short order, the corporate world built out an infrastructure to influence public opinion, legislation, and political candidates, with corporate PACs growing particularly quickly—from 89 in 1974 to 821 in 1978. And the chamber encouraged its local chapters to develop their lobbying capacity. By 1981, the chamber had increased its PACs, known as congressional action committees, from 1,400 to 2,700.[125] And of course the increase in the number of PACs meant that the sheer amount of business giving had grown enormously, with these PACs spending five times more on races for Congress in the late 1980s than they had in the late 1970s, eclipsing spending by labor unions.[126]

Business leaders began to raise money individually, with executives bundling many contributions from other managers in their companies to amplify political clout. They also began to fund cross-industry PACs such as the Business-Industry Political Action Committee and the National Association of Business Political Action Committees, which set up shop in 1977.[127]

Corporate executives coupled the financial support for Republican politicians with "grassroots" activism, organizing internally by cajoling employees, shareholders, allied companies, and those in similar businesses to generate calls and letters to DC politicians in favor of legislation. Companies also worked to ensure that top executives cultivated relationships with elected officials so that they could leverage "friendships" to get special treatment, or at least a private hearing for their point of view. It became a given that running a company required understanding and competing in the arena of lobbying and backscratching.[128]

But straight-ahead corporate donations weren't enough, especially with the limits on donations adopted by Congress after Watergate. So corporate America decided to try to get rid of those limits, funding a strategy to have the restrictions branded as a violation of free speech, pushing wide the door opened by the *Buckley v. Valeo* case in 1976, in which the Supreme Court had acknowledged that giving a contribution was a form of speech, even while it upheld some of the post-Watergate limits.[129] A group of young conservatives immediately saw the benefits to an anti-regulatory agenda of stretching the First Amendment doctrine to accommodate all sorts of business activities, especially efforts to affect elections and influence politicians.

Writing in the *Washington Monthly*, Haley Sweetland Edwards noted that "beginning in the early 1970s, a new crop of conservative think tanks, clubs, and legal funds, like the Pacific Legal Foundation, the Heritage Foundation, and what later became the CATO Institute, funded by the Koch brothers, formed alliances with the U.S. Chamber of Commerce and other powerful trade groups, in an effort to push an anti-regulatory, pro-business agenda, with expanded corporate free speech rights as a key weapon."[130] The culmination of this work, which included scholarly writing, legal advocacy, and a communications strategy, was

Citizens United and a related case, *SpeechNow.org v. Federal Election Commission*,[131] in which the Supreme Court and the DC Circuit Court of Appeals, respectively, dismantled controls on direct donations by corporations and independent expenditures by corporations and wealthy individuals and other special interests. The rulings taken together opened a gusher of spending on campaign ads, social media, and other communications tools to support or oppose candidates, ushering in dark money and super PACs—a form of campaign committee that is allowed to raise unlimited funding from businesses, other organizations, and wealthy people, so long as it doesn't coordinate with parties or candidates—and killing off most of what was left of campaign finance restrictions enacted after Watergate and in the Bipartisan Campaign Reform Act (better known as the "McCain-Feingold Act").[132] Independent spending in congressional elections by nonparty groups was nearly fourteen times higher in 2016 than 2008, the last election before *Citizens United*.[133]

In particular, these cases birthed the weaponized 501(c)(4), the tax code designation for a nonprofit organization that has been established to serve social welfare exclusively. Although they are allowed to participate in some political activity without losing their tax-exempt status, 501(c)(4) groups cannot make those activities their "primary activity,"[134] meaning that their spending on politics must be less than 50 percent of their budget. There's never been much clarity about how to interpret that rule, however, with the result that many of these dark groups exceed those limits with impunity. Some of them may actually do nothing *but* engage in politics, and they've gotten away with it. The Center for Responsive Politics (CRP) has followed the money trail, documenting the explosive growth in these organizations after *Citizens United* and *SpeechNow*. According to the CRP, "These organizations can receive unlimited corporate, individual, or union contributions that they do not have to make public, and though their political activity is supposed to be limited, the IRS—which has jurisdiction over these groups—by and large has done little to enforce those limits. Partly as a result, spending by organizations that do not disclose their donors has increased from less than $5.2 million in 2006 to well over $300 million in the 2012 presidential cycle and more than $174 million in the 2014 midterms."[135] Both parties get some support from these groups, but the scale tips strongly in favor of Republicans. In 2016, the tax-exempt groups—including 501(c)(6) groups like chambers of commerce, business leagues, and trade boards; 501(c)(5) labor organizations; and 501(c)(4)s—favored Republicans by $140 million to $64 million; in 2012 it was $270 million to $58 million.[136]

Dark money has infected state elections and legislative activity as well as national politics. Mississippi Supreme Court Justice Jim Kitchens thought his 2016 race for reelection against Court of Appeals Judge Kenny Griffis was an old-fashioned campaign on the issues and not a character assassination. "I don't know anything bad about him and if I did, I wouldn't tell," Kitchens told his local newspaper. "This race is about two good guys." But soon enough the election was about the agenda of a shadowy outside group, the conservative Center for Individual Freedom (CFIF). CFIF upended the placid judicial election by buying airtime for an ad claiming that Kitchens was on the side of "child predators." The ad attacked Kitchens for rulings in a case involving "three monsters" who "repeatedly raped a 4-year-old girl" and another case where the defendant "pleaded guilty to beating a 2-year-old girl to death," calling on viewers to ask Kitchens to "stop siding with child predators." CFIF also ran ads in other races, including one in Louisiana attacking a candidate for overturning the convictions of "a repeat child molester" and a "man found guilty of attempted forcible rape."[137]

But despite its heavy spending on ads like these, CFIF's real interest was protecting corporations against liability for harming the public, with its initial funding coming from Big Tobacco, which supported Griffis's more pro-business stance. Running ads about child molesters is more conducive to turning voters than spots thanking a judge for letting companies escape the consequences of illegally dumping toxic waste in groundwater.[138]

Conservative "charities" and major donors have allied with political activists to flout the letter and spirit of the tax law with little to no consequence. In a lengthy investigation into the David Horowitz Freedom Center, *Washington Post* reporters Robert O'Harrow Jr. and Shawn Boburg detailed the dense entanglement of allegedly charitable institutions and partisan politics. "The Freedom Center has declared itself a 'School for Political Warfare,'" wrote O'Harrow and Boburg, "and it is part of a loose nationwide network of like-minded charities linked together by ideology, personalities, conservative funders and websites, including the for-profit Breitbart News. Horowitz's story shows how charities have become essential to modern political campaigns, amid lax enforcement of the federal limits on their involvement in politics, while taking advantage of millions of dollars in what amount to taxpayer subsidies."[139]

Horowitz's school for political warfare was funded by the Olin and Bradley Foundations and the Scaife family, all integral in building and sustaining other parts of the conservative infrastructure. The Freedom Center provided a home for those who wanted to wage war against the political left, "multiculturalism," and Islam, including Stephen Miller, Jeff Sessions, Ann Coulter, and Steve Bannon. With a shared belief that immigration was the single biggest problem America faced and that an outside anti-elite candidate could speak to disgruntled white Americans, the Freedom Center stepped up its direct political engagement during the 2016 election, attacking Hillary Clinton, denouncing the "Never Trumpers," and working in tandem with Breitbart News and Bannon's nonprofit Government Accountability Institute. Horowitz chortled later to the *Post* reporters how proud he was to have such an influence on both the staff and the policies of the Trump White House.[140] So much for the requirement that politics not be the "primary activity" of nonprofits.

Under President Obama, the IRS made noises about tackling a rewrite of the regulation to make it clearer what counts as social welfare and allowing the IRS more ability to police groups that become too partisan. But even raising the issue met ferocious resistance from groups on the right, which claimed that the IRS was targeting only those groups that leaned right. In an outrageous maneuver, in addition to squelching the effort to tighten the regulation, some House Republicans tried to impeach Obama's IRS commissioner John Koskinen. Koskinen, a faithful public servant who, among other accomplishments, had successfully ensured that the new millennium—Y2K—would not disrupt computer systems controlling our most sensitive functions, took on the task of managing an agency in disarray. The alleged scandal occurred *before* Koskinen began his service at the IRS, and a subsequent report by the IRS's inspector general found that it actually gave *equal scrutiny to left-leaning groups*. Nevertheless, the Right was so enraged that the House Freedom Caucus demanded Koskinen's head. Ultimately, the impeachment resolution was deflected by the House leadership, but it nonetheless betrays the take-no-prisoners approach of the Right. U.S. history has never witnessed the impeachment of a subcabinet-level official, and there had not been a cabinet member in 140 years who had been subject to an impeachment process. Constitutional law professors warned that the Koskinen impeachment resolution would "seriously injure our constitutional system."[141]

While the vote failed, it nevertheless sent a clear signal to agencies not to enforce the law in a way that inconveniences the Koch brothers. Some House Republicans continue to push for legislation that would actually bar the IRS from clarifying the 501(c)(4) definition; these legislators want to go even further and allow churches to engage fully in electioneering. In May 2017, President Trump signed the Consolidated Appropriations Act, 2017, which included a prohibition on rewriting the 501(c)(4) rules.[142] Because of a parliamentary challenge by Democrats, the Republican tax bill did not include a repeal of the 1954 Johnson Amendment, which until now has barred tax-exempt churches, charities, and foundations under Section 501(c)(3) of the tax code from supporting candidates.[143] But it is still on the agenda. The religious Right has long desired the repeal of that prohibition so they can get even more directly involved in campaigns. The *Washington Post* Editorial Board was appropriately critical of the effort.

> What the House bill really amounts to is throwing open an entirely new channel for campaign money to politicize churches, charities and foundations. Today, so-called super PACs are a massive force in politics, spending more than $1 billion in the 2016 election cycle. Such super PAC donations must be disclosed to the Federal Election Commission and are not tax-deductible. What if these donors are tempted to give their money to a 501(c)3 organization that beckons with a tax deduction and no disclosure? The givers won't hold back. Churches and church-affiliated groups generally don't even have to file IRS returns, so there will be no information about who these contributors are. Other 501(c)3 groups do file, but the donors are not disclosed to the public. The politicized churches, charities and founda-

tions could become the latest vessels for dark-money politics.[144]

The answer to this problem is substantively easy—clarify and
enforce the 501(c)(4) rules and don't change the restrictions on
501(c)(3)s. The politics are harder—but only because the Right
focuses on these arcane provisions and devotes resources to them,
while the Left doesn't provide consistent financial support for
structural battles. If we can muster the willpower to fund a strong
campaign to address these structural problems, donors and activists on the left who care about wealth inequality and climate
change, about abortion restrictions and LGBTQ rights, would
see more success in those areas. But those victories are dependent on us making sure the playing field isn't tilted against us.

Business does not neglect Democrats entirely. To the contrary,
with the fund-raising imperative for political candidates, many
Democrats eagerly solicit business PACs and corporate leaders.
Part of this is to maximize funds: there are lots of business lobbyists in Washington and state capitals, while small donors have
to be recruited retail, one by one, and $100 contributions don't
add up fast. While the business community tends to reward the
Republican Party, it donates to individual Democrats to cultivate
votes on key issues and to gain allies who can help forestall regulatory moves. It's not a secret that Democrats have often cast the
deciding vote against a progressive initiative or for a major tax cut
for millionaires; even more commonly, they derail or water down
good policies and, when they announce support for Republican
measures, help make legislation designed to benefit big business
look bipartisan.[145] Donations by lobbyists and corporate interests
are almost always hiding behind those votes. As a result, Democratic leaders often veer away from strong populist legislation.
They don't want to undercut their fund-raising by chasing away

lobbyists entirely. But they're never going to win this game in the
long run unless they become Republicans themselves. Certainly,
in the short term, corporate contributions provide some of the
gas that runs the campaign engine, and Democrats will take it.
But in the long term, if we want a progressive party, and not two
corporate front groups, we, the grassroots, need to push for other
solutions. And as the Center for Responsive Politics data makes
crystal clear, the Left has been eclipsed in the dark-money game
with the vast sums going to conservative 501(c)(4)s and progressive groups left with crumbs.

In an insightful law review article, U.S. District Judge Lynn
Adelman pondered how Wisconsin Democrats had lost their way
on campaign finance reform, with bitter consequences for their
electoral success. Adelman, himself a former Wisconsin state
senator, asked,

> But why did the Democrats, who had enacted the reforms
> [in Wisconsin] and had been in the majority ever since,
> let the system atrophy? To some extent, it was a case of
> state legislators putting what they believed was in their
> personal interest ahead of any loyalty they may have had
> to campaign finance reform. . . . Many Democratic legisla-
> tors, however, just became too comfortable raising money
> from special interest groups, particularly business interest.
> They failed to recognize that competing with Republicans
> for business campaign contributions was a game they were
> ultimately going to lose. Similarly, they failed to perceive
> that by making special interest money less important, cam-
> paign finance reform was in their party's long-term inter-
> est.[146]

The same must be said for the party on the national level.

THE DEATH KNELL OF PROGRESSIVE CAMPAIGNS

In 2003, the *New Yorker*'s Nicholas Lemann probed Karl Rove on whether it would be "the death knell of the Democratic Party" for the Right to go after three important financial supports for the left: trial lawyers, Jews, and the labor movement. Lemann posited that "one could systematically disable all three, by passing tort-reform legislation that would cut off the trial lawyers' incomes, by tilting pro-Israel in Middle East policy and thus changing the loyalties of big Jewish contributors, and by trying to shrink the part of the labor force which belongs to the newer, and more Democratic, public-employee unions." The Bush administration pursued all three approaches.[147] Republicans haven't deviated from the playbook since then, especially as the attack on unions and trial lawyers aligns so well with their pro-corporate agenda.

To help bring down unions, conservatives took aim at their ability to organize, making it harder to find and keep members. In 2011, Wisconsin governor Scott Walker and the Republican legislature took on public employee unions in an attempt to kneecap the labor movement. Conveniently, labor law scholars Benjamin Sachs and Daryl Levinson note, "the new restrictions exempted all the unions that had endorsed the Republican Governor in the previous election." The GOP regarded the effort as a pilot project for the nation. According to Wisconsin's Republican senate majority leader, "If we win this battle, and the money is not there under the auspices of the unions . . . President Obama is going to have a . . . much more difficult time getting elected."[148] Scholars who have analyzed the data found that so-called right-to-work laws have pushed down the Democratic presidential candidate's vote by 3.5 percent—more than enough to tip the balance to the Right in the last three defeats.[149]

But it is not just through state law changes that conservatives hope to destroy unions. They have also sought to use the Constitution to strike a decisive blow. In June 2018, the Supreme Court decided a case that seeks to put a dagger through the heart of collective bargaining. In *Janus v. American Federation of State, County, and Municipal Employees, Council 31*, the Supreme Court found that public employee unions may not charge a fee to non-union beneficiaries of their representation, even though they receive higher wages and benefits and assistance in workplace disputes because of the union. Right-wing legal groups challenged the fair-share fees as a violation of the First Amendment as a way to impose "right to work" on everyone in the country. Sachs points out that this policy could have "massive implications for the balance of political power in the country. A decision in *Janus* that agency-fee agreements violate the First Amendment . . . foist[s] onto public sector unions a type of free-rider challenge that most organizations cannot withstand. And, as Karl Rove pointed out long ago, if you want to kill the Democratic Party, you can get pretty far by hobbling the unions."[150]

As for trial lawyers, another traditional source of support for progressive candidates and groups, the Right has taken aim at the ability to win lawsuits against corporations. Not only do these restrictions limit trial lawyers' ability to fund campaigns, they harm victims of corporate malfeasance as well: no class actions, no recovery for most low-wage workers whose wages have been illegally docked by an employer, no recompense for a consumer whose cell phone doesn't work as promised.

And while a reflexively pro-Israel policy has become a plank of the Republican platform, this issue has served more to galvanize the Christian Right than the American Jewish community.[151] Other issues, from the anti-Semitism of certain Trump supporters to domestic political issues, have served to keep most Jews with the Democratic Party, where they remain a strong source of funding.[152]

CHRISTIANS AND CAPITAL FORMATION

Richard Viguerie, who pioneered direct-mail fund-raising campaigns to assist candidates and conservative organizations in the 1970s, was a brilliant strategist who helped build a previously unthinkable link between the religious Right and politicians. Along with Jerry Falwell and Paul Weyrich, he set up the Moral Majority to push free market philosophy to evangelicals. Of course, they fulminated against abortion and for school prayer, but these New Right leaders also wanted to engage conservative religious people in the fight against social welfare legislation and government regulation of business and for Milton Friedman's economics.[153]

Viguerie's genius was in recognizing that the white ethnic working class—people of Eastern European stock or from Italian or Irish Catholic families—could be brought into the Right's camp because of their social conservatism. By appealing to them on issues such as crime, sexual mores, and fraying social values, as well as preying on their suspicion of media and cultural elites, Viguerie believed, the white ethnic working class could be severed from their unions and the Democratic Party; the workers would line up with the bosses.[154] Viguerie knew that social issues, not abstract economic reports, win elections even if the goal remained advancing the interests of American corporations. Addressing a business audience, Viguerie's partner Paul Weyrich explained, "We talk about issues that people care about, like gun control, abortion, taxes, and crime. Yes, they're emotional issues, but that's better than talking about capital formation."[155] The Chamber of Commerce got it, putting money into conservative social groups because those organizations' ability to speak to voters about issues such as abortion, prayer, the Equal Rights Amendment, and crime could be a bridge to speaking to them about economic policy.[156]

Ronald Reagan imbibed this lesson. He spoke to white working families about busing, states' rights, and "values issues" like abortion, and when he talked about the economy he avoided abstract or academic language. Racism, cloaked in "traditional values," historian Kim Phillips-Fein says, was a formula first advanced by Barry Goldwater in 1964 to "appeal to white working-class voters afraid of the integration of their schools and neighborhoods by using the language of market idealism combined with resentment."[157] The marriage of social conservatism, racial signaling, and business interests helped birth the Reagan Democrat.

After the 1954 Supreme Court decision in *Brown v. Board of Education* finding segregation of public schools unconstitutional, conservative whites rushed to establish so-called Christian schools that would not have to comply with integration. The number of these private schools, designed to avoid desegregation, skyrocketed: from 150 Christian schools in the early 1950s, the number shot up to approximately 18,000 in the next several decades. But in 1978, the IRS issued regulations to curb those schools, which had been established primarily to avoid enrolling black students. These regulations lit a match under the evangelical movement.[158] Across the conservative movement, from evangelicals to anti-regulatory businesses, leaders came together to challenge the new rules. Weyrich later credited the controversy with being the spark that really set the evangelical movement on fire, more than the Equal Rights Amendment or abortion.[159] This was a formative moment for the Right, which was able to make taxes an issue for social conservatives, to the benefit of the wealthy and corporate America.

The awakening of the evangelical movement over the tax issue helped create a new and powerful ally for the business community. From 1994 to 2002, the magazine *Campaigns & Elections* documented the increasing strength of religious groups in the

Republican Party, reporting that in 1994 thirty-one state Republican parties were under "moderate" or "strong" control of the Christian Right, but by 2002 that had grown to forty-four. And the churches fed bodies into get-out-the-vote efforts.[160] The business leaders saw it was to their benefit to make common cause on social issues to get the evangelicals on board with their economic agenda.

For business, the partnership could not have been more beneficial. The pact did not include addressing the economic needs of these voters, and, as Jacob Hacker and Paul Pierson have written, "political figures . . . could be relied upon to either deflect attention away from economic issues or assure supporters that the threats to their economic security came from liberals and Democrats."[161] This allowed the Republican Party to become quite extreme on the economy without paying a price, as working-class whites became disengaged from the Democrats and shared the social agenda of the increasingly right-wing Republicans. With huge resources pouring in from the extremely wealthy and from corporate PACs to support infrastructure, and the influx of new voters driven by social concerns more than economic ones, the party could cater its economic program to its donors, and its social policy to its voters.[162] A master stroke, by attacking unions' political strength, the Right undermined both Democrats and the fight for economic redistribution. This strategic alliance between business and the Christian Right drove working-class voters into supporting a party antagonistic to their own economic interests.

DRAINING THE SWAMP

The best defense against this massive influx of money into the campaign system and the attacks on progressive sources of financial support would be a different Supreme Court. With that solution off the table for now, several approaches to address-ing this broken system remain. We can change how campaigns are funded by pushing for public financing for federal, state, and local elections. One appealing approach is for a system of matching funds for small-donor contributions. After all, it costs a lot of money to run for office and few people are financially situated to be able to give money. That means that elected offi-cials and candidates spend a lot of time with a few people, who bend their ears on the issues that matter to them—and have fat wallets. With a small-donor match program, politicians would actually have to spend time with a lot of other people who have a stake in the outcome of policymaking but not a lot of cash.

Probably most achievable is greater disclosure of the sources of campaign cash and independent expenditures that fund stealth attack ads. In their book *It's Even Worse Than It Looks*, Norm Ornstein of the American Enterprise Institute and Thomas Mann of the Brookings Institution are emphatic that we must "aggressively try to restore the effectiveness of two provisions of the law the Court affirmed in *Citizens United*—(1) disclosure, and (2) the separation of independent expenditure groups from the candidates and campaigns they support." To do so, we need to know who is actually funding these groups and we need much stronger enforcement of the prohibition on these groups coordi-nating with candidates and parties.[163]

Knowing that corporations are funding anti-gay candidates or that a group called "Americans for Cleaner Air" is actually a 501(c)(4) set up by coal companies would allow progressives to organize counterattacks, including boycotts of companies, or to attack candidates' environmental records if they take money from coal's front group.[164] The Campaign Legal Center describes the rationale for requiring backer disclosure as helping voters evaluate claims made in advertising: "Members of the NRA or the Brady Campaign to Prevent Gun Violence, or any citizen, will have different views about the reliability of an ad if they know that a pro- or anti-gun group paid for it. Ads about ciga-rette taxes may be seen as more or less reliable if you know they were paid for by tobacco companies or anti-smoking groups."[165]

Most of this money does in fact come from groups like the NRA, not the Brady Campaign. The NRA wields its clout in the dark, spending most of its political largesse on ads it runs itself rather than donations to political candidates. Reporters Eric Lip-ton and Alexander Burns explained in the *New York Times* the logic behind the spending.

> The N.R.A. spent $20 million . . . on ads and other cam-paign tactics intended to persuade voters to reject Hillary Clinton and an additional $11 million to support Donald J. Trump—money that is not marked down as a direct contribution to Mr. Trump, because the N.R.A. spent the cash on its own. At the state level, the N.R.A. also spends much more on these independent expenditures than on direct contributions to candidates. Expenditures like these are the area of real growth for the N.R.A.: At the federal and state levels, overall independent spending by the group jumped from $9.3 million in the 2009 election cycle to at least $55 million in 2016, according to an analysis by the National Institute on Money in State Politics.[166]

And the pro-gun candidate doesn't have to report any of that money. Even though it far exceeds the amount the NRA could donate, it's all legal—that is, unless the money turns out to have come in from Russia. It's bad for the Left and it's bad for democracy.

We also need to bar lobbyists from donating to campaigns. Time after time, the media report on special interests who simultane-ously push for favorable legislation and bankroll the campaign of a politician who has oversight on that issue. Lo and behold, the lawmaker supports the bill. While this kind of logrolling isn't illegal yet, Americans are right to consider it corruption. Not surprisingly, economists have shown that contributions skew legislative outcomes because politicians weigh donors' views higher than others' and that "the policy preferences of wealthy individuals and business-oriented interest groups exert a large influence over U.S. public policy."[167] Commentator Steven Strauss described how the financial sector relied on political contributions and lobbying to pull itself out of the Great Recession.

> The Securities Industry and Financial Markets Association (SIFMA) reported that its member firms collectively lost pre-tax $34 billion in 2008 (an amount equal to the prior 2 years' profits). Despite massive and unprecedented losses, the financial industry did not reduce its expenditures on lobbying and campaign contributions. Instead, it increased lobbying and campaign spending by about 40% over the prior presidential cycle—from $690 million in 2004, to $956 million in 2008.
>
> This investment in political advocacy appears to have paid off handsomely! In 2008–2009, the Federal government made up to $7 trillion available to support America's banks—and on such generous terms—that the banking industry's 2009 recorded profits were double those of its best prior year. All while many American small businesses (unable to afford such generous campaign contributions to their elected officials) suffered record losses/layoffs.[168]

More recently, during the push for Trump's tax bill, Republican donors made it clear that funding for the GOP was contingent on the bill passing Congress. Republican congressman Chris Collins from New York forthrightly stated he was feeling pressure from special interests to make sure they came out well in the bill. "My donors are basically saying, 'Get it done or don't ever call me again,'" Collins told a reporter for *The Hill*.[169] Collins chose the Koch brothers over his voters, and the high tax state of New York got screwed by the Trump bill. Former uber-lobbyist Jack Abramoff, whose activities crossed the line into illegality, is now an advocate for reforms. In his book, published after he got out of jail, Abramoff wrote, "If you get money or perks from elected officials—be 'you' a company, a union, an association, a law firm, or an individual—you shouldn't be permitted to give them so much as one dollar."[170] And certainly lobbyists should not be able to bundle contributions to campaigns, making their importance to the politicians even more palpable. And why should our elected officials be able to spend valuable daytime hours dialing for dollars? In some states, politicians can only fund-raise when the legislature is out of session—why not Congress?

In the long term, we need to revitalize our jurisprudence around democracy, explaining why the First Amendment should actually be read to protect people's ability to be heard, whatever their wealth. In his book *Madison's Music*, Burt Neuborne, who was the national legal director of the ACLU during the Reagan presidency and has argued many cases before the Supreme Court, argues that the First Amendment was meant to advance democracy. He contends that the Supreme Court's decision in *Citizens United* turns the First Amendment on its head by giving democracy over to hugely wealthy individuals and corporations, encouraging cynical officials to disenfranchise the weak, and allowing politicians to manipulate the system to stay in power.[171] But it's not just democracy that suffers, as important as that is. All the people whose interests are trampled on by politicians on the right in thrall to their donors suffer too. Some argue that the most effective and lasting solution would be to amend the Constitution to make it clear that money and speech are not the same. With the outrage over the *Citizens United* decision, this approach may not be a fantasy. Already, eighteen states and 727 cities and towns have adopted resolutions supporting a twenty-eighth amendment that would limit corporate money in politics.[172]

Former congressman Jim Leach, an old-style moderate Republican, laments these attacks on representative democracy. By rigging elections so certain groups face growing barriers to voting and making districts conform to partisan aspirations rather than democratic participation, and by fueling campaigns with huge amounts of dark money and corporate cash, these far-right forces are trying to create a single-party regime. "What's at issue is the nature of democracy," said Leach. "It's this nexus of *Citizens United* nationalizing elections, with the redistricting process, and it's created a nefarious and dangerous approach to politics which is out of step with what the Founders envisioned. It takes the competition out, and it plugs the ears of people in the legislative process."[173]

But progressives can't just stand around moaning—we know what the policies are that will make a difference, including updating the Motor Voter Act to move to automatic voter registration, allowing Election Day registration, and increasingly allowing voting at home. We need to fight for nonpartisan redistricting and curbs on money in politics, from low-dollar public financing to broad disclosure laws, as well as the national popular vote and a new jurisprudence of the First Amendment, and if all else fails, a new twenty-eighth amendment to overturn *Citizens United*. All of these reforms have the benefit of melding progressive values with effective politics—that is, not only are they right, but they help the Left win elections. Paul Weyrich, co-founder of the Heritage Foundation, ALEC, and the Moral Majority, understood that rigging elections is good for the Right. But if Republican victories at the polls go up as the voting populace goes down, the opposite is true for progressives.

And the Democratic Party should hear from those of us who want a party of the left, not a party just a little less captured by plutocrats and insiders. Ron Klain, who worked for Presidents Bill Clinton and Barack Obama, set out a list of reforms for the party that would make its own process of selecting candidates more fair and transparent, which would help the Democrats make the case that they're not the same as the Republicans. Describing the current process as "so jerry-rigged as to be incomprehensible to all but the most savvy observers," he calls for Democrats to get rid of party caucuses and use primaries to choose delegates to the convention (notably—and perhaps wrongly—leaving Iowa aside). Caucuses favor people with time who can spend several hours choosing a nominee, disenfranchising those who don't have flexible work hours, are responsible for young children, or don't have transportation options; the sheer difficulty of participating makes them an exclusive club and one that prevents many low-income people from casting a vote. Klain also recommends open primaries, where not only Democrats but also unaffiliated voters could take part. And, most importantly, even if symbolic, he says it is past time to take away the votes from superdelegates, who are mostly elected officials and Democratic operatives. These moves would show that the voters and not the hacks have chosen the candidate in a fair and open way.[174] In August of 2018, the Democratic Party moved to reduce the role of superdelegates so we can hope there's more reform to follow.[175]

4

THE LEAST DANGEROUS BRANCH

When President Obama set about to nominate a replacement for Justice Scalia I coined a hashtag—#NoHearingsNoVotes—that telegraphed a principled opposition to tipping the Supreme Court very hard to the left in an election year, an opposition that Senate Majority Leader McConnell had already resolved upon. It was an opposition independent of the name and qualifications of whomever President Obama would eventually send to the Senate—it would turn out to be the very able jurist, but "living Constitution" enthusiast, Judge Merrick Garland—and that opposition to holding hearings and conducting votes would stick. Only one Republican senator broke with the Leader, Illinois's Mark Kirk, and he was defeated in November.

—Hugh Hewitt[1]

That's conservative commentator Hugh Hewitt explaining how the Right foiled President Obama's effort to fill the final Supreme Court vacancy that arose during his presidency. Opposition to *anyone* whom Obama might nominate, defiantly announced within hours of Scalia's death. They play hardball.

The Right seeks to control both state and federal courts, working with aggressive campaign operatives to run extremist candidates for state judgeships and promoting federal nominees through the Federalist Society, the Judicial Crisis Network, and the Heritage Foundation—an infrastructure funded lavishly by the Koch brothers; the Mercers, another extremely wealthy conservative family; and the Chamber of Commerce. This secretive network has had a demonstrable impact on the nation's courts, resulting in an increasingly reactionary Supreme Court and business-dominated state courts, with far-reaching impacts on social justice. Data shows that elected judges favor contributors and partisan interests, and Republican federal appointees rule for corporate interests over average people. And conservatives infused the importance of the courts into their political strategy, pushing it down so that the base of the Republican Party began to see the judiciary and its rulings as a key voting issue. Donald Trump represents the culmination of this strategy, whereby evangelicals have embraced a philandering sexual abuser because he will give them the judges they want, dedicated to overturning *Roe v. Wade*.

Complacent after years of assuming the courts were a bulwark for liberty and personal rights, the Left blithely ignored the radical change that was happening right before their eyes. During the years of the Warren Court, the liberal justices issued opinions upholding the right to privacy, limiting abuses by police and government officials, and ending legal segregation, allowing many to think the courts would protect us without our needing to *protect them* from infiltration and dominance by the Right. Unfortunately, the Left is still somnolent as well as sanctimonious, with many finding it distasteful to mix politics and judicial selection, even in the face of an ever more conservative judiciary.

In a perfect world, I would favor a détente of sorts between

Right and Left over the courts; indeed, I would vastly prefer a professional judiciary that was immune to politics. But because the Right has gone from conventional to nuclear arms in the battle for the courts, progressives need to deploy an effective counterweight to ensure our courts aren't captured by reactionary zealots. As conservatives have done, we need to develop a pipeline for state court candidates and federal appointees and a well-resourced support system for them. Along with fighting for good judges, we need to advance a vision of the Constitution. Is it one that understands that the document was drafted to serve "we the people" or one that purports, like the Right's originalism, to mind-read the views of eighteenth-century slave owners to determine the "meaning" of a particular vague phrase, with the inevitable conservative outcome? We need to develop and disseminate persuasive approaches and theories to challenge conservative legal arguments and constitutional interpretation, and we need to make sure to educate both elected and appointed judges with seminars, forums, and writings to ensure they are aware of, and can implement, our ideas.

GETTING ON THE WALL

Legal groups were built into the original DNA of the conservative infrastructure. The godfather of the effort to build a battalion of right-wing institutions, future Supreme Court justice Lewis Powell, recognized that the courts were a key battleground. Along with the Heritage Foundation, ALEC, and the other organizations that helped solidify the right-wing hold on our branches of government, the Federalist Society and conservative public interest law groups were created to generate legal scholarship and litigation strategies and, crucially, to build a pipeline of dependable reactionaries to take seats on the state and federal benches.

A supportive legal structure enabled through the appointment or election of aligned judges, the development and normalization of legal theories to justify conservative positions, and the hiring of litigators to move those theories into practice would ensure that the Right's policy goals wouldn't be thwarted by an independent judiciary.

The Left had pioneered the concept of public interest law firms, with the ACLU and the NAACP Legal Defense and Educational Fund (LDF) being among the most prominent examples. Inspired by legal victories of those groups and others, conservative lawyers founded their own organizations to advance their agenda.[2] The Powell Memo contemplated that the Chamber of Commerce would take the lead on pro-business litigation. And while the chamber did quickly move to establish the U.S. Chamber Litigation Center in 1977, other groups such as the Pacific Legal Foundation, the Alliance Defending Freedom, and the Project on Fair Representation also emerged to challenge environmental rules, access to reproductive health care, affirmative action, and public education.[3] These legal groups may have been inspired by the Left's successes, but they were quite different. Unlike the nonpartisan and principled ACLU and NAACP LDF, which sometimes work at cross-purposes with the Democratic Party and sometimes, in the case of the ACLU, even against the progressive agenda, legal groups on the right tracked the Republican platform. Moreover, their work was significantly supported by corporations because their litigation advanced the companies' bottom lines. Exxon, for example, lavishly funded the Pacific Legal Foundation, which has vigorously litigated to undermine environmental policy, including efforts to control global warming.[4]

But conservatives soon recognized that they needed to do more than sue. In a 1980 report, Michael Horowitz lamented that the existing organizations had not met "the great need for vibrant, intellectually respectable conservative law/action centers."[5] To enable lasting and fundamental change, Horowitz said, a strategy was necessary to connect visionary thinkers with legal practitioners to spark radical new approaches to the law and infuse them into the practice of law. Only by making connections between the legal academy and political actors, Horowitz determined, would the movement be able to "redefine what is moral in law."[6] Of course, political parties and elected officials also help drive a constitutional narrative, but they need experts to generate the ideas and provide validation for the media and the public.

The Right's goal was to create a framework to move legal ideas that were "off the wall," in Yale law professor Jack Balkin's useful construct, to "on the wall." Balkin describes the process as one where legal theory interacts with social movements and politics, and he points to conservative scholars' arguments challenging the Affordable Care Act as providing a textbook example of the process. Balkin observes that "arguments move from off the wall to on the wall because people and institutions are willing to put their reputations on the line and state that an argument formerly thought beyond the pale is not crazy at all, but is actually a pretty good legal argument. Moreover, it matters greatly *who* vouches for the argument—whether they are well-respected, powerful and influential, and how they are situated in institutions with professional authority or in institutions like politics or the media that shape public opinion."[7]

Founded in 1982, the Federalist Society epitomizes the type of institution described by Balkin, designed to move controversial or disfavored legal theories into the mainstream by ensuring a powerful network of people willing to endorse and promote them. While there certainly were prominent conservative jurists prior to the founding of the Federalist Society, conservatives had long believed that legal academe and hence the jurisprudence of the courts was dominated by liberals, and that they needed another channel to promote their agenda. And indeed, it is true that law professors lean to the left, just like journalists. But as with the media, just because the personal views of academics skew liberal does not mean they are producing content to serve liberal political goals. Indeed, sometimes liberal law professors exult in upending the progressive agenda by endorsing right-wing judicial nominees because they are "qualified" and by undercutting critical policies through provocative and ill-timed blogs or comments. They are hardly a dependable arm of the progressive movement. Nonetheless, the Right wanted to provide a forum to drive more politically oriented scholarship to counter that perceived liberal academic "bias." The Federalist Society allowed them a venue to meet, network, and support each other's advancement, as well as to disseminate countervailing arguments to what they perceived as the dominant legal discourse.

Originally solely a student organization, the society was the creation of students at the University of Chicago and Yale Law Schools, who organized the group to provide themselves an intellectual home at otherwise allegedly liberal institutions. Lee Liberman Otis and Steven Calabresi, both still active with the society, had spent time on the presidential campaign of Ronald Reagan and felt a particular disconnect with the prevalent law school ideology.[8] Quickly attracting funding and the interest of established conservative academics such as Robert Bork, Richard Posner, and Antonin Scalia, the organization spread to other campuses and from there began to establish lawyer chapters.

Its founding coincided with Republican domination of the federal government, allowing Federalist Society student members to vault into influential clerkships and legal jobs in the Reagan

White House and the Justice Department. The Justice Department became almost an extension of the organization and, under Attorney General Edwin Meese, the agency worked to develop useful legal theories and strategies that would lead to conservative outcomes. When the young Federalist Society lawyers came to the Justice Department, they were seen by some mainstream Republicans as radical. Charles Fried, who served as the solicitor general for the last four years of Reagan's presidency, called the positions society members drafted for Meese's speeches "extreme," including "questioning the constitutionality of independent agencies or suggesting that the president need not obey Supreme Court decisions with which he disagrees."[9] But Fried's views were not shared by the attorney general, who embraced the ideas and the organization.

The synergy between the political appointees in the government and the fledgling legal organization gave it wings as its members became the leaders of the conservative legal movement, handing out jobs and access to high-placed allies.[10] Most law schools now have a Federalist Society chapter, and the membership has grown to approximately sixty thousand students, lawyers, judges, politicians, and others interested in conservative legal thinking. Its budget has also grown to $25 million or more with generous funding from the anchors of right-wing philanthropy: the Koch brothers, the Bradley Foundation, and Richard Scaife.[11] At the society's thirtieth anniversary gala in 2012, Executive Vice President Leonard Leo proudly noted the growth and impact his organization has had through the work of its "citizen-lawyers," who serve in government as lawyers or judges, do pro bono litigation, or help provide intellectual fodder for the movement. In the audience were several senators, over twenty federal appellate judges, and at least one Supreme Court justice.[12]

The Federalist Society has an enormous influence in shaping politics, without being overtly political. Ann Southworth, who devoted a book to the organization, writes, "The Federalist Society pursues its integrating mission indirectly, by sponsoring conferences, generating publications, convening practice groups, promoting lawyers' involvement in public affairs, and *facilitating appointments of judges and government officials.*"[13] Amanda Hollis-Brusky, who has also written a book on the group, similarly relates that "the Federalist Society itself actually does very little in terms of direct legal and political engagement. Animated by the belief that ideas *can* and *do* have consequences, the Federalist Society's focus has been on training and shaping its members through intellectual engagement, networking conservative and libertarian legal elites, and facilitating opportunities for members to put their shared legal principles into practice as 'citizen-lawyers.'"[14] But the society has no need to be obviously political because its work generating legal theories to challenge liberal policies and constitutional values, sharing them with politicians, finding lawyers to bring cases, and getting judges on the bench who can hear those cases serves conservative goals. (I don't fault them for it. The American Constitution Society [ACS] was established to mirror this work but on the left. Much younger than the Federalist Society, ACS was founded after the infamous *Bush v. Gore* decision in which the Supreme Court handed the presidency to George W. Bush. It was an awakening for the Left, when it finally registered at least among a few people that we had been asleep at the switch and the Right had built a formidable network, promoted a conservative constitutional interpretation that had a surface appeal to the public, and begun to dominate the judiciary.)

For the Federalist Society, a key part of the work has been advancing "originalism" as the only acceptable way to understand the Constitution. This approach requires that we read provisions in that document as they would purportedly have been understood at the time. Conservative scholar Johnathan O'Neill describes originalism as holding that "although interpretation begins with the text, including the structure and relationship of the institutions it creates, the meaning of the text can be further elucidated by . . . evidence from those who drafted the text in [the Constitutional Convention] as well as from the public debates and commentary surrounding its ratification."[15] For some parts of the Constitution, this approach works—we still agree that thirty years old is thirty years old. But for others, many scholars argue that the theory doesn't hold water: we can't mind-read, so we often don't know what the exact intentions were behind a particular word or phrase such as "reasonable" or "due process." Even if we could time-travel back to the 1780s to ask James Madison what he meant, those understandings may well be very difficult to apply to current problems; and there's no basis to suggest that the framers actually wanted twenty-first-century Americans to be governed by eighteenth-century worldviews.[16]

In his book *The Living Constitution*, professor David Strauss provides a thorough rebuke to originalism, pointing out the many flaws and problematic outcomes if applied consistently. For example, Strauss explains that under an originalist approach, the Supreme Court could not have found "separate but equal" unconstitutional as it did in *Brown v. Board of Education*. Few people could seriously argue that the nineteenth-century framers of the Fourteenth Amendment meant to attack segregated schools in the amendment.[17] Even Justice Scalia had to admit that his approach didn't always work, calling himself a "faint-hearted originalist." After all, he confessed, "I am an originalist. I am not a nut."[18] Other died-in-the-wool originalists confess that it is a leaky vessel. According to professor Randy Barnett, sometimes the words alone don't answer a contemporary question due to facts that wouldn't have been thought possible by the eighteenth-century authors. The text is often vague—how are we to understand what is a reasonable search under the Fourth Amendment when customs agents grab someone's cell phone? Barnett admits that the Constitution "does not say everything one needs to know to resolve all possible cases and controversies." How judges evaluate cases under these circumstances is something even originalists don't agree on among themselves.[19] But they do tend to agree that all the results should be conservative.

Southworth adroitly observes that the Federalist Society—and the legal Right, generally—have "sacrificed philosophical coherence to achieve political objectives."[20] And those political objectives are what matter. "They believe that the text of the Constitution strictly limits what Congress and judges can do," says Samuel Issacharoff, a professor at New York University School of Law. "So they embrace a whole series of doctrines that say Congress can't do anything unless it's specifically authorized in the Constitution. And then administrative agencies can't do anything unless Congress has specifically authorized it by law. For decades, judges thought it was permissible to fill in the gaps left by the ambiguities in the Constitution and laws. But the current conservatives have an activist agenda to peel back the power of government."[21]

This approach is designed with outcomes—conservative ones—in mind, rather than theoretical coherence or even a textual or historical basis. Professor Geoffrey Stone of the University of Chicago Law School found that the judges following an "originalist" approach dependably reached conservative outcomes. Looking at the twenty most important constitutional cases since 2000, Stone concluded that the conservative justices were on the conservative side in 98.5 percent of the cases. In other words, the outcome is predetermined.[22] Steven Calabresi, Federalist Society founder and law professor, confesses as much with no shame, lauding the consequences of applying an originalist frame to contemporary cases.

> The country would be better off with more federalism and more decentralization . . . with a president who had more power to manage the bureaucracy . . . if we did not abort a million babies a year as we have done since 1973 . . . if students could pray and read the Bible in public school and if the Ten Commandments could be posted in public places . . . if citizens could engage in core political speech by contributing whatever they wanted to contribute to candidates for public office . . . if we could grow wheat on our own farms without federal intrusion . . . if criminals never got out of jail because of the idiocy of the exclusionary rule . . . if our homes could not be seized by developers acting in cahoots with state and local government . . . [and] if state governments could not pass laws impairing the obligations of contracts.[23]

This statement of what originalism could achieve is truly radical: it would undo the New Deal (wage and hour laws, anti–child labor provisions), environmental protections, the right to choose, and most federal regulations providing important limits on corporate malfeasance, not to mention radically reinterpret the First Amendment's ban on the establishment of a preferred religion. It would return us to the eighteenth century.

Before the 1980s, originalism had been a sleepy theory discussed by conservative scholars, but Reagan's attorney general Edwin Meese saw its utility and made it a political force for the Right. Meese commandeered the vast resources of the Justice Department to promote originalism, including publishing a manual of constitutional interpretation and speaking around the country to promote it. Professor Laurence Tribe, a well-known Harvard constitutional law scholar, describes how successful Meese was in "making it look like he and his disciples were carrying out the intentions of the great founders, where the liberals were making it up as they went along. It was a convenient dichotomy, very misleading, with a powerful public relations effect."[24] In July 1985, Meese addressed the American Bar Association's annual meeting, titling his speech "Jurisprudence of Original Intention." Taking on the Supreme Court directly, he successfully brought the theory into the public debate. Meese criticized the court for enabling "a drift back toward the radical egalitarianism and expansive civil libertarianism of the Warren Court." Meese argued that only originalism would prevent this backsliding. Justice William Brennan fired back, describing the theory that we can read the minds of the founders for their intentions as "arrogance cloaked in humility."[25]

On a range of issues, these originalists assert that their view is supported by their unassailable understanding of the Constitution's original meaning, and conservative scholars and activists have used the doctrine as a hammer to attack liberal positions and policy victories. A notable example is how they mobilized to challenge the constitutionality of the Affordable Care Act. With the groundwork laid by the Federalist Society and the promotion of originalism by Reagan's Department of Justice, conservative legal activists created a receptive environment to raise a novel challenge to the Affordable Care Act: that it was not a constitutional exercise of Congress's power under the Commerce Clause.

The Commerce Clause of the Constitution had been the basis for most of the major pieces of legislation adopted during and since the New Deal, a critical undergirding for progressive policy. The Federalist Society and its allies assiduously promoted the radical attack on congressional power, normalizing the idea through programming and writing in legal publications and also more popular magazines and newspapers. During the debate over the Affordable Care Act, conservative legal commentators David Rivkin and David McIntosh wrote a piece in the *Wall Street Journal*—a favorite placement for opinion pieces designed to bring extremist approaches to an audience that will find them persuasive—arguing that the individual mandate would be unconstitutional if adopted. Randy Barnett, a prominent Federalist Society "expert," also pushed the idea that the Affordable Care Act's mandate was unconstitutional in media and public appearances.[26] One favorite talking point was the alleged concern that the principle behind the individual mandate would allow the government to force people to buy any sort of product—including broccoli. Fox News spent many, many hours talking about broccoli, amazed at the supposed overreach of the law. Justice Scalia actually referred to this specious talking point in his opinion. "Everybody has to buy food sooner or later," he said. "Therefore, you can make people buy broccoli."[27]

That bizarre reference to broccoli didn't grow in Scalia's mind organically—it was a plant. *New York Times* reporter James B. Stewart dug into how it grew, writing, "The vegetable trail leads backward through conservative media and pundits. Before reaching the Supreme Court, vegetables were cited by a federal judge in Florida with a libertarian streak; in an Internet video financed by libertarian and ultraconservative backers; at a Congressional hearing by a Republican senator; and in an op-ed column by David B. Rivkin Jr., a libertarian lawyer whose family emigrated from the former Soviet Union when he was 10."[28] Yale constitutional law professor Akhil Amar confessed "grudging admiration. . . . All the more so because it's such a bad argument. They have been politically brilliant. They needed a simplistic metaphor, and in broccoli they got it."[29] Legal common sense says that there are certain items that government can indeed require people to buy; for example, you have to buy an airbag when you buy an automobile. On *The O'Reilly Factor*, I flummoxed Bill O'Reilly by asking about whether the Militia Acts of 1792, requiring militia members to buy muskets and shot, affected his argument that the government had never, ever required anyone to buy anything. He couldn't answer.[30] But broccoli won the day; the Supreme Court found that the Commerce Clause did not actually provide a constitutional foundation for the individual mandate (although the taxing power did). The impact of this radical revision of the power of Congress is still unknown. We must admire what the Right achieved. With its legal network, supported by the Fox News echo chamber, feeding radical dogma to handpicked judges, conservatives undermined a key pillar of progressive policymaking.

THE FEEDBACK LOOP

In her 2015 book examining the rise of the Federalist Society, scholar Amanda Hollis-Brusky notes that theory isn't everything: "To have a serious and lasting influence on the direction of constitutional law and jurisprudence—a constitutional revolution—you need to appoint the *right* cast of characters" and you need to police their work once appointed.[31] The Federalist Society recognizes that judges are a critical audience for its work—its white papers and events are directions on how to apply the law and it critiques opinions it believes deviate from the orthodoxy. To be doubly sure the judges are hearing the right message, conservative organizations have provided judges with seminars and training programs at luxurious resorts—junkets of jurisprudence—where they learn why class actions should be limited and environmental regulations should be subjected to tough scrutiny. Republican

appointees dominate these events, making what Senator Sheldon Whitehouse called a "sort of right-wing judicial jamboree
and team-building exercise." Wined and dined by groups that
have cases in their courts, the judges learn their dinner mates'
preferred outcome and are given a specific understanding of the
factual and legal context of the cases. Whitehouse quotes a newspaper editorial that rightly condemned these all-expenses-paid
trips as "popular free vacations for judges, a cross between Maoist
cultural reeducation camps and Club Med."[32] These judges are
instructed toward "unabashed activism" and told that "the Reagan revolution will come to nothing" if the judges don't uphold a
"libertarian Constitution."[33]

Judges can also send direct messages in these informal settings about what cases they would like to see—and indirect messages in the opinions they write. In 2009, Chief Justice Roberts
famously requested a challenge to the Voting Rights Act (VRA)
in *Northwest Austin Municipal Util. Dist. No. One v. Holder*, signaling that in a subsequent case the court would find the VRA
unconstitutional—and four years later, *Shelby County v. Holder* was the result. Similarly, Justice Samuel Alito made it clear
in his writing in *Knox v. Service Employees International Union*
(2012) that the precedent, *Abood v. Detroit Board of Education*
(1977), which supported the right of public employees to organize
and receive fair-share fees for collective bargaining costs from
nonmembers, deeply offended him. He again critiqued *Abood* in
Harris v. Quinn, two years later, calling it "questionable on several grounds."[34] With the four other conservative justices, he con-
veyed that the court would like to overturn *Abood* in the future.
Alito's request was hardly subtle, and lawyers were ready with the
case, *Friedrichs v. California Teachers Association* (2016). *Friedrichs* almost brought an end to this important regime for working
people, but we were spared at the last minute by the death of

Antonin Scalia, which meant the decision was split 4–4. In 2018, with Justice Neil Gorsuch replacing Scalia on the bench, a new case presenting the same issue came before the court. With this case, *Janus v. American Federation of State, County, and Municipal Employees, Council 31*, the Right won, and it now plans to decimate public employee unions, a critical protector of working people in the last sector where unions have any power. Ruth Bader Ginsburg and Sonia Sotomayor can complain in their dissents about mistaken majority opinions, but they can't signal to the Left that we can win on the next try because we can't—not without a Supreme Court majority that recognizes the progressive values of the Constitution. First, we have to win the court. Nevertheless, these dissents do provide a road map for future majority opinions, and we need to be attentive to the specific directions they send.

The Right has also been adept at creating a self-perpetuating network, with judges promoted by the Federalist Society choosing law clerks and mentoring young lawyers who come out of its chapters. It is no secret that the judges who are moved forward by the Federalist Society or who are active in the group prefer law clerks who have been part of the organization. Judge Alex Kozinski of the U.S. Court of Appeals for the Ninth Circuit—until he was forced to resign due to allegations of sexual harassment in December 2017—was quite forthright in saying that he looked for the Federalist Society on student resumes because it "tells me you're of a particular philosophy, and I tend to give an edge to people I agree with philosophically."[35] (He also said, famously, in a response to a comment that Barbie dolls give girls a distorted body image, that "the only thing wrong that I saw when I held Barbie is when I lift her skirt there is nothing underneath." This might explain why he had to resign.[36])

Hollis-Brusky notes that "taken together, these efforts both inside and outside the legal profession have acted like, to bor-row Federalist Society member Lillian BeVier's language, 'drip-ping water,' slowly wearing away at the dominance of liberal legal thought and effectively changing the dialogue about our Con-stitution and constitutional culture."[37] This feedback loop rein-forces the rightward drift of the law as judges adopt positions that the Right pushed from the outside in and conservative scholars and litigators get hand signals from judges about what litigation would get a positive reception in the court.

The somewhat messy and uncoordinated legal Left hasn't been nearly as effective. While it is true that the academy is more liberal than conservative, conservative scholars have been more tightly aligned with activists and have been more intentional about harnessing legal writing in service of political goals. Pro-gressives have no such camps where judges could learn about why aggregating small claims in a class action allows people to recov-er damages and holds corporations accountable for wrongdoing or why employment discrimination claims are too frequently dismissed before discovery. And why no Left Club Med? While some of the Left are waking up to the fact that generating ideas isn't enough if no one knows about them, most funders are still asleep when it comes to building an infrastructure to advance top candidates into the judiciary and ensure that they are edu-cated on pending legal issues. There's nothing wrong with expos-ing judges to ideas.

Here's the takeaway: liberals need to embrace and promote our understanding of the Constitution. Instead of being cowed by originalism, with all its flaws and inconsistencies—and in the face of the cynical application by the Right that drops the theory when it doesn't work in their favor—the Left needs to forthright-ly advance the position that the document is progressive. It starts with "We the people" and was drafted to embed democracy in our nation as well as to limit the government's power to override minority views. Thus, we have majority rule but protections for freedom of speech and due process. Fair-minded constitutionalists review the text and history to understand how to apply its democracy-advancing goals to current circumstances. That's why we can find protections in the Fourth Amendment for cell phone data even though phones didn't exist in the nineteenth century; and that's why we find that waterboarding violates the Eighth Amendment's ban on cruel and unusual punishment. Maybe it wasn't cruel in the past when whipping was a widespread civil disciplinary measure and we were still arguing about whether nonwhite people were indeed "people," but it sure is now. Originalists can't get there without twisting themselves—and our Constitution—in knots. Originalism wasn't born in a day; it had a long gestation period before it had an impact. But we can now see the damage. We need to take back the Constitution and restore its pride of place for progressive values.

In addition to advancing a better alternative to originalism, we can't shy away from thought leadership and scholarship more tightly aligned with political goals. Young scholars on the left are often frightened that writing articles and advancing theories that help the Left—or worse, Democrats—will harm their chances at tenure. Some of that fear could be mitigated if the big donors who give to universities and law schools were to endow positions that focus on policy and constitutional jurisprudence with a liberal flavor. But we also need more focused think tanks and publications that can do some of this work, just as the Federalist Society and Heritage have done on the right.

The American Constitution Society has taken up this challenge, as have other organizations like Demos, the Constitutional Accountability Center, and the Brennan Center for Justice, but the field needs more funding and more buy-in from our political allies so the ideas can flow as efficiently from the scholars to the politicians as they do on the right.

These think tanks also need funding to provide judicial education so we too can have a process for sharing our best ideas directly with judges. We already work to embed these ideas in opinion pieces and law review articles, share them on social media, and promote them on Capitol Hill, in statehouses, and in the courtroom. But we can't neglect the pipeline, so we need to build out our education program to supply these judges with the best and most diverse law clerks. Unlike conservative Federalist Society judges, liberal judges are unlikely to take direction from any advocacy organization—that resistance is in the Left's DNA. But we can provide critical mentorship, guidance, and networking to law students and lawyers to clerk for and become judges so we can have more fair-minded constitutionalists on the bench.

POWER LASTS LONGER WHEN APPOINTMENTS ARE FOR LIFE

From the beginning, one of the main objectives of the right-wing legal establishment has been to put judges on the bench who will carry out its interests. Amanda Hollis-Brusky describes the approach as understanding that achieving constitutional changes is about more than just appointing judges and justices. It's about "appointing enough of the *right* judges and Justices: individuals who have been shaped intellectually and have been professionally credentialed by a network that will, through its personal and professional ties, hold those judges and Justices accountable for being faithful to a particular point of view of the Constitution and of constitutional interpretation."[38]

Leonard Leo, executive vice president of the Federalist Society, got a call from Donald Trump in the spring of 2016, asking for advice on judicial nominees—specifically a list of vetted candidates. No campaign in history had put out such a list. In an interview with the *New Yorker*'s Jeffrey Toobin, Leo recalled that Trump said, "People don't know who I am on these issues, and I want to give people a sense of that." Leo told Trump, "That's a great idea—you're creating a brand."[39] Leo did indeed provide a list that complied with the president's campaign promise to fill the bench with activists committed to expanding gun rights and overturning *Roe v. Wade*; that's not surprising considering Leo's conservatism is driven as much by his Catholic faith as by free-market dogma. Joan Desmond of the *National Catholic Register* proudly wrote that "when Trump turned to Leo for help with his first nominee to the high court, he was soliciting the advice of a devout pro-life Catholic."[40] To Toobin, Leo asserted that having two children with spina bifida made him more deeply anti-abortion than he had been previously, and that he brings that to his work on judicial nominees. Conservative legal commentator Edward Whelan said of Leo, "No one has been more dedicated to the enterprise of building a Supreme Court that will overturn *Roe v. Wade* than the Federalist Society's Leonard Leo."[41]

In an interview with the *Washington Post*, Hollis-Brusky was asked how the Federalist Society could work so closely with Donald Trump, who seems not closely aligned with its values. Quite easily, she responded, reminding the reporter that "as the late-Justice Scalia . . . wrote in two of his most famous dissents, 'this . . . is about power.' Access to power is key to the Federalist Society's long-term goal of capturing the courts and reorienting constitutional and legal culture to embrace conservative and libertarian ideas. Access to Trump means access to power and because judges and justices serve, on average, 26 years on the bench, the Federalist Society's influence will long outlast this president."[42]

Donald Trump has delivered on judicial nominations, sticking to Leo's list of almost exclusively white and startlingly young men.[43] Where Mitt Romney had "binders of women," Trump apparently has a notebook of white male clones all dedicated to undoing the twentieth century. Neil Gorsuch, who now sits on the Supreme Court, was on Leo's list and fit the bill to a tee: a known quantity and frequent Federalist Society participant, religious conservative, and scion of an extreme conservative, Anne Gorsuch, who had served in the Reagan administration.[44] Brett Kavanaugh, Trump's second nominee to the Supreme Court, also from Leo's list, is cut from the same cloth. Dubbed "polemicists in robes," by *Slate*'s Dahlia Lithwick,[45] Trump's judicial nominees have benefited from the well-honed right-wing focus on the courts, getting confirmed in high numbers. Trump's allegiance to the Federalist Society's list of nominees is keeping many Republican politicians and donors, as well the base of the party, especially evangelicals, in his corner longer than they might otherwise have stayed. Even in the face of White House firings and publicly aired disagreements between the president and his cabinet, Trump's team has moved more nominations and confirmations in his first two years than Obama, and by a lot. "It's just been a win on all fronts," said Carrie Severino, policy director and chief counsel for the Judicial Crisis Network.[46]

THE GIFT THAT KEEPS ON GIVING

Feeling burned by earlier Supreme Court justices who had shown insufficient adherence to the conservative dogma, the Right was ready when Sandra Day O'Connor retired in 2006. Swearing that her replacement would toe the line, a prominent group of lawyers organized a plan to ensure a safe choice. Dubbed the "four horsemen," Leo, former attorney general Ed Meese, White House counsel in the first Bush administration C. Boyden Gray, and Jay Sekulow, from Pat Robertson's American Center for Law and Justice, brought together a broad swath of conservatives to fight for the nominations of Chief Justice John Roberts and Justice Samuel Alito, not to mention a large number of lower-court judges named by George W. Bush. These judges espoused a firmly conservative—and pro-corporate—ideology.[47] The funders who supported these efforts, including lawyer Ann Corkery, real estate magnate Robin Arkley II, the Koch brothers, and the Mercer family, no doubt found the investment profitable as the current Supreme Court has provided a safe harbor for corporate interests and promoted a social agenda that's far to the right, prompting Southern Baptist head Richard Land to call Bush's justices "the gifts that keep on giving" for religious conservatives.[48] From high-profile cases like *Citizens United* to those that fly under the radar, such as *Comcast v. Behrend*,[49] which threw out a class action antitrust suit, the court has reliably ruled for companies over employees, consumers, and government regulators.[50]

The four horsemen were bolstered by a political strategy to pressure senators to support the nominees. In late 2004, Justice Antonin Scalia joined Leonard Leo and several wealthy conservative donors to celebrate the founding of a new organization, the Judicial Confirmation Network (JCN), which could be described as the political arm of the Federalist Society.[51] News reports credit Sekulow, who would later serve as President Trump's lawyer, with the idea to create the JCN.[52] Immediately jumping into the fight for Bush's Supreme Court nominees, the JCN helped secure victories for the two new extremely conservative justices, Roberts and Alito.

Then, with the election of Barack Obama, the Judicial Confirmation Network became the Judicial *Crisis* Network.[53] Obama's election was a windfall for the JCN as its funders doubled down in the interest of limiting the Democratic president's impact on the courts. Obama's first nominee to a federal appeals court, David Hamilton, got the first taste of the JCN in attack mode. Despite his quite moderate record, Hamilton was painted as a "hard-left political activist," and somehow his nomination was cast as Obama's way of thanking ACORN for services rendered. Hamilton had spent one summer in college in the 1970s canvassing for that organization, which was accused by the Right of having tipped the election illegally to Obama in 2008.[54]

Citizens United, decided in 2010, provided rocket fuel for the JCN. Like other 501(c)(4)s, the JCN is not required by law to disclose its donors, but investigative journalists have tracked the organization's money to the shady Wellspring Committee, another 501(c)(4) group, which even shares an address and overlapping officers with the JCN. The JCN's coffers were swelled by a $17.9 million gift from Wellspring; it had only two other donors between 2015 and 2016 in the fight to keep Merrick Garland off the Supreme Court.[55] In 2016, Wellspring put $23.5 million in the JCN's bank account.[56] Wellspring was originally created by the Koch brothers and run by Ann Corkery, who joined Scalia and Leo at the dinner when the JCN was born.[57] The backers, who also support the Federalist Society, have a sophisticated understanding of how both groups support the end goal of packing the courts with far-right jurists. The Federalist Society runs the inside game, meeting with the White House and Republican senators to choose nominees and establish their credentials, remaining superficially above the fray. The JCN works the outside game, focusing on vulnerable Democrats or wavering Republicans, attacking the former to affect their votes on nominees as well as their reelection chances and savaging the latter for any sign of deviance from the hard-right line. To maintain its tax status, the JCN must spend less than 50 percent of its revenue on electoral activities, but, as election law expert Rick Hasen notes, it "may funnel a lot of the rest of the money into Supreme Court–related ads."[58]

On February 13, 2016, Justice Antonin Scalia died. I know exactly where I was at the time and I remember thinking, "Now President Obama truly has a chance to shape the law. Now, perhaps *Citizens United* and *Shelby County* and countless other poorly reasoned—and harmful—decisions can be reconsidered." Within hours of Scalia's death being announced, right-wing commentators and Republican senators declared that Obama would not get to pick his replacement. Enunciating a freshly minted doctrine, and one that conflicts with the Constitution's text and history, they said presidents could not fill Supreme Court vacancies in an election year. The fact that other presidents had done so on numerous occasions (including the appointment of Justice Anthony Kennedy in 1992) did not bother them. It is enough to just keep repeating the lie to make it true—until it is inconvenient, at which point it can be jettisoned (which is what happened when Kennedy's retirement created a vacancy in 2018, also an election year).

Much ink has been spilled about President Obama's decision to pick Judge Merrick Garland of the District of Columbia Court of Appeals to replace Scalia. A fine judge and former prosecutor, Garland was the definition of "moderate"—and white and in his sixties. In the Rose Garden ceremony announcing the nomination, Obama said, "Because of Justice Scalia's outsized role on the court and in American law, and the fact that Americans are closely divided on a number of issues before the court, it is tempting to make this confirmation process simply an extension of our divided politics. But to go down that path would be wrong. It would be a betrayal of our best traditions and a betrayal of the vision of our founding documents."[59] His remarks crystallize the difference between progressives and conservatives—for the latter, the nomination process is not an extension of politics; it *is* politics. Let's remember that when Justice Thurgood Marshall left the Supreme Court, Republicans fought to have Clarence Thomas replace him. Democrats let them.

Curt Levey, of the Committee for Justice and FreedomWorks, threatened Obama with "Armageddon" from the Senate were he to nominate someone to the "left of Merrick Garland."[60] But when Obama responded by nominating Garland himself, the Right went on to unleash "Armageddon" regardless, and all of a sudden the judge went from a moderate to a raving left-wing radical. Speaking to Mike DeBonis of the *Washington Post*, Carrie Severino of the Judicial Crisis Network said the Right was energized to fight Garland's nomination because "at the end of the day, the American people do not want to see the Supreme Court shift dramatically to the left, and that is what would happen if Merrick Garland were confirmed."[61]

Along with thwarting President Obama's Supreme Court pick, Senate Majority Leader Mitch McConnell had worked assiduously to block appointments to the lower courts. Hoping for a victory in the presidential race in 2016, he conspired to hold open as many seats as possible. DeBonis compared how the 2007–8 Democratically controlled Senate had treated President George W. Bush's nominees in his last year in office to what was happening to judicial nominees under Republicans in Obama's last year: "The current Senate's record is particularly dim on judicial confirmations. Obama has seen 17 lifetime judges confirmed in the past 16 months, compared to 45 for Bush in the same time frame, 40 for Clinton, and a whopping 82 for George H.W. Bush (including a Supreme Court justice, Clarence Thomas)."[62] The Democrats had treated Bush's nominees very differently. According to Jay Michaelson of the *Daily Beast*, in 2007–8, "the Democrat-led Senate confirmed 45; in 1991–92, when Democrats controlled the Senate and George H.W. Bush was president, it confirmed 82. In other words, the GOP Senate is confirming just 38 percent as many judges as the Democratic 2008 Senate, and 21 percent of the Democratic 1992 one."[63]

Trump is doing even better than his Republican predecessors, nominating and confirming judges at a record pace. Despite tapping nominees who receive a "not qualified" label from the American Bar Association, describe transgender children as part of "Satan's plan," call Justice Kennedy a "judicial prostitute" (to mention just a few), as of July 2018, no Republican senator had voted against or raised any concerns about any of Trump's picks (except for Senators Ted Cruz and Ben Sasse objecting to a Hawaii nominee as not pro-gun enough and Senator John Neely Kennedy voting against a nominee to the DC Circuit due to conflicts of interest—the only merit-based oppositions from Republicans). The Far Right is practically salivating: "We are thrilled with the nominees," gushed the JCN's Carrie Severino.[64] Trump is primed to fill 20 percent of the federal bench with nominees like these, who will serve for life.

Scholars Lawrence Baum and Neal Devins provide data to show how relentless Republicans have been in putting ideology above all other considerations in judicial selection, as opposed to the Democrats' contrasting weak-kneed approach. Merrick Garland, they argue, embodies this divergence and "reflects the practice of recent Democratic presidents to balance ideology with other goals by appointing moderate liberals. In sharp contrast, our research shows that Republican presidents over the past 25 years have put ideology first by appointing strong conservatives to the court." By nominating Garland, Obama may have hoped Republicans would revert to their prior support for him and reject their commitment to oppose any Obama nominee. But even had the Democrats been in control of the Senate, Baum and Nevins argue, "Obama likely would have chosen a nominee who was roughly similar to Garland in ideological terms."[65]

Republicans were ready to spend a lot of money to keep Obama's nominee off the court. The Judicial Crisis Network went on the offensive, waging preemptive strikes against possible nominees. Jane Kelly, a judge on the Court of Appeals for the Eighth Circuit, was among those targeted. Hailing from Iowa, Kelly might have been a difficult candidate for fellow Iowan, and Senate Judiciary chairman, Chuck Grassley to oppose, but she had worked for eighteen years as a public defender and that made good material for outsider-funded attack ads, especially regarding the fact that she had once defended an accused child molester. Kelly got knocked off Obama's list.[66] When Garland was nominated, the JCN ran ads against him during the Sunday news shows in DC as well as in targeted states, showing a multiracial America, with smiling children and cozy home scenes. A woman's voice intoned that "the American people should decide" on the next Supreme Court justice by voting in the next presidential election, rather than President Obama, although it was his constitutionally assigned role to select a replacement for Scalia. "This isn't about Republicans or Democrats," the woman advised. "It's about your voice."[67] This from a group that ran ads against the nomination of Sonia Sotomayor in 2009, and in 2010 tried to defeat Elena Kagan, even though President Obama had just been elected and these nominations reflected the "voice" of the voters.[68]

After investing more than $7 million to fight Garland's nomination, the JCN spent $10 million in ads attacking Democrats who might oppose Donald Trump's eventual nominee.[69] In addition to the Supreme Court battles, the JCN also spent heavily on ads to support lower-court nominees and attack Democratic senators who might object to their extreme views. Because the JCN doesn't disclose its donors, viewers have no idea that the force behind the organization is a tiny group of extremely right-wing billionaires and multimillionaires rather than average people concerned about the courts. Heritage Action supplemented the JCN's attack ads by telling Republicans, starting in January 2016, that there would be consequences for deviating from the party line and that if they supported any Obama judicial nominees for the rest of his administration, Heritage would use it against them in their election.[70] The Right's strategy featured advertising but also grassroots mobilization and polling, with a focus on defeating Senate Democrats in red states, with conservative organizations like the Tea Party Patriots and the Susan B. Anthony List helping to drive messaging in support of the Republican nominees.[71] The Koch network, which has announced plans to spend up to $400 million in the 2018 elections, has made it clear that judicial nominees are a "huge priority" and that Democrats who stand in the way will pay a price.[72] Well before Justice Kennedy's retirement and Kavanaugh's nomination, the Kochs were already spending to keep the next open seat for the Right.[73] They went all in for Kavanaugh, who could be the vote to overturn *Roe*.

Ron Klain, who served as a senior adviser to Presidents Clinton and Obama, criticizes the Left for neglecting the judiciary. In an opinion piece for the *Washington Post*, Klain noted that Trump "not only put Neil M. Gorsuch in the Supreme Court vacancy created by Merrick Garland's blocked confirmation, but he also selected 27 lower-court judges as of mid-July. Twenty-seven! That's three times Obama's total and more than double the totals of Reagan, Bush 41 and Clinton—combined. For the Courts of Appeals—the final authority for 95 percent of federal cases—no president before Trump named more than three judges whose nominations were processed in his first six months; Trump has named nine. Trump is on pace to more than double the number of federal judges nominated by any president in his first year." Klain also underscored that the relative youth of Trump's appointments means they will serve for many more years than Obama's older nominees.[74] Where the Right put millions into attacking Garland and advancing Gorsuch and Kavanaugh, the Left didn't vigorously fight back. Some of us tried to respond to the attack ads and misleading rhetoric on the right, but support from the Democratic Party and major funders was measly. We brought a knife to a gunfight. They brought AR-15s.

Getting these lifetime appointments was deemed so vital that Senate Republicans upended prevailing Senate practices and constitutional norms. First, they refused to give Merrick Garland a hearing, the first time in history a Supreme Court nominee has been so denied. Then, after successfully keeping the seat open for a year for Donald Trump to fill, they immediately abolished the filibuster for nominations to the high court and moved Neil Gorsuch expeditiously onto the bench. Gorsuch has quickly shown himself to be as conservative as feared. His first opinion involved sending a death row prisoner to be executed by lethal injection. With Gorsuch on the Supreme Court, the Right already expected the court to deliver in cases involving discrimination against gays and lesbians, women's reproductive rights, and more. And with another Trump justice, there is little doubt that the court will veer hard right. The new justices are expected, like Roberts, to come down on the right side when it counts for maintaining Republican power—making it easier to exclude valid voters, draw congressional districts that give a lock for the conservative candidate, destroy the labor movement, and undo any remaining campaign finance restrictions. *Bush v. Gore* should always remain in our minds when we think about how political the court can really be.

The filibuster is not the only rule that was jettisoned. In contrast to the Democrats, who even in the face of Republicans' dug-in opposition continued to honor the "blue-slip courtesy," a Senate Judiciary Committee practice of refraining from scheduling a hearing on a nominee until the nominee's home-state senators have noted their agreement by sending a blue slip to the chairperson of the committee, in 2018, Republicans basically dumped this tradition. During his time as Democratic chairman of the committee, Senator Patrick Leahy would not entertain any discussion of a change to the practice and, predictably, the Republicans refused to turn in blue slips on a large number of nominees, sometimes even blocking those who had been suggested by their own nominating commission. Sarah Binder, a longtime observer of the Senate judicial confirmation process, writes that "Leahy's policy undermined Obama's ability to confirm judges onto the bench in states represented by at least one Republican" and accounts in part for Obama's low confirmation rates.[75]

By contrast, in late November 2017, Republican senator Chuck Grassley of Iowa, the new chairman of the committee, announced he would proceed to a hearing for a judicial nominee over the objections of a Democratic home-state senator—without the blue slip, in other words. This decision was no surprise. In an article for the *New Republic* written prior to the change, David Dayen noted that "if Republicans change the rule, it would be all too typical. When Republicans hold the Senate and want a president to get judges through, they relax blue-slip rules. When the president is a Democrat, they tighten them. Democrats have adhered to blue-slip traditions regardless of who sits in the Oval Office. It speaks to the intensity of the GOP's pursuit of judicial confirmations. Republicans simply want their judges more, and will not let Senate customs get in the way."[76]

Unfortunately, some senior Democratic senators have a strange nostalgia for Senate rules, seemingly forgetting why

they were elected: not to fetishize a tool for committee operations but to advance a progressive agenda. When the base on
the left got energized because of Republican obstruction of certain Obama nominees, the Democrats under Senate Majority
Leader Harry Reid did ditch the filibuster rule for lower-court
nominees, enabling President Obama to confirm some key judges. (Unfortunately, the blue-slip rule remained in effect.) But
the filibuster effort demonstrated that when the base and major
funders work together, we can force passive Democrats to make
getting judges confirmed a priority.

Control of the judiciary is so important to the Right that at
a private gathering hosted by the Koch brothers in early 2017,
Koch officials handed out a document explaining the blue slip
and why it needed to be abolished (at least while there was a
Republican president). Speaking to a USA Today reporter, Koch
executive Mark Holden stated, "Having a home-state senator
have the ability to slow down the process, in our opinion, doesn't
make sense under the Constitution." At the Koch retreat, high-
level donors and influential conservatives were asked to push
Republican leaders to abandon the rule. The document asked
participants to "tell them not to allow needless delay tactics and
obstruction of the process."[77] And in an article in Time, Holden
chastised Democrats for holding up nominees. Under the byline
Mark Holden, chairman of Freedom Partners Chamber of Commerce, he disguised his day job as senior vice president, general
counsel, and corporate secretary of Koch Industries, Inc. (He
also serves on the board of directors of Americans for Prosperity,
another Koch group.) In the article, Holden fulminated against
the blue slip; while admitting that "Republicans did it to President Obama," he argued that "it's this sort of tit-for-tat that needs
to be dispensed with."[78] Of course. Until there's another Democratic president, that is.

ENDING PARTISAN ASYMMETRY

On the left, we periodically pay attention when the Supreme Court has an opening. When Scalia died, leaving a hole on the court that should have been Obama's to fill, Obama decided that his best play was to assume that the Republicans would cooperate if he nominated a moderate who had won Republican support in the past. Despite all the evidence from his seven years as president—efforts to win Republicans over on the Affordable Care Act and the stimulus bill, naming Republicans to his cabinet, all of which got the back of the hand from the GOP—Obama fell into the trap of thinking he could get Republican support for a centrist move. He found no support from the GOP and also failed to ignite the Democratic base. A sixty-three-year-old white man, moderate to a fault, Garland did not ignite the grassroots.

While Republicans fight for radical nominees, Democrats select moderate lawyers—but they tend not to fight hard even for them. I experienced this disparity myself, working in Democratic politics. During the Clinton administration, I was on the staff of Democratic Senate leader Tom Daschle, with a portfolio that included judicial nominations. Daschle, who recognized the importance of getting judges through the process, helped shepherd many Clinton nominees onto the bench—as the Democratic leader should do. This role was not controversial in South Dakota, until the right-wing donors decided to make it so. When Daschle ran for reelection in 2004, he was targeted by the Right for his role in supporting Clinton judges and opposing Bush judges, who fit the pattern of middle-of-the-road nominees versus hard-right activists. JCN donors Robin Arkley II and Ann Corkery set up a PAC to take down Daschle through an ad campaign that spotlighted his role in judicial nominations.[79] It was called "You're Fired Inc."[80] He lost.

None of this bubbled up from the electorate, but the fact that the topic had been used as a bludgeon against the Democratic leader both encouraged Republicans to fight on judges and made Democrats leery of fighting back. Democratic operatives now counsel senators to stay away from the issue, suggesting that their voters don't care and that the other side will punish them, so why engage? In fact, Senator Harry Reid ran for Democratic leader after Daschle lost his reelection by promising he wouldn't make his fellow senators fight on judges the way Daschle had. And so Democrats ceded more ground to the Right, with a real impact on our courts. With a record number of vacancies to fill, President Trump is benefiting from Democrats' absence from the fray. Journalist David Dayen says, "This imbalance means that the judicial branch inexorably drifts right, toward a constrained view of the Constitution and a limited federal government. It creates a judiciary that favors big business and puts big legislative advances at risk. And its impact stretches over decades, well beyond Trump's presidency. After eight years in the wilderness, Republicans in Congress and their backers in think tanks and super PACs don't want to stop that forward momentum."[81]

So what can we do to ensure that our courts aren't simply an extension of Koch Industries? Just as the JCN and the Federalist Society have long understood that judicial selection is a political process, so must we on the left. Already, some of us have begun to build that counterforce. First, we need to get Democratic senators to care by getting their donors to care, shaming senators in the press when they do the wrong thing and rewarding them when they do the right thing. Organizing those with close relationships with senators (in other words, donors) to demand senators engage has already made some difference. Even outside of a campaign fund-raiser, funders have sway—their opinions matter. Our task is to build this group, educating those progressive funders already involved—from those fighting for LGBTQ rights to the environment and on across the progressive spectrum—to recognize how central legal decisions are to their interests so they too can use their influence to impress on senators the importance of the courts. This project is ongoing.

Second, we need to be ready for when Democrats again have control of the Senate. Activists and donors must fight against the Democratic senators' tendency to be "holier than thou." Rather than reinstating antiquated practices like the blue slip or deferring to the minority by once again instituting the filibuster, Democratic senators need to aggressively fight for good judges and against right-wing zealots, without deferring to practices that will undercut that effort. The current Republican leadership has made several moves that should be emulated: abolishing the blue slip; prioritizing court of appeals nominees, since they have the most power to influence the direction of the law; picking young lawyers as nominees (as young as possible); and (if there's a Democratic president) working closely with the White House to swiftly nominate candidates. Rather than worrying that each nominee has an unblemished record, Democrats need to be willing—as Trump has been—to see a few go down. As one expert said to me privately, "Trump has sent one hundred soldiers over the hill; he thinks if ninety make it back, he's going to win." Contrast that with the typical liberal flyspecking, which results in delays and vacancies—and we still don't get our ninety to come back over the hill.

We must also make sure senators and candidates for the Senate feel both pressure and pain, as well as love, for doing the right thing on judges. That has to include direct campaign support for champions of good judicial candidates. Already, some progressive lawyers in DC have begun to bundle small checks from many donors into one donation to reward the few sena-tors who grasp the need to fight. But this effort needs far more funding to be effective. When senators and presidential can-didates begin to see the federal judiciary as deeply important to donors, they will make it a priority. And, though some find this repugnant, we need a robust analog to the Judicial Crisis Network that will channel high-dollar donations to run inde-pendent expenditure campaigns for nominees, with targeted paid advertising to thank and spank friends and foes. That's happening and needs to be supported. Demand Justice, an orga-nization formed by veterans of Capitol Hill and Obama's White House and presidential campaigns, hopes to motivate progres-sive voters on issues related to the federal judiciary. Demand Justice's executive director, Brian Fallon, a former spokesperson for Hillary Clinton's campaign, researched the backgrounds of those individuals on Trump's short list. Brett Kavanaugh and Amy Coney Barrett were particularly targeted for their posi-tions on dismantling the Affordable Care Act and overturning *Roe v. Wade*, as well as because they would be a rubber stamp for Trump on issues relating to the Russia investigation. In the campaign against Kavanaugh, Demand Justice went after con-servative Democrats as well as liberals who should know bet-ter but have supported Trump nominees. A sign that it works: Senator Bob Casey joined a growing list of Democrats who will not vote for any nominee on Trump's list.[82]

Just as conservatives understand the value of a deep bench, we also need to cultivate and support young progressives who want to become judges. The American Constitution Society has begun this painstaking work of running a job bank and clerkship train-ing programs, and assisting potential candidates with applying, but we are still catching up. This kind of leadership development needs funding. While some on the left are starting to grasp that policy needs personnel, it hasn't taken root like on the right.

Kristine Lucius, who served for many years as a senior staff person on the Senate Judiciary Committee, emphasizes that this investment cannot be for just one election cycle. "All of our civil rights and freedoms depend on judges to uphold these hard-won protections," Lucius told me. "We the people must demand that senators not rubber-stamp Trump's extreme judicial nominees and his plans to make our courts unrecognizable." And not just now but in perpetuity. Otherwise we will get more judges like John K. Bush of the Sixth Circuit, a "birther" and homophobe whose first published opinion ripped a hole in the Fourth Amendment's protection against unreasonable searches and seizures.[83]

And progressives must do a much better job of informing the public about the rightward turn of the federal courts. Despite decisions like *Bush v. Gore* and *Citizens United*, Democratic voters still believe the Supreme Court to be a moderate institution. While Republicans believe the court to be too liberal, even with its GOP-appointed majority, progressives think it is centrist. Writer Sean McElwee argues that this "partisan asymmetry" explains why the Right engages its base so much more successfully in the fight over the courts. "Republican voters," McElwee argues, "believe the court is working against them and are willing to fight against it, while Democrats mostly see it as a neutral arbiter of law."[84] In addition to informing voters that the Republicans have blocked women, minorities, and LGBTQ individuals from serving on the bench, progressive organizations need to make court transparency an agenda item: the Supreme Court should be pushed to televise proceedings, or at least release same-day audio, and justices should be subject to the same type of ethics rules—such as recusal when they have a financial interest in a case—that other judges are subject to. Sunshine is called the best disinfectant; even if some greater transparency doesn't fix the right-wing drift of the court, it might help show the Left that this is no moderate institution.[85]

STATE COURTS FOR SALE

While federal courts may dominate media coverage, state courts have a more direct impact on people's lives. State courts may seem sleepy, but fully 95 percent of cases go through the local courts—that's over 100 million cases in front of almost thirty thousand state court judges.[86] They rule on issues from contract disputes and custody battles to the rights of gays and lesbians and voting rights challenges, as well as on consumer product liability, malpractice, and, notably, criminal justice, including the death penalty. But progressive activists who can barely register a yawn over the U.S. Supreme Court battles have not engaged in the states much at all. Only labor unions and trial lawyers have paid attention, and these players, competing against special interests spending vast sums on campaign contributions and advertising, are easily outgunned. Eric Lesh, the former Fair Courts Project director of Lambda Legal, says, "Progressives have taken their eyes off the ball when it comes to judges. Many of us have taken comfort at the fact that, thus far, the courts have stopped some of the worst actions of the Trump administration and of over-reaching state legislators." He warns, however, that "we shouldn't expect that to continue. For years, far-right groups and powerful special interests have been working to game the system by stacking state courts with judges who will rule in accordance with their agenda."[87]

Soon after being launched to help conservatives pack the federal courts, the JCN turned to the state judiciary, pouring huge amounts of money into formerly dull races. The *Sacramento*

Bee found the JCN's interest unsurprising, noting it was "part of an effort by the GOP and business groups to spend big to create a friendlier legal environment, one that often is couched as 'judicial restraint,' is sympathetic to small government and limits tort liability for business."[88] The JCN has partnered with other dark-money organizations, including Club for Growth affiliates and other arms of the Koch empire, to provide deep pockets for state races in key parts of the country like Wisconsin and Michigan, where courts' rulings on redistricting and union dues have helped tip the states into the GOP column. In 2012, the JCN made an investment of over $2 million in Michigan state court elections alone.[89] And the JCN pumped money into the Republican State Leadership Committee, the campaign arm that focuses on state legislative elections and redistricting, to bring them into state court elections in 2014.[90]

"The first time I ever met Karl Rove was in Alabama, in a meeting of funders and operatives working on state Supreme Court races," said Chris Jankowski, a Republican consultant and strategist. "Karl had spotted this in the nineties and would go into each state and set up the machine that was needed. To get the judges, you had to recruit good lawyers. It's a really soft-touch process. You're not recruiting guys who want to run for Congress. You've got to do it subtly, you've got to move the money in the right way, you've got to fight the trial lawyers."[91] It is no coincidence that the evil geniuses behind the great ratfuck of 2010 also saw the importance of state court races early on. The two are intertwined—control redistricting, and you control the electoral prospects of your party. Control the judges, and you control whether the redistricting—or voter suppression laws—withstand judicial scrutiny. Not coincidentally, Jankowski has gone from the redistricting project he ran with the Republican State Leadership Committee, REDMAP, to work as a consultant for the JCN.[92]

Wisconsin provides a sad example of what happens when a state's judiciary becomes the target of the Far Right. Once a state with a respected judiciary, Wisconsin now has a fiercely partisan conservative majority. Since 2007, dark-money groups, including the Wisconsin Club for Growth and Wisconsin Manufacturers & Commerce, have plowed nearly $8 million into races to capture the state supreme court for conservatives. Lincoln Caplan of the *New Yorker* called these groups "central players in turning Wisconsin into solid evidence of how judicial elections corrode public confidence in state courts."[93] Behind the allegedly home-grown Wisconsin Club for Growth was the JCN, which gave the group over $500,000 in 2012–13, to be plowed into the campaign of Justice Patience Roggensack, who was seeking a second ten-year term on the Wisconsin Supreme Court.

Progressive reform groups attacked Wisconsin governor Scott Walker, who faced a recall in 2012, for illegally coordinating with these outside groups. The story of how the case against Walker developed, and then was thwarted, illustrates the impact of a judiciary captured by conservative interests. When the case against Walker came before the Wisconsin Supreme Court, prosecutors requested that several of the justices recuse themselves since their campaigns had been recipients of the same outside groups' financial backing. The justices declined and the court not only dismissed the charges, it blessed secret coordination between candidates and dark-money funders. The Madison-based Center for Media and Democracy condemned the ruling, saying, "No other court in the land has taken such a step, and the move took Wisconsin from being one of the most transparent systems in the nation to one of the worst." Or at least, the least transparent. The prosecutors appealed the decision but the United States Supreme Court declined to review it.[94] Prosecutor Francis Schmitz, who had served as a Republican appointee, lamented that "as a result of the [Wisconsin Supreme Court] decision and subsequent action by the legislature, a wealthy corporation or individual can make an anonymous and disguised political contribution through certain groups. The public will never know if those donations influenced the decisions of elected officials," including judges.[95] Why these anti-coordination rules exist, explained Judge Lynn Adelman in a law review article, is because "if a candidate can coordinate with an independent group that, under the United States Supreme Court's decision in *Citizens United v. FEC*, can accept secret, unlimited contributions, then contribution and disclosure rules that apply to political candidates are meaningless."[96] So with the sotto voce blessing of the United States Supreme Court, the JCN, the Club for Growth, and other right-wing groups have free rein to buy judges and legislators in Wisconsin, and no one is the wiser about the funders because they can remain secret. "Equal justice under law" needs a footnote: "If you are a donor."

Where was the Left while this was going on? Apart from the challenges to the electioneering of Walker and the conservative justices, the Left was largely quiescent. While the push for legal consequences for Walker's lawbreaking was a useful tactic, one that encumbered the GOP, it was not embedded in a broad strategy to advance progressive judges and a truly fair court system. What happened in Wisconsin has been mirrored in states across the country, and well-financed efforts have moved many courts far to the right, with the expected outcome—conservative victories in lawsuits and a growing cynicism about judicial impartiality. In one of the 2016 races, the JCN and the RSLC crowed after their win in electing a new chief justice in Arkansas who promised voters he would rely on "prayer, not politics" to make his decisions.[97] On the left, we have been splintered, with a few groups (labor, trial lawyers) putting some money into state supreme court races but with most progressives horrified by the very idea of electing judges and therefore staying out completely. This asymmetry of funding and interest have ceded a tremendous advantage and a major area for policymaking to the Right, with dire consequences.

It's not a coincidence that the Right has been pouring money into these races. Seventy percent of independent expenditures on judicial elections come from conservative groups, and it's been a good investment for them—the candidates with the most financial backing tend to win. Indeed, 90 percent of those candidates get elected.[98] These judges' votes can be counted on to harm consumers, reduce women's access to abortion, erect hurdles for gays and lesbians trying to marry, disfavor criminal defendants, and uphold barriers to the ballot box. Money talks, even to judges. In several studies, the American Constitution Society has demonstrated how campaign donations from business entities lead to business-friendly decisions, how attack ads insinuating candidates are soft on crime cause judges to rule against defendants, and how Republican-aligned judges are much more likely to vote their partisan interests in election cases. One study, *Justice at Risk*, examined the impact of *Citizens United*, finding that the Supreme Court has truly unleashed a flood of money into the state court systems, severely undermining the fair administration of the law. The report documented "a significant relationship between business group contributions to state supreme court justices and the voting of those justices in cases involving business matters. The more campaign contributions from business justices receive, the more likely they are to vote for business litigants appearing before them in court. Notably, the analysis reveals that a justice who receives half of his or her contributions from business groups would be expected to vote in favor of business interests almost two-thirds of the time."[99]

Another report, *Skewed Justice*, shows that attack ads run by dark-money groups to favor corporate candidates have a decidedly negative impact in the criminal justice arena. The study found, "The more TV ads aired during state supreme court judicial elections in a state, the less likely justices are to vote in favor of criminal defendants. As the number of airings increases, the marginal effect of an increase in TV ads grows. In a state with 10,000 ads, a doubling of airings is associated on average with an 8 percent increase in justices' voting against a criminal defendant's appeal."[100] A third study, *Partisan Justice*, found that in election cases, there is some partisanship on both sides, but "Republican judges systematically favor their own party in election cases by a statistically significantly greater margin, controlling for other things, than do Democratic judges."[101] In other words, *Republican judges chose party interests over fair outcomes.*

All of these reports demonstrate that the Left is losing in an important arena. Corporate contributions skew outcomes and attack ads make justices fearful of ruling in favor of criminal defendants. Eric Lesh, formerly at Lambda Legal, urges the Left to be more proactive in this key arena: "Progressives must mount a well-coordinated response to this extreme takeover of our courts in order to prevent extensive damage to our democracy and the further erosion of our constitutional rights. We are in danger of losing the courts for a generation."

Just as with federal courts, we need both a short- and a long-term plan. First, we need to contest elections, putting up good progressive candidates against corporate stooges and right-wing zealots. The Left has rediscovered the states, remembering how important they are not only as an incubator for policy development but also as a pipeline for diverse talent. So far, however, that has meant only more funding for state legislative candidates and attorneys general, both important, but not sufficient. With state court races remaining relatively inexpensive, progressive funders could make a real impact. We need a national hub, similar to the Democratic Legislative Campaign Committee, which raises money for state candidates, to identify the most promising races, such as those where having more progressives on the state courts would affect critical policy battles including redistricting and voting rights disputes. With an investment of $30 million, similar to what Karl Rove raised for redistricting in 2010, leading funders could dramatically influence the direction of our state courts and the outcomes of all of the battles that will play out in those arenas. Unlike the Right, where financial rewards for corporations and the wealthy align with their donation strategy, the big donors on the left don't see a personal gain from a progressive court system. But what has brought them to progressive politics in the first place is very much at issue in these judicial elections—the challenge and opportunity is to harness this ideological commitment (to choice or racial justice or fair elections) to the court battles where abortion rights or police reforms or voting rights stand or fall depending on who sits on the bench.

In the long term, financial asymmetries between Right and Left militate for building mechanisms to shield courts from moneyed interests. Moreover, these types of reforms are consistent with progressive values of transparency, fair rules, and an independent court system, and they build trust in government, which furthers our long-term mission. Labor unions, Democratic activists, and other groups on the left with power at the state level must put building an impartial court system on their legislative agendas, even as they battle to elect progressive judges. These reforms range from getting rid of elections for judges altogether and instituting a nonpartisan merit selection process, or passing a public financing law, as well as developing mechanisms to ensure that the state courts, which are overwhelmingly white

and male, become more diverse. In addition, the judges themselves can promulgate robust recusal rules (which some progressive judges have advanced). Parties appearing in court shouldn't
worry that the other side's lawyer spent the previous evening at a
fund-raiser for the judge.

But in the short term, we must take back the state court
benches. As Lesh recognizes, "The powerful, organized threat
to fair and impartial state courts requires a dedicated, aggressive
and well-coordinated response to prevent extensive damage to
our democracy and the further erosion of our constitutional right
to due process."[102] First, win elections, then fix the courts.

5

THE RULES OF THE GAME

When the rules get in the way of winning, change them. That's been the way the Right has operated when it comes to the courts, local control, and even the constitutional system. When it comes to seizing control and keeping it, nothing, it seems, is beyond the pale. Representative John Dingell, a Democrat from Michigan, famously once said, "I'll let you write the substance on a statute and you let me write the procedure, and I'll screw you every time."[1] We've been screwed for too long. It's time to grab the pen and write our own rules. Engaging foundations and donors, leading advocacy groups and politicians as well as the grassroots, we must track, expose, and challenge rules narrowing court access through media, legislative advocacy, and litigation. We must monitor and participate in courts' rulemaking bodies, ensure local governments' progressive policies aren't thwarted by state procedural maneuvers, and derail conservative efforts to use a constitutional convention to achieve the ultimate nationwide gerrymander of our rights. These efforts will never grab major headlines or light up Twitter, but without them we will remain "screwed."

LOCKING THE COURTHOUSE DOORS

Mention civil procedure, even to a group of lawyers, and people look at their watches or their phones or yawn. Dry and technical, the topic doesn't have the sexy attraction of voting rights or immigration to progressives in the legal world, but it's essential knowledge for successful legal advocacy. By focusing on a set of rather unexciting provisions, the federal courts, led by the Supreme Court, have whittled away at the ability of average people to have their day in court. Activist right-wing judges, assisted by legal scholars funded by the Chamber of Commerce and other corporate interests, have created a rule book that blocks progressive interests at every turn, forcing plaintiffs to jump a high hurdle to get into court, limiting class actions, and letting companies push conflicts into private arbitration, out of litigation and away from juries. By shutting down access to the courts, the Right has effectively obliterated statutory rights without legislative action and has made it extremely hard to challenge government actions like giving money to religious groups or stripping accused criminals of their rights. In his recent book *Closing the Courthouse Door*, noted constitutional scholar Erwin Chemerinsky asks,

> Why have conservative justices so embraced limiting the power of the federal courts to enforce the Constitution? I believe it is a way to achieve the substantive results they desire. They think many constitutional rights have been broadened beyond their desirable scope, and one way to limit them is through procedural doctrines that prevent people from being heard in court. . . . To select just a few examples, one way to allow more government aid to religion—which conservatives favor—is to restrict who has standing to challenge it. One way to limit the rights of criminal defendants is to deny review on habeas cor-

pus. Businesses can be protected from lawsuits by imposing heightened pleading standards and restricting class action suits. In other words, the restrictions on jurisdiction . . . reflect a desire for a particular outcome.[2]

The New Deal–era authors of the Federal Rules of Civil Procedure wanted to make it easier to hold government and companies accountable. Progressives in the early twentieth century, skeptical of corporate power, believed average folks should be able to go to court to challenge actions that violated statutory and constitutional rights. So they favored something called notice pleading that allowed a case to move forward based on a simple statement of harm and allowed discovery, or the exchange of information between the two sides, to get evidence, recognizing that most people who are suing someone do not possess all the facts at issue at the start.[3] Progressives believed that lawsuits would help hold big businesses accountable and make them pay for wrongdoing, providing an incentive for safer products and workplaces, and force government to change policies that undermined rights.

Starting in the late 1960s, Democrats in Congress made sure that new federal civil rights laws, including the Voting Rights Act, allowed individuals to sue to enforce the law. The executive branch, they feared, especially when in the hands of Republicans, would not pursue cases helping minority voters or victims of discrimination.[4] Thus, they drafted strong provisions in statutes like the Civil Rights Act of 1964 to ease access to courts, recover attorneys' fees, and get damages. They wanted to make sure the law would work to help victims and deter bad actors.[5] It wasn't just civil rights statutes that provided avenues to recovery not dependent on government agencies, but also environmental and consumer protection laws. Indeed, it was Ralph Nader's successes suing on behalf of consumers for safer cars, and conservation groups' litigation to attack polluters, that so aggravated Lewis Powell.

The Right organized to push back. At the top of their agenda was getting judges on the bench who would be hostile to plaintiffs. By successfully stocking the judiciary with conservative judges, the Chamber of Commerce and its allies ensured that the courts were a favorable route to limit lawsuits. Scholars Stephen Burbank and Sean Farhang analyzed extensive data that reveals how corporate America turned to the legal system to win the victories it had been denied through lobbying. "Recognizing that, as Lewis Powell had written in 1971, the courts were fertile and unploughed territory for such a campaign," wrote Burbank and Farhan, "those seeking to retrench private enforcement turned to that institution and were well rewarded. Litigation seeking to narrow private rights of action, attorneys' fee awards, and standing, and to expand arbitration, achieved growing rates of voting support from an increasingly conservative Supreme Court, particularly over the past two decades."[6] Big business appreciated that it was more efficient to have the courts themselves slip in rule changes in seemingly abstract or complex legal decisions than fight legislative battles under the bright lights.

Political scientist Paul Pierson called this approach purposefully "subterranean," designed to be "invisible at the surface" but leading to "long-term erosion," like "termites working on a foundation."[7] With a sleight of hand, the court has hollowed out Americans' ability to pursue legal remedies with no one the wiser.[8] The scholars' statistical analysis shows that "in the period 1970 through 2013, Supreme Court justices have increasingly forged majorities for anti-private-enforcement decisions and that the justices' votes on those issues have been increasingly influenced by ideology, leading to a wide gap between the Court's liberals and conservatives."[9]

As deep as the divide is between the Republican and Democratic appointees over substance, it is a chasm over decisions interpreting procedure.[10] Unfortunately, these decisions are often overlooked, both by Congress, which could overrule many of them, and by the public, because they seem abstract with little relationship to everyday life. We on the left need to remember that people mobilize over broad policy battles—health care and immigration—but not over the minutiae of court procedure that blocked a suit or allowed it to advance; we should be bolder in fighting these battles because the consequences are enormous for policy and the cost is low in terms of political capital (it's hard to make an attack ad out of civil procedure changes).

TERMITES IN THE COURTHOUSE

While most of us were unaware, beneath the surface, the termites were at work, eating away at the supports for our justice system. At its most basic, corporate America and its allies have slammed the courthouse door on "we the people": by limiting *who* can bring a case, by setting unrealistically high standards to even make a complaint, and by making it harder for people who have suffered similar harms to join a case together.

Created by judges, the "standing doctrine" has defined and constrained who can bring an action in a court of law. Someone filing a lawsuit thus has to say, "I have been hurt (*sustained an injury* in the language of the judicial system) or will be hurt soon (*imminently*) by the defendant (*traceable to the defendant's conduct*) and the court can stop the harm or give me money or other damages to compensate me." That makes a certain amount of sense, but conservatives have interpreted the terms "injury," "imminent," and "traceable to the defendant's conduct" in such a way as to turn away many valid claims.[11] The Constitutional Accountability Center's David Gans credits Justice Antonin Scalia for advancing this cramped view. Gans writes, "Scalia argued that the Constitution strictly limits Congress's authority to give individuals a right to sue to enforce federal rights." Quoting legal scholar and poverty advocate Gene Nichol, Gans explains how Scalia's approach put a thumb on the scale, using standing doctrine to "'fence out disfavored claims,' repeatedly invoking the 'toughest standing hurdles' in cases in which racial minorities had been victimized by the government. As a result, individuals who had previously turned to the courts to remedy systemic injustices—whether housing discrimination or the use of chokeholds by the police—were thrown out of court."[12]

Scalia also had a significant impact on environmental law, and hence in protecting corporate polluters by advancing the view that individuals may not bring a case on another's behalf but only for injuries they have personally suffered. Nor may they sue over a general grievance common to many taxpayers or citizens—like drilling in a national park or killing off an endangered species. In the controversial 1992 case *Lujan v. Defenders of Wildlife*, Scalia severely constrained the ability of environmental groups to litigate as representatives of their members, a decision Justice Harry Blackmun in his dissent described as a "slash-and-burn expedition through the law of environmental standing."[13] When it came to companies that wanted to challenge environmental regulations, however, Scalia had a much different approach. In an overview of Scalia's legacy for the environment, reporter Patrick Parenteau characterizes it as almost uniformly destructive: "To establish standing, a plaintiff must show how it is injured by the action being challenged. Scalia applied a more liberal test of injury for industry plaintiffs than for environmental plaintiffs. Standing was presumed whenever industry alleged that a government action might cause undue economic harm but not when an environmental organization alleged that the same action would cause undue environmental harm."[14]

Plaintiffs who make it over the standing hurdle must describe a plausible set of facts to establish a legal claim. This is the "pleading" component of litigation. Recent Supreme Court decisions have taken a sledgehammer to the concept of notice pleading, in which the injured party had only to state a claim generally to move forward. With the adoption of the Federal Rules of Civil Procedure, a plaintiff would describe her claim in simple terms in her complaint. If the allegations were sufficient to state a legal claim, the parties would begin discovery to find out the facts sufficient to prove or disprove the allegations.[15] With facts in hand, judges and juries could make decisions about whether to dismiss a case or let it go to trial and assess damages. The basic process was fairly simple: the victim would allege that she was a woman, had been fired, had all the skills necessary and good work performance, and that she'd been replaced by a man. But now, after two Supreme Court cases, plaintiffs must have a "plausible" claim, that is, they must state more facts about what happened than had been required before.[16] Thus, a victim of employment discrimination, for example, would have to know facts about her firing before she files a claim; for example, she would have to have the documents or emails or witnesses who could directly speak to the allegation and evidence that in the past she would have been able to acquire through the discovery process.

For civil rights plaintiffs, in particular, the discovery process, which allows access to an employer's documents or to witnesses, has been the only way to find out the truth. It isn't surprising that in most cases where employees believe they have been fired or paid less because of their sex or race, the boss is not likely to make a public announcement saying, "I fired her because she's black" or "I demoted her because I think women should earn less." Instead, when a woman strongly suspects her wages are lower than those of her male colleagues, she needs access to information about her supervisors' private meetings, any meeting notes, documents dealing with salary issues, and who might have been party to the decisions or know something about them. Unsurprisingly, employers take great care not to share this information with anyone. The upshot is that if a woman who has been paid less has good cause to believe the unfairness is due to sexism, a court can nonetheless dismiss her case if she doesn't yet have a smoking gun as evidence. Erwin Chemerinsky points out that now "the chance of a meritorious complaint being dismissed is high because many plaintiffs do not have the necessary facts prior to discovery. . . . The approach adopted by the Court meant that many plaintiffs, including in constitutional cases, will never get to that point."[17] Finally, if a plaintiff climbed over these two high hurdles, she must now usually go it alone rather than suing as part of a class action. In *Wal-Mart Stores, Inc. v. Dukes* (2011), the Supreme Court made it significantly harder for workers to join class action lawsuits to pursue their rights by giving a very narrow reading to the Federal Rule of Civil Procedure number 23. The Court's "interpretation" of rule 23 was dubbed "undemocratic legislation" by scholars because what the court did was, in fact, rewrite the rule.[18] When the decision was announced, *SCOTUSblog*, the website pored over by Supreme Court followers from both the Right and the Left, had this comment: "For large companies . . . the ruling offered a . . . message: the bigger the company, the more varied and decentralized its job practices, the less likely it will have to face a class-action claim." These limits to access to class action suits for employees facing widespread and systematic discrimination make it literally impossible for low-wage workers to seek justice.[19]

These court decisions didn't come out of nowhere. A coalition of banks and retail companies had joined together in a decade-long effort to develop a strategy to deflect lawsuits and immunize themselves from having to pay damages to harmed consumers and workers. In a deeply researched three-part series, the *New*

York Times exposed the history and the impact of this corporate effort to privatize our civil justice system. Reporters Jessica Silver-Greenberg and Robert Gebeloff explain how the coalition's efforts "culminated in two Supreme Court rulings, in 2011 and 2013, that enshrined the use of class-action bans in contracts. The decisions drew little attention outside legal circles, even though they upended decades of jurisprudence put in place to protect consumers and employees. One of the players behind the scenes, the *Times* found, was John G. Roberts Jr., who as a private lawyer representing Discover Bank unsuccessfully petitioned the Supreme Court to hear a case involving class-action bans. By the time the Supreme Court handed down its favorable decisions, he was the chief justice."[20]

Conservative activists—judges and lawyers—have also crafted doctrines that limit suits against the government for civil rights and constitutional violations. In most circumstances, court doctrine now prohibits any suit against a state, no matter how egregious the violation of rights has been. Despite the fact that there's no historical basis for reaching the conclusion that the Constitution precludes such suits, the Supreme Court has nonetheless found states immune when they are accused of violating someone's federal rights, including their constitutional rights. Chemerinsky argues that the Supreme Court's support of the sovereign immunity doctrine has no basis in the text or history of the Constitution.[21] Indeed, he writes, "the idea that a state can violate the law and nowhere be held accountable is inconsistent with the most basic notions of justice and with the view that federal courts exist to enforce the Constitution and laws of the United States."[22] Originalism, supposed to be content with finding support in the explicit text of the Constitution or clearly implied understandings, cannot make a case for sovereign immunity—but conservatives have no problems with this outcome. It is dismaying that those who claim to know what the

founders thought have forgotten the wise words of our fourth
chief justice, John Marshall, who observed, "To what quarter will
you look for protection from an infringement on the Constitution, if you will not give the power to the judiciary? There is no
other body that can afford such a protection."[23]

TERMITES ON COMMITTEES

In addition to the court decisions scaling back access to justice—
and even less visible to the public—conservative jurists have
other tools to short-circuit the ability to sue, such as by using
the rulemaking process that Congress assigned to the Supreme
Court in the Rules Enabling Act (REA) of 1934.[24] The REA
established the judiciary's authority to draft and issue the Federal Rules of Civil Procedure and also bestowed on the Supreme
Court the power to name members to the Advisory Committee on Federal Rules, which proposes amendments to the rules
for the justices to review. These rules address the basic operations of the courts and have an enormous impact on whether a
lawsuit will be successful. In 1971, Chief Justice Warren Burger,
who shared the concerns of the Chamber of Commerce and his
colleague on the court Justice Lewis Powell that there was an
explosion of litigation in the federal courts, saw the committee
as another avenue to achieve his goal of limiting lawsuits. While
the cases that troubled Powell were the consumer and environmental cases, he also fretted that the success of civil rights litigation resulted in significant "business expense."[25]

Burger and the subsequent chief justices, all Republican
appointees, have been able to drive changes through the appointment of like-minded judges to the advisory committee, with the
result that Republican appointees have served at a rate 161 percent higher than Democratic appointees.[26] Professor Alan Morrison, then at the Public Citizen Litigation Group, critiqued the

committee for being dominated by judges, and for the fact that
the few practitioners on the committee were all lawyers whose
work involved defending corporations.[27] According to a statistical analysis by Stephen Burbank and Sean Farhang, "the pre-
dicted probability of a proposal favoring plaintiffs went from
highly likely in the 1960s to zero in 2011."[28] It is no surprise that
the rulemaking process has provided corporations with more
and more power to operate without liability for wrongdoing. The
by-product, if not the direct intent, of closing off recovery for
victims of bad products and employment discrimination is an
elimination of remedies for those whose voting rights have been
harmed. Fewer voters means fewer people who can elect legislators who might change those rules back.

Even as the conservative judges dominate the advisory committee, corporate interests have funded an outside effort to push
interpretations of the rules that would further limit court access,
most recently focusing on cutting back on discovery. Suja Thomas, a law professor who has attempted to bring attention to the
impact of corporate efforts to influence the rules, describes how
the companies have helped to fund a purportedly independent
center at Duke University to train judges in how to understand
the rules. The Duke Law School Center for Judiciary Studies'
advisory council convenes private meetings between judges and
corporate lawyers, Thomas writes, "under rules of secrecy protecting the identity and affiliation of the speakers." The participants
work to draft an "interpretation" of the rules issued by the federal
advisory committee to ensure that they will be read in a business-
friendly way. The Duke Center then organizes "trainings" around
the country for federal judges. "These guidelines are trumping the
federal rulemaking process," Thomas says. In the normal course,
the federal advisory committee drafts rules and the Supreme Court
reviews them. Congress has the power to veto them, although that
rarely happens. It is only then that judges would interpret the rule.

But with the corporate-funded training of federal judges, the judges get their interpretation already "baked in," allowing the Duke Center's cramped, pro-business understanding of the rules to gain near-official status.[29]

UNRIGGING THE RULES

The courts themselves, the rulemaking process, and the Duke Center are all working diligently to prevent those harmed by corporate or government malfeasance from seeking relief. But we can't cede this ground, and indeed there are many consumer and worker advocates, civil rights lawyers, and others who are trying to make sure the rules are fair. Here's how: First, and most importantly, the progressive legal community must pay attention and publicize—and politicize—rules changes. Second, we have to prioritize mobilizing real people to file comments in the rulemaking process to contest the corporate interests, something that is critical *and* achievable. Connecting court rules to outcomes in court cases that affect people's lives is also essential and again is doable. Last, organizations and individuals beyond the traditional players need to speak up. It is up to the lawyers to organize this effort, but engaging leaders and members of faith communities, civil rights and environmental organizations, and voting rights advocates would really reframe the narrative and help rewrite the rule book.

Paul Bland, the executive director of Public Justice, an advocacy group that fights predatory corporate conduct and governmental abuses, offers these words of advice to those who want to make a difference: "The rules that govern the procedures followed in federal and state court are generally amended through public processes, where committees of judges and lawyers consider proposals by reviewing comments from lawyers and the general public and then hearing from interested persons who come to testify at live hearings. While the vast majority of the comments that the rules committees receive tend to come from lawyers and professionals, there have been times when members of the general public have spoken out in powerful and important ways and had an influence on proposals." He recollects how, with respect to the discovery rule changes, civil rights lawyers worked to get members of the public to write and say things like "I was discriminated against based on my gender, and my lawyers found these great documents that proved my case. But if I'd had to pay tens of thousands of dollars, I couldn't have afforded them." This effort "helped moderate the language of the final proposals. The final language was definitely a lot better than where they were starting."[30]

Advocacy groups, he notes, did a much better job in protecting access to class actions (rule 23) than they had done in the discovery rules fight because the civil rights groups and other new players got engaged much earlier. "At the outset," Bland says, "there were all these proposals that were clearly aimed at slamming plaintiffs, making it harder for plaintiffs to get class actions certified. But this time, the civil rights and consumer groups were all very engaged right from the outset." Progressive organizations invited members of the federal advisory committee to participate in conferences and discussions that included "listening to a bunch of consumer lawyers talk about what the proposals would mean for their cases, and also hearing a bunch of people talk about positive proposals to change the rules to enhance access to justice. Anyhow, the process ended up leading to a small package of proposals that were not partisan in either direction—meaning, they didn't slam the plaintiffs' bar and our clients, which in this context was a huge victory!"

Law professors Suja Thomas and Alan Morrison echo Bland's suggestions. What's really important, they both say, is to systematically track and respond to changes proposed by conservatives.

"It's not a plebiscite," Morrison cautions. Our side needs to do its work, he says, filing comments and testifying at times; progressive legal groups need to make sure they read the minutes of meetings and talk to participants and try to learn what they might be planning. "We need to get ahead of it before the train has left the station," Thomas reiterates. For example, progressives were late in proposing revisions to a 2017 proposal on litigation financing. The legal elite, as well as consumer and worker advocates and politicians, "should have been talking about it, but now it's too late." Morrison adds that the corporations in favor of restrictive rules brought together a disparate set of allies to weigh in, while those defending access to the courts have been less successful at getting diverse groups to file comments.

We are making progress, though, concludes Bland, writing that "historically, the process of amending the rules was more dominated by lawyers for large corporations, but in recent years, consumer and civil rights advocates have played a larger and larger role in influencing proposals to change the rules, and that has led recent amendments to be much more balanced."[31] Progressive legal groups like the NAACP Legal Defense and Educational Fund, the ACLU, and the American Constitution Society are doing their part by demonstrating diversity of support for court access—from civil rights advocates and environmentalists to women's rights lawyers and civil libertarians. Beyond that, these groups are organizing legal strategies and amicus briefs and explaining our side to the media, something the business interests do without fail. Collectively, we need to bring in our supporters, from major foundations to wealthy liberals, to fund a hub that can aggressively challenge what the Right is doing. We need to hire dedicated staff to track, analyze, and draft comments; we need to mobilize lawyers and others to file those comments and litigate when necessary; and we need to educate Congress, which can always overturn those rules. All of this costs money. And of course, recommends Thomas, "we need to initiate changes; we can't always be on the defensive. We have to figure out what we want and what we can do to protect rights."

VOYAGE TO THE CENTER OF THE EARTH: KEEPING STATE COURTS SAFE FOR CORPORATIONS

If rulemaking in the federal courts takes place under the radar, what happens in the state courts is truly invisible to almost all of us. But the conservative termites are equally busy there, chewing away at the vital supports to our democracy by blocking court access and controlling judges. Approximately 95 percent of all cases in the United States are filed in state courts, with state courts handling the cases that are most likely to directly touch people's lives: child custody, divorce, consumer disputes, and criminal prosecutions, but also lawsuits against companies for harm caused by pollutants or dangerous products as well as challenges to electoral districts and voter suppression.[32] Similar to their efforts on the federal level, corporate interests and conservatives have worked through state legislatures to move bills limiting damages or cutting off lawsuits as well as to retaliate against judges who don't cooperate.

A particularly noxious example—literally—of using the legislative route to change court rules is the North Carolina hog industry's plot to block lawsuits for environmental degradation brought by members of the mostly low-income and minority communities that live near the industrialized operations. The coastal plain, home to most of the state's hog farms, is where the majority of slave families lived before the Civil War, and it continues to have the densest rural population of African Americans in the state. In 2013, homeowners sued, claiming that the hog farms are "nuisances" and the companies ignored irrefutable scientific data proving the harm to nearby residents. Seeking damages and a jury trial, the residents also wanted the court to require the company to clean up the site. Research published in 2014 shows that these hog operations "disproportionately affect Black, Hispanic and American Indian residents." UNC epidemiologist Steven Wing and public health professor James Merchant of the University of Iowa filed affidavits describing the copious research documenting the harms to the inhabitants, including burning eyes, high blood pressure, trouble breathing, headaches, and an increase in anxiety.[33]

The hog industry decided that it would be better off if these cases would just disappear. So the companies worked with lawmakers to bar these mostly African American victims from protecting their property and their health in court. Over the veto of the governor, the North Carolina legislature passed legislation to ensure that the industry would not have to pay damages to property owners who live near "agricultural or forestry operations." The main sponsor of the bill, Republican state legislator Jimmy Dixon, a retired hog farmer, pooh-poohed allegations about the legislation. He said opponents of his bill were making claims that were "at best exaggerations and at worst outright lies," and he suggested that the victims who had brought the lawsuit were "being prostituted for money" by opportunistic lawyers.[34] Observers might question who is being "prostituted," considering Dixon's war chest was filled with hog-farming contributions.[35]

North Carolina is no outlier. Amid the Right's general efforts to make corporate America immune from liability by restricting class actions, imposing caps on damages, and instituting arduous requirements to file a case, agricultural interests have been particularly successful at exempting their businesses from generally applicable rules through a series of regulations known as "ag-gag laws." According to the Humane Society, these provisions serve to "make it difficult or impossible for whistleblowing employees or animal advocacy groups to expose animal cruelty or safety issues. These bills can take a variety of forms, but the intent is the same: to punish those who expose patterns of animal abuse or food safety violations on factory farms, and therefore conceal these abuses from the public."[36] The laws go so far as to impose criminal penalties on people who simply collect evidence.

Ag-gag laws are only one example of corporate efforts to preclude civil liability by changing the rules for litigation against business. In writing his memo, Lewis Powell had been particularly concerned about tort suits that imposed liability on corporations for polluting or selling dangerous products. Powell counseled business to invest not just in fighting back against litigation but also in scholarship, lobbying, and public relations to defend efforts to limit access to the courts. The Law & Economics Center at George Mason University has become a center for this work, running programs to indoctrinate judges and other officials in the harms associated with civil litigation. In addition to its judicial "education" project, George Mason has an Attorneys General Education Program and the Searle Civil Justice Institute, which has churned out reports and promoted "experts" to validate attacks on civil justice, calling lawsuits against corporations irrational and dangerous to the economy, when, in fact, the institute's real interest is protecting corporate profits at the expense of product safety and a clean environment.[37]

The Civil Justice Reform Group (CJRG) helps fund the lobbying and litigation that rely on the type of scholarship produced at George Mason and other tort reform think tanks. Made up of the general counsels of major companies, the participants include BP, Bristol-Myers Squibb, Chevron, Exxon, GlaxoSmithKline, Johnson & Johnson, and Koch Industries, among others. The CJRG provides resources to the front lines, without leaving fingerprints. According to the American Tort

Reform Association's Victor Schwartz, the CJRG is able to "do things in a quiet and effective way without fanfare."[38] The American Association for Justice, a group made up of plaintiffs' lawyers, sums up the common interest that welds this group together: "These companies produce vastly different products and services—such as Merck's Vioxx, W.R. Grace's asbestos products, Ford's Pinto, and BP's oil spill in the Gulf of Mexico— but they share the common goal of making it harder for injured plaintiffs to hold them accountable for their actions. Their com bined resources and coordination make the CJRG one of the most powerful tort 'reform' groups."[39] Its partners include the Chamber of Commerce Litigation Center, which serves as the legal flank, while the American Legislative Exchange Council provides legislative heft.

The civil justice system, however, is not just for tort suits. It's also the system that adjudicates our political rights, and the more the courts are controlled by the Right—through judges who are compliant, rules that are rigged—the more they deny civil rights plaintiffs their day in court. That includes discrimination claims but also efforts to enforce laws that guarantee political partic ipation; few Americans are aware of the fact that state courts decide the vast majority of significant voting cases.[40] While the expressed intent of these think tanks is to cut off corporate lia bility for unsafe products, the impact is widespread. And when corporations find that they no longer have to pay damages to victims, they have more money in the till to reward right-wing legislators. And the more these legislators protect corporations from paying for their wrongdoing, the more these corporate spe cial interests invest in the tools to keep their friends in power: voter suppression laws and gerrymandered districts. Why kill the golden goose? Better to feed it.

THROW OUT THE JUDGES—FOR THE
SAKE OF THE KIDS

But sometimes, even after passing legislation barring lawsuits against industry, companies still find that judges are standing in their way. Their answer: change the judges or intimidate them into changing how they decide cases. When *Citizens United* unleashed corporate money in elections, a surprising amount of it went into spending on state judicial races, where costs were low but benefits great—for business, having a friendly judiciary is a cheap way to buy immunity from lawsuits. In the 1989–90 campaign cycle, state supreme court candidates raised less than $6 million, but by the 2007–8 cycle, candidates had raised over $45 million for their campaigns. And after *Citizens United*, more of the funding is coming in the form of independent expenditures. For example, in the 2011–12 campaign cycle, independent expenditures accounted for almost half (43 percent, or $24.1 million) of the $56.4 million spent in judicial elections during the cycle. Alicia Bannon, an expert on state courts at the Brennan Center for Justice, explains, "Who sits on state courts can have a profound impact on the legal landscape in a state, and special interest groups and politicians are increasingly paying attention."[41]

Arkansas provides a chilling example of the danger to judges who buck conservative interests. Despite an otherwise conservative bent, Arkansas has been a state without limits on punitive damages when a business commits a serious wrongdoing. Unhappy with the potential for liability, certain business interests worked to pass legislation to cap damages, but their success was thwarted by a court decision that rejected provisions of the law.

Like waving a red flag in front of a bull, the court decision infuriated conservative forces, which decided to throw the judges out. With over $1 million invested in 2016, several dark-money groups, including the Judicial Crisis Network, used television ads and direct mail to attack the two allegedly liberal candidates in the state supreme court races. The TV spending more than doubled previous expenditures for advertising in what used to be dull campaigns. Justice Courtney Goodson, who committed the unpardonable error of writing the majority opinion in the case limiting the tort reform law, was attacked as being in the pocket of trial lawyers and an ally of President Obama, both unpopular in Arkansas. Goodson had also written the opinion that struck down the state's photo ID law. Strike two. Another candidate who was judged too friendly to plaintiffs also faced attack ads financed by the Chamber of Commerce, tobacco company Reynolds American, Walmart, and other major corporations. The candidate they favored was the state legislator who had drafted the bill to limit punitive damages for victims.[42] Goodson and the other "liberal" candidate lost.[43] In 2017, the state legislature passed a bill to put a cap on lawsuit damages on the 2018 ballot—this time around, the court is unlikely to find a problem.[44]

What often gets lost in the coverage of campaign mudslinging is the damage being done to average people. With the ads largely financed by corporations and conservative groups, judges are moving to the right to preempt any efforts to criticize them on the air. Although the true interest, at least for the corporate parties, is to defeat candidates who might hold them accountable for pollution or harm to workers, they don't want voters to know their true motivation. Instead, they camouflage their interest in liability protection behind racially charged ads accusing candidates of being soft on crime—with a demonstrable impact on how judges handle criminal cases. Whether it is intended or not, the attack ads are undermining criminal defendants' chance at a fair hearing in court. The "Willie Horton" approach works in state court races just as it did in George H.W. Bush's campaign against Michael Dukakis.

In one famous example, described by Justice Ruth Bader Ginsburg, "coal executive Don Blankenship lavishly funded a political action committee called 'And For The Sake Of The Kids.' That group bought advertisements accusing Justice Warren McGraw of freeing a 'child rapist' and allowing that 'rapist' to 'work as a janitor at a West Virginia school.'"[45] Blankenship's agenda, however, had nothing to do with protecting children and everything to do with overturning a large damage award against his company. Citing a study by the American Constitution Society on the impact of such advertising, Ginsburg wrote that "disproportionate spending to influence court judgments threatens both the appearance and actuality of judicial independence. Numerous studies report that the money pressure groups spend on judicial elections 'can affect judicial decision-making across a broad range of cases.'" Quoting from the American Constitution Society's *Skewed Justice* report, Ginsburg noted that the "explosion in spending on television attack advertisements . . . has made courts less likely to rule in favor of defendants in criminal appeals."[46]

For those who think the Left might just plunge in and run our own ads challenging judges who rule too harshly, think about the fact that the Right's ads play to fear—fear for family and children, worries about child molesters and dangerous cities, anxiety about crime and loss of property. Our ads would require empathy; it would be a rhetorical battle between a nightmare for me and my family versus an altruistic concern for someone I don't know. Unfortunately, human nature tells us which ad is more powerful. But as I am an optimist, I hope that renewed efforts at criminal justice reform will give the Left a new language that appeals to the broader public, challenging judges who are too quick to incarcerate and too harsh in sentencing.

Another avenue the Right has exploited for punishing

uncompliant judges is to change their terms or the court's juris-diction. Republican lawmakers have been pushing changes to systems of electing, appointing, or retaining judges and trying to limit the power of state courts to overrule the legislature. Alicia Bannon and Nathaniel Sobel of the Brennan Center report that "many bills reflect apparent attempts to increase political influence over the courts, entrench partisan interests, or respond to unpopular judicial rulings. They also align with broader trends toward the heightened politicization of state courts, raising concerns that it will become increasingly difficult for judges to put aside partisan and ideological preferences when deciding cases."[47] What Bannon and Sobel leave unstated is that all of these efforts come from the Right—to help corporate interests and ensure that courts won't protect workers or gays or side with Democrats and minorities when the legislature blocks them from participating fairly in the democratic process.

North Carolina once again illuminates the playbook of the Right. In 2016, after Democrats won the governorship and hence the ability to appoint judges, the Republican-controlled state legislature quickly moved to keep the conservative majority in the courts. They raised the retirement age of judges so that the new governor, Roy Cooper, couldn't fill the seats that were about to open up with the imminent departure of several judges. The legislators also adopted a law to shrink the intermediate appeals court, eliminating three seats so Governor Cooper could not fill them and add liberals to the bench. They wanted to make sure that the legislators' partisan and racial gerrymander—of the statehouse, congressional seats, and judicial districts—would not be overturned by the courts.

By stripping courts of the ability to hear cases against corporations, limiting damages, and punishing judges who don't toe the line, the Right has turned our state court systems into tools to control government. Progressives cannot simply sit back and allow our "least dangerous branch" to become a subsidiary of Koch Industries and an enormous weapon against liberal values. We need to include in our plans a resourced campaign to take the rules back so that good judges can apply them. Because if those whose rights have been violated can't get into the court-room, it doesn't matter if the judges are fair or whether they're biased—we lose.

Taking the rules back in state courts is primarily a legislative battle. As the Left builds more capacity for state policymaking, through groups like the State Innovation Exchange (SIX) that provide substantive support for lawmakers, a focus on court rules must be a critical piece. Just as at the federal level, lawyers and legal policy advocates must educate and engage a diverse con-stituency who will explain to voters how barriers to the court-house limit their rights to clean water and political participation. Trial lawyers are a wealthy constituency who can help provide resources to diverse groups to engage in rulemaking, allowing those voices to frame the agenda rather than the traditional players. We need a set of model bills, draft hearing testimony, a grassroots organizing plan, and political campaigns to elect receptive litigators—it's not a difficult plan to understand, but it needs money.

In addition to getting better rules, we have to select or elect, depending on the state, judges who believe that courts exist to allow people to enforce their rights. We need to overcome any antipathy to electing judges in states where that happens, getting political donors and organizations to make these races a priority. The Judicial Crisis Network is a small group with an enormous reach—it channels donations from anonymous funders not only to pressure U.S. senators on federal judicial nominations but also to fund right-wing judges' state campaigns. These races are not expensive and there's no reason that the Left could not go toe-to-toe with the JCN by reminding voters of that organization's agenda—corporate immunity for environmental disasters and worker injuries, barriers to reproductive rights, and harsh criminal justice policies.

SHUTTING DOWN CITY HALL: PREEMPTION IS TURNING FEDERALISM ON ITS HEAD

With marked success in controlling both federal and state courts, the federal government, and statehouses, conservative interests could be expected to feel that they have earned the right to relax. But there is one level of government that has not been so easy for them to dominate—cities and municipalities, which often lean left. Across the country, some of these jurisdictions have passed legislation to raise the minimum wage or to provide workers with paid sick leave or to ban fracking. Rather than battle these provisions one by one, the Right has developed a much more efficient approach: preempt them. Speaking to an Austin-based conservative think tank, Texas governor Greg Abbott explained the rationale: "As opposed to the state having to take multiple rifle-shot approaches at overriding local regulations, I think a broad-based law by the state of Texas that says across the board, the state is going to preempt local regulations, is a superior approach."[48]

North Carolina, thanks to mini-Koch Art Pope, provides a microcosm of the varied Republican tactics to destroy the democratic process: gerrymandering, vote suppression, rigging the courts, but it doesn't stop there. While much of the attention was focused on it being the "bathroom bill," the state's SB 2 had more to it than that. Even as the Republicans in the legislature were attacking Charlotte's ordinance making it illegal to discriminate against gays and lesbians and protecting the rights of transgender people, they also prohibited every city in North Carolina from adopting any similar rules *and* from raising the minimum wage.[49] Gerald Frug, a Harvard Law professor who writes about localism, told David Graham of *The Atlantic*, "Most people think, *We have an election here, we elect a mayor and our city council, we organize our democracy—we should have a right to control our own city in our own way.* You go to any place in America and ask, 'Do you think this city can control its own destiny?' 'Of course it can!' The popular conception of what cities do runs in direct conflict with the legal reality."[50]

Working with state legislators, the American Legislative Exchange Council has provided model preemption bills and served as a cheerleader and strategic adviser, with great success.[51] Cities are seeing their power usurped by state legislatures on issues from safe working conditions, fair pay, sick days, and family leave to anti-fracking rules to public health. By May 2017, 24 states had moved to preempt minimum wage increases, 18 had blocked paid sick days, 3 had stopped provisions to protect LGBTQ individuals from discrimination, 17 had put a stop to local efforts to set up municipal broadband service, and 6 had overridden fracking bans. And that was just the beginning.[52] "We are about to see a shit storm of state and federal preemption orders, of a magnitude greater than anything in history," says Mark Pertschuk of Grassroots Change, a group founded to fight preemption and to protect local health and safety legislation.[53]

When Birmingham, Alabama, raised its minimum wage, it provoked a swift and fiery reaction from the statehouse. Legislators quickly passed legislation stripping local governments of the ability to raise the local minimum wage. The law, though applicable to every city in the state, was clearly designed to target Birmingham, the only jurisdiction that had increased its minimum wage—and one that is 72 percent African American. The NAACP, residents of the city, and the Alabama Legislative Black Caucus decided to fight back, suing the state for constitutional violations. In the complaint, they argued that the law preempting local wage increases demonstrated "racial animus" due to its reliance on the 1901 state constitution, which had been adopted to institute segregation and white supremacy. Citing violations of the Equal Protection Clause of the Fourteenth Amendment and the Voting Rights Act, the city's residents complained that the law denies them a local government when it comes to their economic interests by taking authority from those they elected and giving it to state legislators.[54] The head of the National Employment Law Project, Christine Owens, called the state legislature's action a usurpation of local control driven by racist politics: "The days of a Jim Crow economy should be long-gone, but sadly, the refusal of Alabama's legislature to allow Birmingham to meet local needs through appropriate local measures signals the past persists."[55]

Birmingham lost in district court in 2017 but successfully appealed the dismissal of its Equal Protection claims to the United States Court of Appeals for the Eleventh Circuit, which sent the case back to the district court for further proceedings.[56] Whatever happens, the suit underscores the true intent behind advocates of preemption and why ALEC and the Right have been pushing it (and, might I add, why who sits on the court bench matters desperately). Cities tend to be more diverse and more progressive than the rest of their states. This is true across the country, with most white Americans living outside of cities and only 10.5 percent of them residing in the country's largest twenty cities. African Americans also support a minimum wage increase by 89 percent, while whites oppose it by 54 percent.[57] In the midst of controversy over Confederate monuments in 2017, some states banned any local action to remove them or even to rename public spaces. Laws that have been on the books in North Carolina and Tennessee prohibiting local governments from moving statues were subsequently proposed in Alabama, Louisiana, Mississippi, and Virginia.[58] Preemption, and the determination of rural and suburban whites to trump the desires of urban voters, has more than a whiff of racism—it stinks of it.

Not only do these preemption laws tie the hands of local leaders to respond to local problems, they also often impose serious penalties on mayors and city councils who don't sufficiently conform to the rules. In Florida, a gun law adopted in 2016 allows aggrieved gun owners to sue local officials, subjecting the officials to fines and penalties and even removal from office if they adopt gun restrictions. Two pro-gun groups brought an aggressive lawsuit against then Tallahassee mayor (and current gubernatorial candidate) Andrew Gillum, not because he urged passage of gun control ordinances but because he did not work to undo those still on the books. Gillum, defending himself without the city's legal team—because the preemption law bars reliance on any public resources to contest such lawsuits—argued that no action was necessary since the city's provision was null and void after passage of the state law. Gillum won in court, but it was a narrow decision and the fines are still in state law. Laws like these not only restrict local control but also intimidate local leaders so that they are scared to defend the interests of their communities.[59]

Taking a rare stand for consistency, commentator Max Bloom criticized his fellow conservatives for pushing to strip authority from local governments. In *National Review*, Bloom suggested his readers examine their commitment to federalism as a bedrock principle.

> Suppose that we have on our hands a federalist-minded conservative. It comes to his attention that, say, Hawaii has done something silly. Perhaps the well-meaning folks in Honolulu have increased the minimum wage to $15 an hour; perhaps they have decreed that rents cannot increase faster than inflation; perhaps they have decided that what the University of Hawaii at Manoa really needs is another three dozen gender-studies professors. Ours is a good conservative, so he shakes his head in dismay and suppresses

a chuckle—but he is a good federalist, too, so he accepts that, strange and unfortunate though the ways of others may sometimes be, Hawaii is Hawaii's to ruin.[60]

For the Right, however, the commitment to federalism has been cast aside in favor of the desire to prohibit local control and progressive policymaking. Indeed, the trend is getting worse. Preemption of specific laws is giving way to "blanket" or "super" preemption, which allows a governor by fiat to find a local ordinance or regulation out of compliance with state law. In 2016, Arizona adopted legislation dubbed the "mother of all preemption bills" that would cut off state funds for any cities or towns that adopt policies in conflict with state legislation, a decision made by the Republican attorney general.[61] Gone are the days when conservatives were sentimental about local control and the need for Main Street, and not just K Street or Wall Street, to have a say in the policies governing people's lives. Today, conservatives are deeply cynical about federalism, continuing to support it only when it advances a right-wing vision for America. Ohio Republican state senator Keith Faber made this clear: "When we talk about local control, we mean state control."[62]

Donald Trump's America is one where state Republicans feel empowered to snatch away local powers, making it harder to address community challenges and imposing legal and financial penalties for any hint of deviation from the state's corporate-friendly policies. Sometimes, the citizens push back and use the ballot-initiative process to advance their views in defiance of the state legislature. But the Right has an answer for that too: after seeing several successful referenda providing minimum wage increases and paid sick leave, ALEC has been pushing to cut off this work-around. In a 2006 resolution, ALEC stated, "The legislative process should be the principal policy-making vehicle for developing state law."[63] It is no surprise in polarized and racist America that suburban and rural white legislators are silencing black, brown, and liberal white voters, even when the latter are in the majority.

The Right is operating at the subterranean level; taking whacks at city self-government doesn't get much attention and so few people understand the effect it has or the intent behind it. But there *is* resistance. A determined group of lawyers and activists around the country are tracking the efforts and working on strategies of opposition. Housed at Fordham Law School's Urban Law Center, the scholars and advocates at the Local Solutions Support Center (LSSC) are advancing ideas to bolster the ability of cities to enact science-based, inclusive, fair, and innovative laws. Working across issues, from the environment to labor to anti-discrimination, they are developing legal theories to protect local control based on federal and state constitutions.

For those concerned about protecting urban jurisdictions against state overreach, there are several promising avenues for litigation by which lawyers and nonlawyers alike can make a difference, including establishing a thorough record as preemption legislation is being considered by testifying about the negative impact of the law or, better, by drawing out supporters of the preemption bill to speak to their real intentions about why they don't trust "urban" voters to make decisions about their own welfare. When legislation is based on animus against gays or certain religions or races, or advances a religious agenda, this work can help prepare the constitutional lawsuits. Advocates are also developing proactive approaches such as drafting anti-preemption provisions to insert in state bills and initiatives.[64] LSSC's legal memorandum acknowledges that the Right has a jump on progressives.

> There is no denying it was the long-term commitment to
> reframing the legal debate and training judges and lawyers
> made by conservative funders starting three decades ago

that has helped define and given rise to the current, daunt-ing legal and legislative environment. To prevail ultimate-ly, a similar investment of resources over time will need to be made in progressive localism. While the LEAP [LSSC's former name] research, tools, and legal strategies . . . are an important first step, especially to counter the escalating threat of preemption, it is important to consider how this work could constitute a start on a long-term law reform movement. Through strategies like constitutional and leg-islative reform, work with think tanks, training of judges and state/local government attorneys, and linking with broader progressive local movements, such an effort could ultimately transform the legal and legislative landscape and support adoption of a robust, progressive view of local authority.

The work we do to build a progressive judiciary and adjust court rules will also build our legal bench and advocacy capacity. Preemption is a cross-cutting problem—like the Right's domi-nation of the courts, it harms all of the Left's priorities and we must attack it in the same systemic way, not piece by piece but by addressing the system, not the issues.

REWRITING THE BIGGEST RULE BOOK OF ALL

In one last grand dirty trick, to make their lock on power unas-sailable, conservatives are moving to change the rules that count the most: the provisions of the Constitution. With increasing control of state legislatures, many conservatives think it is a propitious moment to convene a constitutional convention and jam through all the changes they cannot implement through legislation because they are now unconstitutional. Historically, changes to the United States Constitution have been made by amendment, approved by at least three-fourths of the state legislatures—thirty-eight states—after receiving the support of a two-thirds majority in both the House and Senate. But under Article V, the Constitution also allows two-thirds of the state legislatures to demand a constitutional convention. Republicans now control thirty-three state legislatures, putting victory in their grasp. The governors play no role in this process and cannot block it. This process has never been used in U.S. history.

"Various activist groups have sought to amend the constitution on specific points through an Article V convention before," writes journalist Brendan O'Connor, "but few have been as well-funded or as ideologically driven as the Convention of States Project, steeped in evangelical Christianity and backed by millions of dollars in dark money. Between 2011 and 2015, the group's budget more than tripled to $5.7 million—buoyed by donations from the Mercer Family Foundation and various donor-advised funds linked to the Koch brothers."[65] The Convention of States Project is a special program of Citizens for Self-Governance, with Jim DeMint, former South Carolina senator and former head of the Heritage Foundation, as its senior adviser. The group's objective is to use a convention to "impose fiscal restraints on the federal government, limit its power and jurisdiction, and impose term limits on its officials and members of Congress."[66] This approach would rewrite the most important rules of all, set down in the Constitution, with grave consequences, particularly for vulnerable people—minorities, women, the LGBTQ community, children . . . everyone. While the group seems extreme—it calls the IRS, the EPA, and the U.S. Supreme Court "abuses of power"—it is deeply embedded in the conservative infrastructure, with close alliances with the Tea Party and ALEC, and funding from the Koch brothers.

Speaking to a group of ALEC members, DeMint touted all the accomplishments that could be achieved by invoking Article V. "So many look to Washington to make America great again,"

DeMint told an ALEC panel at the group's 2017 policy conference. "Washington cannot do it and it will not do it."[67] In his
speeches, DeMint rallies his audience by suggesting that the
constitutional convention would overturn *Roe v. Wade* and
Obergefell v. Hodges, the 2015 decision on gay marriage.[68] Mike
Huckabee, former Arkansas governor and two-time GOP presidential candidate, plugged the Convention of States initiative at
ALEC's July 2015 conference in San Diego. Article V, Huckabee
advised the audience, is the "only way" to cut back on federal
powers and would serve to overturn U.S. Supreme Court rulings
with which ALEC conventioneers disagreed. "It is not the law
of the land because five unelected lawyers in black robes said it,"
Huckabee argued. "They don't have that power."[69]

Some on the left have embraced Article V efforts with the
naïve hope that a convention would overturn the Supreme
Court's *Citizens United* decision, but so long as power remains
definitively in the hands of Republican-dominated state legislatures, they are on a fool's errand. Led by Harvard law professor
Lawrence Lessig, their call for a convention channels frustrations
with a nonresponsive government similar to those heard on the
right. In 2011, Lessig teamed with the right-wing Citizens for
Self-Governance to host a conference promoting the idea of a
new constitutional convention.[70]

Most legal scholars, however, believe that the idea of limiting
a convention's scope is a pipe dream. At a 2011 event examining constitutional convention proposals, Harvard law professor
Laurence Tribe, a renowned constitutional scholar, argued that
a "runaway" convention could easily occur because there is no
agreement or legal authority on what any constitutional convention would look like in the first place. There are numerous
unanswered questions, Tribe said, regarding the constitutional
convention process under Article V. Ultimately, a constitutional

convention would essentially "put it all up for grabs," and his doubts about a convention overcame his desire to try for progressive amendments.[71]

That's why most groups that want to see *Citizens United* reversed oppose joining in the Article V process. Common Cause, one such organization, "strongly opposes an Article V convention, even as we strongly support a constitutional amendment to reverse *Citizens United*. We oppose a constitutional convention because we believe there is too much legal ambiguity that leads to too great a risk that it could be hijacked by wealthy special interests pushing a radical agenda that poses a very real threat to American democracy."[72]

The danger is great. With ALEC's leadership, state legislators are moving legislation to force an Article V convention. Such a convention would very likely adopt constitutional amendments that would make it impossible for Congress to enact social welfare legislation and could attack fundamentals of democracy, such as the right to vote. The Koch brothers have eyed the convention process as another avenue to deconstruct regulations on their businesses and taxes on their vast wealth. And imagine the uber-gerrymander that would come out of such a gathering—there's no doubt that these extremists would try to lockdown power for an eternity.

With partners like Common Cause and the Center on Budget and Policy Priorities, however, progressives are pushing back on what the Right had hoped was an inevitable march to a convention. Joining with conservative state legislators who fear what might be unleashed in a chaotic convention, these groups have so far been able to stall the progress of the pro-convention forces. During the 2017 legislative session, Republican-led legislatures in Idaho, South Dakota, North Carolina, Utah, and Wyoming rejected efforts to support a convention and several Democratic legislatures scrubbed calls for a convention that had been passed long ago.[73] Still, we are too close for comfort, and progressives must remain vigilant.

Procedural rules may be dry, but they set the terms for whether progressives will win or lose. Affecting everything from whether children are harmed by dangerous toys, farmers whose crops are destroyed by a toxic chemical can bring a lawsuit, or victims of sexual harassment can have their day in court, they also can hinder whether the Left can challenge voter suppression laws or districts that lock in Republican victories. That's why we cannot abdicate the fight over the courts but need to advance and elect our own judges. And, more than that, we also need to fund a campaign to draft the rules these good judges will apply. It is also incumbent on us to organize against stealth efforts to rob urban areas of their legislative powers and to upend our constitutional structure—all of this is at stake in statehouses. We must provide the resources for our own version of ALEC, which would advance procedural as well as substantive legislation and educate progressives on why the Article V convention won't solve our *Citizens United* problem but in fact could make it far worse.

The Left has woken up recently to the fact that there are fifty states in the United States and that in many, if not most, we have an opportunity to advance a progressive agenda but only if we fund leaders, policy development, and courts to devise and protect those efforts. Jay Cost, writing for a conservative audience in the *Weekly Standard* about the rise of Donald Trump, puts it plainly, and we on the left should heed him: "Changing the rules of a game can change the outcome of the game."[74] It's hard to say it more clearly than that.

6

THEY GO LOW

When Judge Gonzalo P. Curiel ruled against Trump University in a fraud case, then-candidate Trump said, "They ought to look into Judge Curiel because what Judge Curiel is doing is a total disgrace. Okay?" Trump suggested that Indiana-born Curiel's Mexican heritage was a "conflict of interest" in light of Trump's anti-immigrant platform. After his Muslim travel ban lost in various courts, Trump called one of the judges a "so-called judge." When another judge found Trump's executive order on sanctuary cities unconstitutional, the president issued a statement accusing him of giving a "gift to the criminal gang and cartel element in our country, empowering the worst kind of human trafficking and sex trafficking, and putting thousands of innocent lives at risk." Trump's tweets and statements seemed designed to intimidate judges and weaken the credibility of the judiciary. "Presidents have disagreed with court rulings all the time. What's unusual is he's essentially challenging the legitimacy of the court's role. And he's doing that without any reference to applicable law," Indiana law professor Charles Geyh told the *Washington Post*. "That they are blocking his order is all the evidence he needs that they are exceeding their authority."[1]

The undermining of a co-equal branch of government by the

president is extraordinary, but upending the conventional wisdom and the constitutional order seems to be Donald Trump's modus operandi. Calling for a criminal investigation of his general election rival Hillary Clinton, personally attacking average Americans on Twitter, casting aspersions on the media for writing stories unfavorable to him, Trump is testing the outer limits of our democracy with his toxic brew of fake news, big lies, and deconstruction of government. But this strategy isn't unique to him; it's the logical outcome of long-standing right-wing attacks on the pillars of our pluralistic and multiracial democratic society.

UNFAIR AND OFF-BALANCE

Roger Ailes may no longer be with Fox News but he certainly left his mark. Described as the "quintessential man behind the curtain," Ailes was the powerful puppeteer who helped make fake news a major force in American politics.[2] Ailes took the conservative news industry, which predated him, to a new low by turning the idea of "fair and balanced" reporting on its head. Explicitly attacking other news outlets as being hotbeds of liberal bias, Fox and Ailes sought to portray their version of the news as not only right but Right. Fox News was birthed in 1996 by Rupert Murdoch, who placed Ailes at the pinnacle of the organization. Having grown fabulously wealthy publishing extreme right-wing fodder, including the *Weekly Standard*, and empty-headed celebrity twaddle like *TV Guide*, and through his ownership of the movie studio 20th Century Fox, Murdoch wanted to control even more channels of communication.

Greed and gutter tactics are at the heart of Murdoch's business model, concluded muckraking journalist Russ Baker in 1998 after a lengthy investigation for the *Columbia Journalism Review*. "Murdoch uses his diverse holdings," wrote Baker, "to promote his own financial interests at the expense of real news gathering, legal and regulatory rules, and journalistic ethics. He wields his media as instruments of influence with politicians who can aid him, and savages his competitors in his news columns. If ever someone demonstrated the dangers of mass power being concentrated in few hands, it would be Murdoch."[3] Finding a natural alignment between supporting extreme right-wing viewpoints and advancing his own interests, Murdoch envisioned the news industry as a public relations scheme for an anti-regulatory and low- or no-tax regime, which puts even more money in his bulging pockets. Starting off in his homeland of Australia, Murdoch brought his highly partisan, self-serving model to the United States when he began to do business here in the mid-1970s with his purchase of several newspapers, including the *New York Post*.[4] Murdoch's approach was bare-knuckled. In his fight to dominate the Sydney tabloid market, Murdoch outmaneuvered another newspaper for the rights to a printing plant. When the "rival tried to occupy the building," wrote *Time* magazine in a 1977 profile of the magnate, "Murdoch allies rounded up a gang of hammer-wielding thugs and recaptured the plant after a bloody fight. At the same time, Murdoch turned *The Mirror* into a catalogue of crime and cheesecake, and it battled the rival *Sun* to a standstill."[5]

His American targets, and a remaining focus, include the Clintons. He pioneered the approach of running highly questionable attack stories in foreign papers he owned, giving his U.S. papers an excuse to treat those articles as newsworthy. The *New York Post* led the way in the 1990s, observed Baker, picking up foreign news items and repurposing them as well as trafficking in rumor and innuendo about President Clinton and his family. The headlines would stress the most inflammatory charges, even when the evidence was thin or nonexistent.[6] While savaging Clinton, Murdoch's *Post* passionately boosted Mayor Rudy Giuliani, applauding his use of a racially charged white supremacist narrative—dubbed "exposing the bad Negro wherever he or she may be" by Jim Dwyer, who wrote for the *Post's* rival paper, the *Daily News*.[7] John Hope Franklin, the highly respected African American historian who served in the Clinton administration, provided a perfect target. After he lamented the continuing problem of racism in America and the nation's unwillingness to address "its own Holocaust, its own violence," the *Post* called this "a slander against the United States and its white citizens," concluding, "Now it's long past time for him to shut the hell up."[8]

In the 1990s, Murdoch saw an opportunity to bring his vicious brand of attack journalism and racial signaling to cable TV twenty-four hours a day. Roger Ailes had crafted the Willie Horton attack ad for the reelection campaign of George H.W. Bush, invoking age-old racist tropes of the dangerous black man who attacks white women, and had helped launch Rush Limbaugh's (happily short-lived) foray into television.[9] Who could be better for Murdoch's new project, Fox News? Together, Murdoch and Ailes began the "fair and balanced" news reporting that Fox has become known for and that has taken the preexisting right-wing media into the cable and digital fake news era.

SPIN CYCLE

David Brock, before repudiating his conservative credentials, worked as an operative for the worst offenders in the rise of the fake news/political conservative complex. In his book *Blinded by the Right*, he recounts how he manufactured stories about Bill and Hillary Clinton, including "Troopergate" and other would-be scandals. Richard Mellon Scaife generously funded both the

"research" and the right-leaning "journalism" covering these
stories in publications like the *Public Interest* and the *American
Spectator*, with resulting synergies between the source and the
reporter, following the Murdoch model.

Here's how they moved the stories: Brock and his ilk would
help spread false, even defamatory information about the Clintons (favorites included Hillary Clinton's lesbianism, Bill's com-
mandeering of the CIA and the Contras to bring in cocaine
to feed his addiction, and so on). These "news" stories would
first appear in the least reputable right-wing publications. A
less-respected outlet like the *American Spectator* would first get
it into circulation and then more credible organizations like the
Wall Street Journal could begin to report on it. The *Wall Street
Journal* alone ran dozens of editorials about the alleged murder
of Vince Foster by the Clintons, despite the conclusion of two
independent counsels that Foster had taken his own life.[10] From
right-wing financiers to stealthy operatives, a rumor disguised as
news makes its way "into the radical-right fringe press (*American
Spectator*), over to the thinly disguised radical right-wing media
(*Washington Times* and Fox News Channel), and onto the quasi-
respectable right-wing press (*Wall Street Journal* editorial page).
Gathering strength, the tone finally vaults into the mainstream
media (*LA Times*, *Newsweek*, ABC, CNN, et cetera), where it is
disseminated into the homes of millions of unsuspecting Americans," wrote then comedian Al Franken.[11]

The result of this cycle of sleaze is that important stories that
the public should be aware of are overshadowed by scandalous
rumormongering. In the 2000 election, for example, attacks on
Al Gore, who was accused of a variety of made-up nonsense, got
more coverage than George W. Bush's shady business dealings,
both because there was a lot of money behind the anti-Gore narrative and because of the intentional and long-standing effort

to undermine the power of good reporting. Real scandals, like Bush's financial entanglements and questionable business dealings, which resulted in an SEC investigation, were exposed by dedicated investigative journalists including Molly Ivins. In her book *Shrub*, written with Lou Dubose, Ivins detailed the questionable deals that allowed Bush to fail his way upward, increasing his wealth at each juncture.

Journalist Michael Kelly similarly dug up sordid facts behind Bush's success: "His insider-status investment of $500,000, which derived from his insider-status Harken [Energy] stock, which derived from his insider status as a Bush son, eventually nets him a decent-sized fortune of $14 million."[12] This real scandal, consisting of "a president's son who flipped his oil companies faster than a Texas S&L can daisy-chain a Dallas condo; as a corporate board insider, unloaded his corporate stock shortly before its price plummeted; and walked away from the whole mess with more money than Bill Clinton ever dreamed of making on a little real estate deal now known as Whitewater" got little attention from the public despite Ivins's efforts.[13]

Unlike the stories about Gore, apocryphal as they were, the investigative reporting on Bush didn't make it to the front page, because there was no left-wing media engine allied with politicians to drive it. Some might argue—and many on the right do—that the media is already biased toward the Left since most reporters tend to be liberal. But this critique misses the mark just as it does when lobbed against academia; while academics and journalists may philosophically align with liberals, they don't believe it is their job to support progressive advocacy. On the right, however, the media and the professoriate are indeed focused on winning political battles and they shape their work product to achieve that goal.

WEAPONIZING THE LIE

Nicole Hemmer, a close observer of conservative journalism, pinpoints the moment when the Right began to challenge the objectivity of the media and offer an "alternative" take on current events. In 1969, the fringe arguments of publications like *Human Events* and *National Review* got a powerful boost from Vice President Spiro Agnew, who shared their view that the news was filtered through a liberal lens. Agnew attacked journalists for being unfair to conservatives, putting a high-ranking elected official on record saying that news coverage was slanted and couldn't be trusted.

Many Americans, whose belief in government and the accuracy of reporting had been shaken by the Vietnam War, were more cynical about the media, and so even those who didn't consider themselves conservative became more open to the suggestion that the newspapers were not objective.[14] Hemmer concludes, "That widespread suspicion of mainstream journalism created a space for conservative media to grow while promoting the notion of liberal media bias. This is how we wound up where we are today, with a plurality of Americans believing media are biased toward liberalism, and conservative media stronger than ever."[15] James Carville and Paul Begala once said that the media's effort to appear "balanced" often obscures how misleading or false one side's arguments really are. "We get the feeling that if a Republican said the moon was made of green cheese, and a Democrat said no, it's rock, the media would cover it with a headline saying, LEFT, RIGHT CLASH ON LUNAR MAKEUP," they wrote in their book *Take It Back*. "The press ought to call Neil Armstrong and ask him; he's been there."[16] There's a clear imbalance: the mainstream media bends over backward to present a "neutral" stance, while the Right presents demonstrably false stories that move their way from the fringe to nightly news. Among conservatives, the "lamestream" media no longer has any status because the Trump-enabling *Breitbart*-dominated fake news engine has ensured that three-quarters of Republicans now share the view that "journalists and the media are the enemy of the American people."[17]

The conservative press did not simply stop at attacking the mainstream media as liberal; it also began to align itself vocally with politicians, becoming overtly partisan along the way. Many sophisticated observers of politics were nonetheless confounded when Donald Trump hired a new campaign CEO in August 2016 who came from the *Breitbart* news site. But this only made explicit what has been clearly happening under the radar: *Breitbart*, Fox, and radio talk show hosts including Rush Limbaugh and Hugh Hewitt have jumped into the tank for Republican candidates and elected officials feetfirst. The partisanship has become so overt that the Right, long known for its anti-Russia stance, has developed an allergy to addressing one of the biggest issues in fake news—the efforts by the Russians to destroy confidence in the Western liberal system of government by reaching voters through bots and fraudulent news stories.

President Trump clearly benefited from Vladimir Putin's multi-pronged strategy of stealing secrets from the Clinton campaign, selectively releasing the information through WikiLeaks, and generating fake news stories attacking Clinton that were widely distributed on social media by bots and then reported by Fox. The partnership established between partisan operatives and the right-wing media has created a situation where "the political lie is being weaponized to increasing effect,"[18] says University of Chicago law professor Aziz Huq. Seeing the Russians as useful collaborators in their effort to claim all branches of government,

Fox and its ilk decided to treat the "enemy of their enemy" as their friend.

The Trump campaign brought this unholy alliance of party and propaganda to new heights—or depths. Hunt Allcott and Matthew Gentzkow, economics professors and research associates at the National Bureau of Economic Research, sifted through data to show the impact of fake news on political outcomes in the 2016 election. The two academics concluded that an individual with a large social media following can reach as many people as an established journalist despite lack of a reputation for accurate or evenhanded reporting. And they also confirmed how biased these sources of information were in favor of Trump: "Fake news was both widely shared and heavily tilted in favor of Donald Trump. Our database contains 115 pro-Trump fake stories that were shared on Facebook a total of 30 million times, and 41 pro-Clinton fake stories shared a total of 7.6 million times." With the high number of readers finding the spurious stories credible, Allcott and Gentzkow note that "a number of commentators have suggested that Donald Trump would not have been elected president were it not for the influence of fake news."[19]

The president himself has played a large role in the circulation of fake news and in the related denigration of reporters and the "mainstream media," now a pejorative term. When it came out that his son Donald Jr. had helped arrange a meeting with Russians during the campaign to discuss dirt they had gathered on Hillary Clinton, President Trump helped craft a misleading statement to the media. The *Washington Post* broke the story that Trump had dictated the language, keeping his lawyers out of the discussion and providing a story to the media that was completely at odds with the facts.[20] Instead of admitting that the scion had met with the Russian lawyers to discuss the campaign and to find out if the information on Clinton was actionable, the president's version stated that the meeting was to discuss "Russian adoptions." Unfortunately for the president, emails uncovered by journalists showed the reality: the Trump campaign was hoping to use the meeting to gather useful opposition research from lawyers connected with the Russian government.

Fake news also gets weaponized when one communications outlet, like Twitter, takes a story from another, like Fox News. Much as Murdoch's papers normalized false allegations by quoting an overseas journal or David Brock worked stories from the fringes toward the middle, different media rely on each other to source their questionable stories. Fox News and Twitter worked synergistically to spread the lie that a Democratic National Committee staffer, Seth Rich, was killed because *he* had provided WikiLeaks with the Clinton campaign emails—rather than the truth, which was that the Russians had hacked the DNC computers. The *Sacramento Bee* called the stories "irresponsible and breathtakingly cruel to the family of Seth Rich, whose July 2016 slaying on a Washington, DC, street is still unsolved. Twelve days after his death, WikiLeaks dumped thousands of emails embarrassing to the DNC. The timing and circumstances fueled conspiracy theories, but it was Fox News that brought them into the mainstream."[21] And then the bots took over. *New York Times* technology reporter Farhad Manjoo described how easy it is for bad actors to boost a story on Twitter. Users can create numerous anonymous accounts, making it look like the same story is being shared by lots of different people, causing a fringe viewpoint to look mainstream, wrote Manjoo. Once a group decides on what story they want to promote, they use bots to overwhelm Twitter with thousands and thousands of tweets retweeting the initial story and add a "branding hashtag" to allow people to join a conversation. Journalists are slaves to Twitter, following breaking news and gossip, allowing themselves to be manipulated by those behind the bots. Alice

Marwick, a communications expert who spoke to Manjoo, said, "When journalists see a story getting big on Twitter, they consider it a kind of responsibility to cover it, even if the story may be an alternate frame or a conspiracy theory."[22]

Trump's role should surprise no one. His history of spreading rumors and falsehoods has been well documented. Famously, he helped spawn and foster the "birther" movement that accused President Obama of having been born in Kenya, and thus not eligible to be president. Starting in 2011, Trump began to speak at conferences and in the media in preparation for running for president, using the platform to question President Obama's legitimacy to be president. On *Fox & Friends*, Trump accused Obama of spending "millions of dollars in legal fees trying to get away from this issue," and he suggested to his friend Bill O'Reilly that, if they got the birth certificate, it would list Obama's religion as Muslim.[23] He even went on to say that the death in a plane crash of the Hawaii state health director who authenticated President Obama's birth certificate was suspicious.

Pressed by ABC News's Jonathan Karl on why he had continued to reiterate the lie, Trump said, "I think it made me very popular."[24] On September 16, 2016, Donald Trump finally acknowledged that Barack Obama had, in fact, been born in the United States, but did so, with inordinate guile, in accusing Hillary Clinton of having been the source of that falsehood. "Now, not to mention her in the same breath, but Hillary Clinton and her campaign of 2008 started the birther controversy," he said. "I finished it. I finished it. You know what I mean. President Barack Obama was born in the United States period. Now, we all want to get back to making America strong and great again."[25]

While not all of Trump's lies have been about race—he has said many objectionable and false things about women as well—racism underlies many of his tweets and statements.

In 1989, several young Hispanic and African American men were accused of raping and beating up a jogger in Central Park. Trump spent $85,000 on full-page advertisements in New York City's four daily newspapers, demanding the death penalty for the alleged perpetrators, known as the Central Park Five. "Muggers and murderers," he wrote, "should be forced to suffer and, when they kill, they should be executed for their crimes." It is hard to miss the echo of George H.W. Bush's Willie Horton ad. Worse though than Trump's gut racist reaction was that even fourteen years later, after the defendants had been cleared of any guilt through DNA evidence and the confession of a serial rapist, and after their sentences had been vacated, Trump continued to insist they had committed the crime. "They admitted they were guilty," said Trump in a statement he provided to CNN in October 2016. "The police doing the original investigation say they were guilty. The fact that that case was settled with so much evidence against them is outrageous."[26] What is outrageous is the blitheness with which our now-president expresses his hateful, racist, and false ideas. The young men had served six to thirteen years despite being innocent and received a $40 million settlement from the city of New York. But that story, as horrific as it was, got drowned out by Donald Trump's pussy-grab and cable news moved on.

Stories of crime and delinquency that focus blame on people of color and attribute lower morals to their communities are a regular trope in the far-right media, which is increasingly just the conservative media. Fox News and *Breitbart* are not so dissimilar in their choice and framing of stories. Along with crime, these outlets have highlighted allegations of voter fraud. These memes are distributed with purpose: birtherism to discredit Obama and make him less effective as president; crime stories to paint people of color as the "other" who must be kept separate and who are described as dependent on government handouts; and voter fraud, which has the obvious aim of providing a reason to make it harder for certain communities to participate in the electoral process. Ultimately, that's the goal: to discredit the mainstream media and advance policies that undermine electoral democracy.

We have to understand the motivations behind this president's declaration of war on the value of a free press. In a society where plutocrats own so many channels of communication, progressives depend on independent journalists to get the truth out. With Congress sitting on its hands rather than doing oversight, reporters have been the ones who have unearthed how the administration is systematically plundering the federal treasury for private gain; dismantling key protections for workers, women, and the poor; destroying our health care system; and poisoning our water. During his campaign and now his presidency, Trump has attacked the media and incited his supporters to revile and harass reporters, even tweeting a picture of a train running over CNN's logo. *New York Times* columnist Jim Rutenberg warned that "to dismiss Mr. Trump's rhetoric would be to disregard the risk of violence that comes with the kind of presidential incitement we saw Tuesday night [at a campaign rally in Phoenix] . . . Yes, mistrust of the media was growing even before Mr. Trump emerged on the political scene. But this much is unmistakable: The president is significantly adding to what is, without question, the worst anti-press atmosphere I've seen in 25 years in journalism, and real, chilling consequences have surfaced, not just in the United States, but around the world."[27]

Flexing his autocratic muscles, Trump lashed out at NBC for covering the allegation that Secretary of State Rex Tillerson called the president a "fucking moron," threatening to get the network's license pulled.[28] Trump even went so far as to accuse the press of fomenting racial tension and being unpatriotic for not respecting American history in its coverage of efforts to bring down Confederate memorials. As Rutenberg reminded readers, "Anyone with a passing interest in history knows that the founders viewed an independent press as essential to democracy. Talk about heritage."[29]

But that doesn't mean we should simply hope that the *New York Times* will do our work for us or that Rachel Maddow will always be on point. Despite the fact that the entertainment industry is dominated by liberals, with "nearly three times as many liberal- as conservative-minded people in the creative arts," according to a 2015 study, the Left is losing the message wars.[30] Liz Rose, then the communications director for the Economic Policy Institute, with long experience on campaigns and in progressive advocacy, told me, "We need to learn to use Facebook like the Russians. We don't have big talent working for us and we don't have smart social media funded by big money."[31]

Air America, a radio network founded in 2004, was meant to be a liberal response to the right-wing echo chamber. Designed to compete with Rush Limbaugh on talk radio, it quickly folded, going into bankruptcy in 2007 and shutting down completely in 2010. Media analyst Nathan Harden diagnoses the problem as twofold: the radio audience is older and skews right; and National Public Radio, a softer alternative for the Left, took all the audience that might have gone to Air America. Writing a postmortem in the *Huffington Post*, he noted, "NPR . . . produces, on the whole, better and more varied programming than Air America ever did. NPR exudes an understated but very real leftward tilt. . . . Ultimately, they offered consumers of left-leaning radio more appealing options than Air America did."[32] Alison Dagnes, a scholar who has written extensively about media on the left and right, gave me her take on why Air America failed, saying, "What makes talk radio really good is that it is vicious—and entertaining. And it is really hard to do for three hours a day, five days a week. You have to throw shade at your political opponents, use nicknames, express outrage."[33] And Air America did not do that. The Left, it seems, doesn't like the harsh tone of radio polemics but was also bored by Air America's blandness. Even more significant is what this says about the state of play: NPR vs. Fox is not a fair fight; in fact, it's not a fight at all but a surrender.

In her diagnosis, Dagnes finds that conservative news, like the movement generally, is very top-down and hierarchical versus the scattershot Left. All you have to know is that the number one news source for conservatives by far is Fox; for liberals, it's "all of the above."[34] Dagnes described to me the smooth handoff of talking points from the Bush administration to Fox News. It was obvious how they flowed, she said, because as soon as the officials had sent them to the news outlets, each one was on message— Fox, Limbaugh, and so on. Immediately, offices on Capitol Hill would start getting calls from the Fox audience, parroting the White House message. By contrast, she told me, when asked early in Obama's presidency if CNN would be using White House talking points, former Democratic operative and news anchor Paul Begala replied, "That's not how we fly." Instead, he said, they threw them away. The Trump administration, more like a pinball machine than a smooth message operation, hasn't been able to build the same distribution system, but since Trump gets all of his information from Fox, they are still all on message—it's just incoming rather than outgoing. Even more so now, with former Fox News executive Bill Shine's hiring in the White House communications department .

Our response to this message machine is twofold: attack their message and offer our own. For the first effort, we are well equipped. Probably the most important group that Democrats and the Left generally should focus on is not the NPR demo-graphic but the younger activists, who tend to be more tuned in to political satire if they are going to watch TV.[35] Comedy may be our answer to Fox, at least in part. With Trevor Noah, John Oliver, Samantha Bee, Bill Maher, and others, there's no question that the Left is just funnier than the Right. And those comics offer a brilliant takedown of Republican politicians and politics as well as a cathartic expression of our collective out-rage. Fox News made a few efforts to put comedians on the air, but their routines were dull and didn't seem to push the audi-ence's buttons as effectively as straight-up diatribe.[36] If younger people are the best hope for real progressive change in Ameri-ca, and they are more attuned to comedy than Limbaugh-style expostulation, the Left must do more to distribute Samantha Bee and her colleagues and promote new and diverse political satirists.

But comedy has its limits. Designed to attack the establish-ment, it can't offer a positive vision for what the Left is fighting for, nor can it serve as a channel to organize our constituency. As Alison Dagnes said to me, "It's the jester who speaks truth to the king." That is very valuable because part of the project is identifying and undercutting the Right's message. But it is not enough. Importantly, we need our own hub for viral con-tent. David Brock, who created Media Matters for America, which tracks and refutes conservative news inaccuracies, has now founded Shareblue Media. I talked to Katie Paris, Share-blue's CEO, about the organization's goals. First set up to ensure good coverage for Hillary Clinton amid a barrage of bot-driven negative press, Shareblue is trying to take a page from Donald Trump's book. Using a very sophisticated digital strategy, Trump connected with supporters through Facebook and other social media channels in a continuous conversation, said Paris. "Digital communications can enable the ability to create a community and provide meaningful engagement for the audience," she explained. To reach people, Shareblue uses very tailored messages based on what issues already interest people, who they voted for, and other information to build a relationship, and "not just to throw up ads." This allows liberal politicians and advocacy organizations to understand what is concerning voters and then connect with them on specific policies and actions. Paris calls this "finding real-world stories about heroes fighting for American values."[37] Another positive development is the creation of a new group, Tech for Campaigns, which is organizing volunteers to contribute their social media expertise to Democratic campaigns. Working by day at companies in Silicon Valley, these 4,500-plus tech specialists are training campaign staff in how to run a twenty-first-century political campaign with sophisticated email, social media, and digital fund-raising strategies.[38]

Digital technologies allow for a better and cheaper—and far more personalized—mode of communication than television and radio. Paris's hope is that the Left can jump ahead of the Right by taking advantage of our real strengths. For once, our more diverse and individualized constituency can be organized in a new way, while the Right's top-down infrastructure will be at a disadvantage. Add to that our surfeit of creative types adept at new technology, advertising, and entertainment, and we can leapfrog the media loop. Shareblue is avowedly liberal, not neutral, and is fighting to win. It is both an advocacy group and a media organization, providing information to its audience but also helping liberal partners use digital media more effectively. We know we have more creative talent than the Right; now we need to invest in more projects like Shareblue to get those liberal artists, writers, and programmers to turn their focus to politics.

POLICING FAKE NEWS

Technology can exacerbate the problem of fake news, but technology can also help address it. Europeans have grappled with the problem of fake news and found some effective responses. Most important to the effort, their experts say, is educating the public. They don't focus only on voters but also work through school programs and deploy aggressive anti-propaganda task forces. The European Union has created a well-staffed task force that relies on hundreds of volunteer experts to monitor and expose fake news. These countries' governments, of course, are more able to shut down speech they find misleading than is the American government, but that doesn't mean our government couldn't play a much bigger role in combating fake news, and particularly fake news designed to subvert our elections. A tactic embraced by other countries is to warn the public in advance of releases of misleading documents and information, when intelligence services have picked up signals and sources that indicate a planned fake news dump, including calling on the media not to report on them until they are verified, as happened in France during the election of Emmanuel Macron.[39]

Former dean of Columbia Journalism School Nicholas Lemann argues that government involvement in media doesn't have to be all or nothing, that is, state-run propaganda or a totally hands-off approach. Advocates should push to reinstate the Federal Communications Commission's rules that limit media consolidation, recently rolled back under Trump FCC chair Ajit Pai,[40] and demand that the Federal Trade Commission regulate false information in media as we do in other spheres, such as in advertising about prescription drugs or other products.

MSNBC host Ari Melber argues that some fake news sites use fabricated stories to drive up traffic and thus ad revenues. Rec-

ognizing that there's a right to make false statements under the
First Amendment, Melber nonetheless thinks some types of false
statements could be restricted. "A simple way to put it would be:
If a site has even 10 percent political expression by Americans,
the Supreme Court suggests it's protected," Melber told the *Washington Post*. "But if a site is 100 percent Macedonian commerce
and is fraudulently counterfeiting a protected American product,
it may not have the protection of the First Amendment."[41] That
is, foreign-generated fake news, produced for pay and designed
to expose more eyeballs to advertising, is not American political expression but rather a product that can be regulated. Part
of our problem on the left is that we are so sensitive to claims
of violating free speech that we refrain from taking action when
necessary. Speech, like other rights, is not absolute and must be
balanced against other values like protecting our democracy and
fair elections. Melber is right when he says that "it's a worthwhile
challenge to explore, rather than preemptively surrendering and
saying, 'Well, if we can't stop all of it or some of it's protected speech
for good reason, then nobody should do anything about it.'"

In addition to exposing fake news, we need more hard-driving
investigative journalism. Journalists have been critical in expos-
ing corporate corruption and the malfeasance of elected officials.
Even if the government were in Democratic hands, we would
need a free press because Democrats too sometimes choose
money over morals. "Trust, but verify," as Ronald Reagan said.[42]
That's why we need to support more quality journalism such
as that produced by the independent ProPublica, which documents right-wing groups like ALEC and political corruption;
InsideClimateNews, which broke open the story about Exxon's
early awareness of climate change; and the Marshall Project,
which focuses on criminal justice. And we should reinvest in and
expand our public news infrastructure.[43]

Lewis Powell was correct: to advance substantive goals requires building up scholars and experts to deliver the message; providing them access to television, radio, the printed press, and now social media; monitoring news and attacking coverage or analysis that is unfair or biased; and ensuring a supply of content to both our audience and those who might be persuaded. This road map is as valid for the Left as it was for the Right.

WE GO HIGH, OR, "LUCY AND THE FOOTBALL"

While Republicans go low, Democrats go, well, high. Take President Obama, who came into office pledging to work in good faith with Republicans and reestablish bipartisan collaboration in Washington. Met immediately with a stiff arm from the GOP, Obama swore he would continue to try. "You know, when I made a series of overtures to the Republicans—going over to meet with both Republican caucuses; you know, putting three Republicans in my Cabinet, something that is unprecedented [one of the Republicans, Judd Gregg, did not agree to serve in the Cabinet]; making sure that they were invited here to the White House to talk about the economic recovery plan—all those were not designed simply to get some short-term votes," Obama said. "They were designed to try to build up some trust over time. And I think that as I continue to make these overtures, over time hopefully that will be reciprocated."[44] I have nothing against tactical alliances that enable progressive policy changes, but it is time to reject the false bipartisanship that values working together just for the sake of working together. It's an illness that afflicts only Democrats.

Steve Bannon vowed to deconstruct the government and tear down institutions supported by both Republicans and Democrats. Though his bomb throwing was particularly jarring after

President Obama's bipartisan overtures, his methods were presaged by prior actors on the right, from Newt Gingrich as House Speaker to the Tea Party, which forged a tight alliance of elected leaders, oligarchs, and right-wing news outlets. Of particular relevance was the move by Republican leaders, immediately after Barack Obama's historic election, to plot a way to respond to the furor of alt-right donors and activists at the massive 2008 losses. Right after the election, conservative elected officials and activists gathered at a small dinner organized by Republican pollster Frank Luntz. In addition to members of the House and Senate leadership, Luntz asked Gingrich to join in their discussion of how to regain power. After four hours, they agreed that the best plan was to put all their energy and resources into the upcoming midterm election to wrestle back control of Congress and then fight Obama every way they could to deny him any legislative successes. "If you act like you're the minority, you're going to stay in the minority," said Kevin McCarthy, then House chief deputy whip. "We've gotta challenge them on every single bill and challenge them on every single campaign."[45] No one would suggest that the party of opposition should just fall in line, but it was unprecedented to suggest that *no matter what Obama would propose, they would oppose him*. Writing for the blog *Lawyers, Guns and Money*, Daniel Nexon describes the efforts as "a scorched-earth campaign geared toward delegitimating not only Obama and the Democrats, but the entire system of governance."[46]

Democrats haven't operated this way—and we can't, even if we wanted to. Progressive victories are those in which government is strengthened and expanded. The Children's Health Initiative Program (CHIP), Deferred Action for Childhood Arrivals (DACA), Obamacare—all of these require establishing and funding programs that serve people. The Left wants

Dreamers to be able to stay in this country, children and adults to have health care, and clean air and water in perpetuity—so we can't just blow things up. But we can and must resist cheap and diversionary attempts at bipartisanship. The Right has no qualms that sick children won't be able to see a doctor, because they believe the greater good is in killing off Obamacare. Even if a few elected Republicans may differ in their scorched-earth rhetoric, progressives and Democrats must realize that any promises the politicians on the right make to meet us in the middle are of limited credibility because of the blowback they will face from *Breitbart*, the Tea Party, and Koch Industries.

Take for example the way the Obama administration approached the passage of the Affordable Care Act (ACA), which could be characterized as slow, deliberative, and awash in hopes for bipartisanship. Putting considerable energy into trying to drum up GOP support for his legacy initiative, Obama decided on a bill that was closely modeled on a *Republican* proposal developed by the Heritage Foundation.[47] It was not just energy but also valuable *time* that the Democrats spent trying to win Republican backing. The White House held a health care summit, inviting members of Congress from both parties, insurance executives, union members, medical professionals, and hospital administrators, among others.[48] *New York Times* reporter Robert Pear describes the lengthy back and forth beginning in June 2009, when "House Democratic leaders unveiled the first draft of legislation that would ultimately become the Affordable Care Act. A month later, three House committees began formally drafting the bill ahead of a House vote that came well into the fall, after the summer heat had dissipated and the leaves had begun to change."[49] Obama enlisted Senate Finance Committee chairman Max Baucus, a Democrat from Montana, to try to entice Republican support, forswearing the speedy "reconciliation process"—a mechanism that allows certain types of legislation to avoid a filibuster in the Senate—that Bush had used to jam his tax cuts through.

But the Republicans would have none of it, sticking to their pledge to deny Obama any legislative victory. Mitch McConnell told *The Atlantic* in 2009 that no one from the GOP would support the bill. If it won even limited Republican support, he said, the bill would gain credibility. Instead, he argued, "the only way the American people would know that a great debate was going on was if the measures were not bipartisan. When you hang the 'bipartisan' tag on something, the perception is that differences have been worked out, and there's a broad agreement that that's the way forward."[50] And even though the Democrats held multiple days of hearings and posted versions of the bill online for several days before the votes, they were still accused by Republicans of "jamming the bill through." The deliberative process had consequences. The passage of a year spent in fruitless pursuit of bipartisan support saw the growth of the Tea Party and protests that upended Democrats' town hall meetings. Inevitably, Obama and his allies on Capitol Hill had to use reconciliation. But the damage had been done. The Tea Party, with the backing of the Koch brothers and other right-wing funders, had made the bill toxic—and the Democrats extremely unpopular as a result. The election of 2010 was a debacle for the party.

Contrast President Obama's approach to passing the ACA in 2009 with the legislative sprint in spring 2017 to undo the ACA, when two house committees scheduled markups on a bill a day after making it public and planned to move to a full House vote and then to the Senate, all within the space of a few weeks. Pear notes the hypocrisy, writing that "Republicans excoriated Democrats for rushing passage of the Affordable Care Act . . . blasting 'back-room deals' and cheering on the nascent Tea Party movement, with its hostile chant 'Read the bill, read the bill.' But Republicans have adopted a much more aggressive timetable for repealing the law and remaking Medicaid, the health program for more than 70 million low-income people."[51] Republicans admitted frankly that they had not read the Trump bill. And they were not embarrassed by that.

But the ACA is just one small example of how Obama reached out only to have his hand slapped. The same was true on his judicial nominations. Rather than jamming through ideological young lawyers to move the courts decisively in a leftward direction, the president first dithered, failing to nominate candidates in a timely way and choosing older, moderate nominees. His focus, when he did finally start nominating judges, was to diversify the bench demographically, but he did not place as high a value on how his nominees would influence the law jurisprudentially. A president's legacy, sometimes the only legacy, is his imprint on the federal bench. Obama's was a light touch.

Obama made an unprecedented effort to make almost half his cabinet members of the opposing party; he kept Robert Gates on as secretary of defense, added Congressman Ray LaHood of Illinois as secretary of transportation, and offered Senator Judd Gregg of New Hampshire the job of secretary of commerce (Gregg said no). This effort was met with nary a gesture of goodwill from across the aisle. Political scientists Jacob Hacker and Paul Pierson comment that "even GOP leaders acknowledged the administration's unusually intensive efforts to open channels of communication in the early days. The administration's opening proposals on its crucial economic stimulus bill included a less symbolic gesture: a very large tax-cut component designed in part to garner GOP support."[52]

But the Republicans were united in opposition right from the beginning. They believed, rightly, that denying President Obama any victories would harm his political brand and undercut the Democrats' ability to hold on to Congress. And as the Republican Party became increasingly conservative and mean-spirited, there were no longer any moderates who would "triangulate."[53] Hacker and Pierson ask, "Why had Democrats spent so long in futile search for bipartisanship? They had the largest majorities in Congress in three decades. Republicans, for their part, had the lowest party approval ratings in memory. On issue after issue, polls showed dramatically higher support for Democrats."[54]

THIS AIN'T NO PARTY

It's time to chuck the Marquess of Queensberry rules; let's stop playing croquet when conservatives are fighting a war. While we are engaged in a genteel game, they are fighting bare-knuckled over everything that matters in our society, from controlling the courts and the media to locking in control over elected bodies. No longer can we think of bipartisanship as an end in itself—it is a *means*. If Republicans want to support a Democratic or progressive objective, fine. But we have to stop writing legislation to meet them in the middle, negotiating against our left wing to win over some hypothetical conservative votes. Even for those Democrats who are congenitally moderate, it is better dealmaking to start strong. Read *The Art of the Deal*—on this and probably this alone, Donald Trump is right. We should assume we are on opposite sides and let them prove the contrary.

While President Trump has stoked racial enmity and crass nationalistic impulses, progressives have prided themselves on reaching across the aisle. President Obama named several Republicans to his cabinet and appointed James Comey, a high-level aide to John Ashcroft, as head of the FBI. He waited a year for Republican support to materialize on the Affordable Care

Act, while Senator Mitch McConnell announced off the bat that his goal was "to make Obama a one-term president." President Obama picked Judge Merrick Garland, an older white male moderate judge, as his Supreme Court nominee while President Trump picks young far-right ideologues. These actions gained the Left little or nothing and simply gave the Right more time to organize and oppose the president.

The Left needs to abandon empty gestures of bipartisanship and instead fight strategically for our values. We have to think systemically and invest the time and effort to address the rules that underlie the administration of government—and not just the policy preferences we wish for. Progressives have spent a long time debating the nuances of legislation and the details of policy but not enough time or energy in constructing institutions and mechanisms to gain and wield power. As the maxim goes, "Insanity is doing the same thing over and over and expecting different results." Well, let's prove that we are not crazy.

7

HOW PROGRESSIVES CAN WIN BY REWRITING THE RULES OF THE GAME

Some might remember a time when Republicans embraced the science behind climate change. It wasn't so long ago—indeed, John McCain, running for president in 2008, was unembarrassed to stand with scientists and embrace evidence-based policy (at least on climate). But a combination of right-wing funders, hackers, and fake news destroyed any rational thinking in the Republican Party on issues relating to our global future. The Koch brothers drove much of this change, working to protect their large holdings in fossil fuels, including major refineries and pipelines for crude oil. Oil money fueled research in right-wing think tanks to discredit climate science, and hackers grabbed emails from academics that were released selectively to seed doubt about the accuracy of the research. Once *Citizens United* let loose an avalanche of dark money, the Kochs were able to launch what the *New York Times* describes as "an all-fronts campaign with television advertising, social media and cross-country events aimed at electing lawmakers who would ensure that the fossil fuel industry would not have to worry about new pollution regulations."[1] From fringe websites to national newspapers like the *Wall Street Journal*, climate deniers disseminated their false narrative. Former *National Post* reporter Jonathan Kay witnessed how that Canadian newspaper's coverage had suffered, commenting that "global-warming denialism turned the *Post* into a weird hybrid: a beefy entrée of genuine information, with a 1 percent garnish of fake news—a situation that persists to this day. And since many conservatives have an enormous hunger for respectable-seeming news sources that confirm their ideologically motivated skepticism of environmentalism, this tiny slice of fake fare accounted for a massively disproportionate share of our most popular stories."[2]

A Koch operative laid out the strategy to a group of conservative bloggers: "If we win the science argument, it's game, set, and match."[3] Each piece—an attack on science reporting; a charm campaign for susceptible judges; "scholarship" to support the fossil fuel lobby; a legislative, lobbying, and electoral strategy to produce bills and grab legislative seats for the climate deniers—added up to a big victory for the Koch brothers as Donald Trump pulled the United States out of the Paris climate agreement and is tearing down President Obama's environmental legacy brick by brick. Game, set, match indeed.

Lewis Powell was a visionary. Where some in corporate America might have seen the advances in environmental, consumer, and workplace regulation as a reason to make accommodation with a protective welfare state, he called on business and conservative leaders to fight back, to advance a new and aggressive battle plan. What was needed, he believed, was a strategy not only to reverse these losses but to make advances that would be difficult, if not impossible, to undo. To regain and hold power required significant and sustained investment in a conservative infrastructure that would capture and keep the rulemaking process for our society.

Where has the Left been? Everywhere and nowhere, it seems. With no mechanism for choosing the most effective strategy, progressive leaders aggressively defend diffuse and multiple ideas rather than focused and tangible strategies and tactics. Major funders support an array of advocacy groups, most without members or an organizing mission, that often work at cross-purposes and in competition. There's no collective focus or discipline on the essential building blocks of power—elections, foundational legislation, the justice system. Each piece is addressed singly and idiosyncratically without consistent and lasting support or coordination.

Back to North Carolina—if the Left had our own plan, it would be a state where the legislative and congressional districts are not manipulated by parties and where the government helps rather than hinders eligible voters to participate in elections. The state legislature and the congressional delegation would look a lot different and African American and Latino voters would find that their votes had more impact—and that would translate into different priorities for the state's delegation in Congress and the statehouse. And in a system that no longer equates speech and money, which basically gives the person with the fattest wallet a bullhorn to drown out other voices, North Carolinians would see *their* policy preferences reflected in the votes of their representatives, not those of the biggest campaign contributors. Instead of big tax cuts for oil companies, the Tarheel State would have better funding for schools and improved infrastructure.

If North Carolina did not have an elected judiciary or gerrymandered districts for judges, the court system would not favor special interests over injured people, polluting hog farms, for instance, over neighboring African American homeowners. And were court rules structured to allow plausible cases to move forward, victims of discrimination or consumers harmed by faulty products would get into court, be able to join together with others, and get some recovery—and those cases would provide a disincentive to other wrongdoers. And these courts, no longer awash in special interests' campaign cash, would try to rule impartially. These courts would evaluate election rules to see if they unjustifiably restrict voting or impose barriers. These would be courts of justice.

And people might begin to have faith again in their government. And that's good for the Left.

8

PUBLIC MEMORANDUM

ADVANCING AMERICAN DEMOCRACY

Date: April 2019

To: Progressive Americans
From: Caroline Fredrickson

It is time we progressive Americans spelled out our own vision for restoring American democracy. While Lewis Powell wrote in his memo of 1971 to business executives about their responsibilities, my message in this memo is to all Americans about our responsibilities as citizens. Our democracy is in peril; we must act boldly to ensure democratic survival. All people in the United States must be concerned with protecting and preserving the American system of democracy. To do that we must recognize that to win and keep power, leaders on the left—activists, funders, and politicians—need to ensure large-scale and long-term investment in a progressive infrastructure to control and create the rulemaking process for our society, including think tanks to generate ideas, media to disseminate them, lawmakers to enact them, and judges to uphold them. This work of defending our democracy is rarely either exciting or glamorous, but it is essential.

Six ideas provide the foundation to protect and preserve American democracy for progressive values. They are:

1. Embrace small-d democracy
2. Invest financial resources in progressive outcomes
3. Win elections through long-term constituency building and presence in statehouses
4. Work for the greater good rather than personal gain
5. Reform voting laws to energize democratic participation and win elections
6. Elect and appoint good judges by acknowledging that the process is political—and engaging in the process

Collectively, these six actions can transform our current system, which increasingly gives power to the plutocrats, and return it to the engaged, vibrant American democracy where power is in the hands of the people.

EMBRACE SMALL-D DEMOCRACY

For our ideas to take hold and remain strong, we need to understand that long-term victories will require locking in democracy with a small *d*. That means embracing nonpartisan redistricting commissions and state constitutional changes to protect the right to vote, and it means building capacity to get good, progressive judges elected and/or confirmed—judges who can overturn terrible precedents like *Citizens United* and *Shelby County* and protect core victories like *Obergefell* and *Roe*. Democrats are not the same as progressives, and vice versa. Democrats' interest is in personal preservation, sometimes at the expense of liberal values. That's why we need to push Democrats to adopt nonpartisan redistricting plans and move constitutional amendments to protect the right to vote, because the Left can't be beholden to politicians—who care more about incumbency than progressive policy—to draw representative districts or to anchor the right to vote in something stronger than what benefits them on any particular day. Moreover, we need and should *want to support* a system that is fair and democratic. What makes us progressive is our belief in democracy as a value; we won't win by abandoning what sets us apart. Since the Left embraces the role of government, we need to show that government can and does work. If most Americans think there's no difference between "all those politicians in DC," the Right wins. They're the ones who want to tear down government; we need to make it worth supporting.

INVEST FINANCIAL RESOURCES IN PROGRESSIVE OUTCOMES

Progressive change requires progressive capital investments. Despite the gains in the 2018 midterm elections, the Left must take stock of how and why it has been losing for so long. Some have recognized the asymmetry in funding strategies. In 2005, Rob Stein, founder of the progressive donor network Democracy Alliance, set out to organize funding for infrastructure analogous to Powell's vision for the Right.[1] But, as current Democracy Alliance president Gara LaMarche admits, "liberal values aren't command and control. It's a steep climb to get donors to consider collective aims. The Right believes in long-term funding and general operating support while the Left requires groups to perform against metrics in project grants and cuts them off after a short time to fund something new." At an event for philanthropists, LaMarche had a conversation with James Piereson, formerly of the conservative Olin Foundation. "Piereson said to me that he would read the newspaper to find out whether groups are performing." LaMarche thinks that sums up the difference.[2]

Major funders, elected officials, and advocacy groups have the responsibility of sorting the wheat from the chaff. We need a major and undivided focus on elections (that means not just on the candidates but on the electoral system), on the courts, on core legislative priorities, and on an effective communications infra-structure. Large donors, including progressive foundations, need to take a page from the right-wing philanthropists and coordinate funding so that these priorities get substantial resources. They need to agree on a sustainable and long-term commitment to a smaller set of organizations that work in collaboration and not, as they do now, in competition for funders' dollars. Fewer groups with more money will make a difference. Funders have a unique ability to make the advocacy community play nice. In research-ing the conservative attacks on unions, Columbia University political scientist Alexander Hertel-Fernandez acknowledged that liberal donors sometimes work together, but emphasized that the Right shows far more unity. Calling it a "multipronged, multitiered strategy," Hertel-Fernandez found that, while con-servatives funded differing projects on the state level, nationally "they're all working with one another. You don't see the same thing on the left."[3]

It is time for those liberal billionaires who think their vanity projects are more important than the future of our democracy to get behind these efforts. On the left, individual ego often bests col-lective advantage. As a friend said to me, "The Right wants power, but the Left wants to be right." But even if they go big on democ-racy, these wealthy liberals have more than enough in the bank to support their pet causes. And foundations, sitting on huge pots of money, have got to stop being afraid that certain projects are too "political." The rights to vote and to participate in a democracy are indeed political rights. What could be more central to the mission of a progressive or even moderate foundation than that?

WIN ELECTIONS

In order to implement these changes to energize our democracy, we need to win elections. This requires broadening and deepening the right to vote for constituencies on the left—minorities, women, young people, urban voters. In blue states, we need an aggressive campaign to pass legislation to expand early voting and automatic voter registration; in red states, well-funded litigation will be necessary to attack each and every law that threatens the right to vote as well as a political strategy to target the legislators behind those bills. And that will require the Left not to shy away from bare-knuckled tactics. Those lawmakers have to feel some pain, whether that entails losing voter support or having to defend their actions in public from a vigorous attack. Several states already have stronger protections for the right to vote in their constitutions, which has allowed the Left to challenge some voter suppression efforts successfully—for example, the Pennsylvania voter ID law that was found unconstitutional in 2014.[4] In other states, like Michigan, progressives are trying to emulate Pennsylvania by passing a constitutional amendment to protect the right to vote, including early voting, no-excuse absentee ballots, and straight-ticket voting.[5] And we need to emulate Florida and restore the right to vote for the formerly incarcerated. Funders and leaders need to coalesce around a group of states where existing constitutional provisions can support a litigation strategy and those where a ballot initiative might be the first step.

Similarly, of immediate importance, progressive donors and activists need to fight for Democratic control of statehouses before the 2020 census, which precedes redistricting. Part of this effort will be constitutional challenges to the districts that were heavily gerrymandered in favor of the GOP after the

2010 census. These lawsuits are beginning to find some success, with some lawsuits focusing on state constitutional provisions, others on federal. This approach perfectly melds our strategic imperative with progressive values. According to Jessica Post, the executive director of the Democratic Legislative Campaign Committee, new rules restricting partisan gerrymandering would put "10 to 12 more chambers in immediate play" in six or seven states. Democrats would then have a role in the map drawing post–2020 census. "We still have a shot on the current map, but if we have fair maps, we could see real progress," Post said.[6] But fair maps are only step one. Without powerful recruitment and support for Democratic candidates for state offices, Republicans will retain control. Washington, DC, and national politics hold the Left in thrall, but it is the towns and cities across the country that hold our hopes for future gains.

WORK FOR THE GREATER GOOD

The Left has to end temper tantrum politics. Paul Booth, a real hero of the Left who died early in 2018, left an important message. Recalling Ronald Reagan's "eleventh commandment—Thou Shalt Not Speak Ill of Any Fellow Republican," he added one for Democrats that goes further. What we need, Booth wrote, is another mandate: Thou Shalt Support the Primary Winner. We are not just a "Big Tent" but "a battalion in which each wing does its part."[7] Booth was interested in getting and holding power, which can't be accomplished with narrow majorities. In order to really lock in gains, the Left needs numbers—that means sometimes living with candidates who may not be perfect. In fact, it means more than just holding one's nose and voting but actually getting behind the candidate for the greater good. Witness Tom Perriello, the hero of progressives who lost the Virginia gubernatorial primary to current governor Ralph Northam: immediately after losing, he tweeted, "Congratulations to Ralph Northam. Let's go win this thing—united." And they did; Northam won with Perriello working hard on his side. Folks, that's how we do it.

REFORM VOTING LAWS

And of course, we can fix all the election rules in the world, but if people don't vote, we won't win. So that's where changes like voting by mail and same-day registration come in. We need to make it easy to vote. And donors and the Democratic Party need to invest in a ground game that reaches out to low-propensity voters—minorities and young people—over a period of time. It can't just be the day before the election but needs to be a continuous engagement over time that gets them invested in the outcome. In an analysis of Obama voters who stayed home in 2016, a group of political scientists found that these voters have strong progressive values and "four out of every five . . . identify as Democrats, and 83 percent reported they would have voted for a Democrat down-ballot. A similar share of Obama-to-nonvoters said that they would have voted for Mrs. Clinton had they turned out to vote. In short, while reclaiming some Obama-to-Trump voters would be a big help to Democratic prospects, re-energizing 2012 Obama voters who stayed home is a more plausible path for the party going forward."[8] But that takes money and a strategy that can't be cooked up right before the election.

GOOD JUDGES

It's time to recognize that creating a good justice system—criminal justice reform and fair procedures for low-income people—means we need to get good judges. Black lives matter *more* when judges aren't racist, and good judges can help the environment, choice, and workers' rights. To get those kinds of judges, we need to admit that the nominations process is political. Not just when it entails elections for state judges but also when it involves presidential nominations in the federal system. It is politics and we need to embrace it. We need to recruit and then support good candidates using campaign tactics—paid advertising and social media as well as lobbying and donations. That means helping our "friends," politicians who grasp the importance of judicial power, and "spanking" those Democrats and Republicans who get in the way through attack ads and a strategy to penalize them at the ballot box. The selection process must have an electoral component including 527 electoral organizations and PACs that will force Democratic politicians to make choosing judges a priority. So long as progressives consider it unseemly or bad form to wallow in this "muck," those who need a justice system that is not biased toward powerful interests will continue to be denied their day in court. We need to continue to push for tools to limit the power of plutocrats' money in winning elections—but the best way to achieve that end would be to have a Supreme Court that would overturn *Citizens United*.

POWER TO THE PEOPLE

It is a cliché but it rings true: progressive policymakers have missed the forest for the trees. But there is no better time than now to grapple with how to win power and develop the strategies and tactics for long-term success. We too must be ruthless in thinking through which procedures and rules will make it easier for us to win electoral, legal, and legislative victories. The difference is that systems that favor transparency and fair dealing and that are accessible to all ultimately lead to better outcomes and outcomes that are sustainable—a virtuous circle for progressives. None of this is easy. Lewis Powell himself did not see his plan come together all at once, but on the right, there was quick recognition that he had correctly analyzed the problem and proposed the only solution. To their credit, they kept their eyes on the prize—power—and have not turned away. We progressive Americans have the same opportunity to pursue with passion and determination a world that is more just, more democratic, and more equal for all people. These six areas for action, when pressed with persistence over a number of decades, can transform our democracy, returning power to people to act with care and compassion for all.

ACKNOWLEDGMENTS

This book, written in the era we are in, owes everything to the inspiration of countless people around the county doing things big and small to defend our democracy against an onslaught of attacks and to challenge the pervasive racism and xenophobia behind many of those assaults. Without this engagement by grassroots organizations, movement leaders, and others, we would be in far worse shape than we are in. I long for the time when their energy and brilliance can turn to the project of advancing progress.

I could not leave out of my appreciation my family, friends, and colleagues who gave me many ideas and challenged my assumptions. That being said, all opinions in this book are my own and not attributable to the American Constitution Society or any other organization or individual.

NOTES

1: THE FIX

1. Vann R. Newkirk, "The Battle for North Carolina," *The Atlantic*, October 27, 2016.

2. Matea Gold, "In NC, Conservative Donor Art Pope Sits at Heart of Government He Helped Transform," *Washington Post*, July 19, 2014.

3. Ari Berman, "How the GOP Is Resegregating the South," *The Nation*, January 31, 2012.

4. Ari Berman and Pema Levi, "Don't Blame Black Voters if Roy Moore Wins. Blame Alabama's Secretary of State," *Mother Jones*, December 11, 2017.

5. Rusty Jacobs, "Under Pressure, North Carolina Draws New Voting Maps," NPR, August 30, 2017.

6. *North Carolina NAACP v. McCrory*, 831 F. 3d 204, 215 (2016), www.ca4.uscourts.gov/Opinions/Published/161468.P.pdf.

7. Sheldon Whitehouse, *Captured: The Corporate Infiltration of American Democracy* (New York: The New Press, 2017). Also "May It Please the Corp.: How the Conservative Wing of the Supreme Court Delivers for Republican Special Interests over the American People," PowerPoint presentation to the Senate Democratic Steering and Outreach Committee, March 15, 2017 (on file with author).

8. "Roberts: "My Job Is to Call Balls and Strikes and Not to Pitch or Bat," CNN.com, September 12, 2005.

9. Jacob S. Hacker and Paul Pierson, *Winner-Take-All Politics: How Washington Made the Rich Richer—and Turned Its Back on the Middle Class* (New York: Simon & Schuster, 2010), 305.

2: THE WILL TO POWER

1. Charlie Cray, "The Lewis Powell Memo—Corporate Blueprint to Dominate Democracy," Common Dreams, August 25, 2011, www.commondreams.org/views/2011/08/25/lewis-powell-memo-corporate-blueprint-dominate-democracy.

2. Kim Phillips-Fein, *Invisible Hands: The Making of the Conservative Movement from the New Deal to Reagan* (New York: W.W. Norton, 2009), 153.

3. Robert W. Patterson, "What's Good for America . . . ," *National Review*, July 1, 2013.

4. Phillips-Fein, *Invisible Hands*, 157.

5. "PowellMemorandum:AttackonAmericanFreeEnterpriseSystem"(hereafter "Powell Memo"), August 23, 1971, p. 2, law2.wlu.edu/powellarchives/page .asp?pageid=1251.

6. Powell Memo, 11.

7. Letter of August 25, 1971, from Eugene B. Sydnor to Lewis F. Powell, p. 4, Lewis F. Powell Jr. Archives, Washington and Lee University, law2.wlu.edu /deptimages/Powell%20Archives/PowellSpeechResearchAOFESMemo.pdf.

8. Cray, "The Lewis Powell Memo."

9. Letter of September 13, 1971, from Lewis F. Powell to Ross Malone, p. 7, Lewis F. Powell Jr. Archives, Washington and Lee University, law2.wlu.edu/deptimages/Powell%20Archives/PowellSpeechResearchAOFESMemo.pdf.

10. Phillips-Fein, *Invisible Hands*, 162.

11. Phillips-Fein, 163.

12. Bill Blum, "The Right-Wing Legacy of Justice Lewis Powell and What It Means for the Supreme Court Today," *Huffington Post*, August 16, 2016.

13. Cray, "The Lewis Powell Memo." See also Powell Memo, 31.

14. Phillips-Fein, *Invisible Hands*, 165.

15. Thomas Byrne Edsall, *The New Politics of Inequality* (New York: Norton, 1984), 114.

16. Phillips-Fein, *Invisible Hands*, 162.

17. Sally Covington, *Moving a Public Policy Agenda: The Strategic Philanthropy of Conservative Foundations* (Washington, DC: National Committee for Responsive Philanthropy, July 1997), p. 5, www.ncrp.org/publication/moving -public-policy-agenda (describing presentation of Richard Fink to Philanthropy Roundtable's 1995 annual conference).

18. Ann Southworth, *Lawyers of the Right: Professionalizing the Conservative Coalition* (Chicago: University of Chicago Press, 2008), 24.

19. Jeff Krehely, Meaghan House, and Emily Kernan, *Axis of Ideology: Conservative Foundations and Public Policy*, (Washington, DC: National Committee for Responsive Philanthropy, March 2004), p. 5, www.ncrp.org /publication/axis-of-ideology, citing (and reaffirming) Sally Covington, *Moving a Public Policy Agenda: The Strategic Philanthropy of Conservative Foundations*, (Washington, DC: National Committee for Responsive Philanthropy, July 1997), www.ncrp.org/publication/moving-public-policy-agenda=.

20. Powell Memo, 26

21. Michael Perelman, *The Confiscation of American Prosperity: From Right-Wing Extremism and Economic Ideology to the Next Great Depression* (New York: Palgrave Macmillan, 2007), 64.

22. Powell Memo, 22.

23. Phillips-Fein, *Invisible Hands*, 169, 171.

24. Molly Ball, "The Fall of the Heritage Foundation and the Death of Republican Ideals," *The Atlantic*, September 25, 2013.

25. Jacob S. Hacker and Paul Pierson, *Winner-Take-All Politics: How Washington Made the Rich Richer—and Turned Its Back on the Middle Class* (New York: Simon & Schuster, 2010), 123.

26. Mark Schmitt, "The Myth of the Powell Memo," *Washington Monthly*, September/October 2016.

27. Hacker and Pierson, *Winner-Take-All Politics*, 123–24.

28. Schmitt, "The Myth of the Powell Memo."

29. Letter of William Baroody to Harvey Peters, July 17, 1959, quoted in Phillips-Fein, *Invisible Hands*, 63.

30. Phillips-Fein, *Invisible Hands*, 176.

31. Phillips-Fein, 66.

32. Nathaniel Ward, "John Bolton Sports a Heritage Necktie on Fox News," Heritage Foundation, www.myheritage.org/news/john-bolton-sports-a-heritage-necktie-on-fox-news.

33. Nicole Hemmer, "How Conservative Media Learned to Play Politics," *Politico*, August 30, 2016.

34. Nicole Hemmer, "The Conservative War on Liberal Media Has a Long History," *The Atlantic*, January 17, 2014.

35. Eric Miller, "Before Breitbart: How Right Wing Media Transformed American Politics," *Religion Dispatches*, October 31, 2016.

36. Krehely, House, and Kernan, *Axis of Ideology*, 32.

37. Letter of August 20, 1971, from William J. Gill to Lewis F. Powell, p. 3, Lewis F. Powell Jr. Archives, Washington and Lee University, law2.wlu.edu/deptimages/Powell%20Archives/PowellSpeechResearchAOFESMemo.pdf.

38. Miller, "Before Breitbart."

39. Hemmer, "The Conservative War on Liberal Media."

40. Letter of September 13, 1971, from Lewis F. Powell to Eugene Sydnor, p. 9, Lewis F. Powell Jr. Archives, Washington and Lee, University, law2.wlu.edu/deptimages/Powell%20Archives/PowellSpeechResearchAOFESMemo.pdf.

41. Powell Memo, 21.

42. Hemmer, "The Conservative War on Liberal Media."

43. Krehely, House, and Kernan, *Axis of Ideology*, 32–33.

44. Powell Memo, 27.

45. Blum, "The Right-Wing Legacy of Justice Lewis Powell."

46. Erwin Chemerinsky, *Closing the Courthouse Door: How Your Constitutional Rights Became Unenforceable* (New Haven, CT: Yale University Press, 2017).

47. Southworth, *Lawyers of the Right*, 12–14.

48. Krehely, House, and Kernan, *Axis of Ideology*, 25.

49. Sheldon Whitehouse, *Captured: The Corporate Infiltration of American Democracy* (New York: The New Press, 2017), 65.

50. "About ILR," Institute for Legal Reform, www.instituteforlegalreform.com/about-ilr.

51. Stephen B. Burbank and Sean Farhang, "Litigation Reform: An Institutional Approach," *University of Pennsylvania Law Review* 162, no. 7 (June 2014): 1552.

52. Nancy Bowen, *Ralph Nader: Man with a Mission* (Brookfield, CT: Twenty-First Century Books, 2002), 80–86.

53. Burbank and Farhang, "Litigation Reform," 1551–52.

54. Burbank and Farhang, "Litigation Reform," 1568.

55. Krehely, House, and Kernan, *Axis of Ideology*, 11.

56. Roger M. Williams, "Sustaining Ideas on the Right," *News & Comment* 1 (2006), available at foundationnews.org.

57. John J. Miller, *Strategic Investments in Ideas: How Two Foundations Reshaped America* (Washington, DC: Philanthropy Roundtable, 2003), www.issuelab.org/resource/strategic-investment-in-ideas-how-two-foundations-reshaped-america.html.

58. Michael Avery and Danielle McLaughlin, *The Federalist Society: How Conservatives Took the Law Back from Liberals* (Nashville, TN: Vanderbilt University Press, 2013), 2–3.

59. Steven M. Teles, *The Rise of the Conservative Legal Movement: The Battle for Control of the Law* (Princeton, NJ: Princeton University Press, 2008), 142.

60. Report to the Attorney General, *Original Meaning Jurisprudence: A Sourcebook* (Washington, DC: U.S. Department of Justice, Office of Legal Policy, March 12, 1987).

61. Charlie Savage, *Takeover: The Return of the Imperial Presidency and the Subversion of American Democracy* (New York: Little, Brown and Co., 2007), 45.

62. Avery and McLaughlin, *The Federalist Society*, 2.

63. Alex Swoyer, "Federalist Society Becomes Progressives' New Bogeyman," *Washington Times*, June 18, 2017.

64. Ryan Lovelace, "Trump Adviser Leonard Leo Details Plans to Overhaul Judiciary," *Washington Examiner*, May 12, 2017.

65. Avery and McLaughlin, *The Federalist Society*, 12–13.

66. "The Roberts-Alito Court: Thank You, Ted Kennedy and Ralph Neas," *Wall Street Journal*, January 26, 2006 (emphasis in original).

67. John Nichols, "ALEC Exposed: Rigging Elections," *The Nation*, July 12, 2011.

68. Jessica Desvarieux, "ALEC Turns 40, but Who's Behind It?" Transcript of interview with Brendan Fischer, Real News Network, August 5, 2013, therealnews.com/stories/bfisheralec0805.

69. Bruce Weber, "Paul Weyrich, 66, a Conservative Strategist, Dies," *New York Times*, December 18, 2008.

70. ALEC website history page, alec.devhm.net/about-alec/history.

71. Alan Greenblatt, "What Makes Alec Smart?" *Governing*, October 2003, www.governing.com/topics/politics/What-Makes-Alec-Smart.html.

72. Lisa Graves, "ALEC Exposed: The Koch Connection," *The Nation*, August 1–8, 2011, and Lisa Graves, "A CMD Special Report on ALEC's Fund-

ing and Spending," PRWatch, July 12, 2011, www.prwatch.org/news/2011/07
/10887/cmd-special-report-alecs-funding-and-spending.

73. Jessica Desvarieux, "ALEC Turns 40, but Who's Behind It?"

74. Molly Jackman, "ALEC's Influence over Lawmaking in State Legislatures," Brookings Institution, December 6, 2013, www.brookings.edu/articles
/alecs-influence-over-lawmaking-in-state-legislatures.

75. Greenblatt, "What Makes Alec Smart?"

76. Lois Beckett, "Our Step-By-Step Guide to Understanding ALEC's
Influence on Your State Laws," ProPublica, August 1, 2011.

77. John Nichols, "Michigan Adopts the ALEC Model for Diminishing
Democracy," *The Nation*, December 12, 2012.

78. Lee Fang, *The Machine: A Field Guide to the Resurgent Right* (New York:
The New Press, 2013), 213–16.

79. Nichols, "Michigan Adopts the ALEC Model."

80. David Daley, *Ratf**ked: The True Story Behind the Secret Plan to Steal
America's Democracy* (New York: W.W. Norton & Co., 2016), xviii.

81. Daley, xviii.

82. Fang, *The Machine*, 218.

83. Daley, *Ratf**ked*, xvii.

84. Olga Pierce, Justin Elliott, and Theodoric Meyer, "How Dark Money
Helped Republicans Hold the House and Hurt Voters," ProPublica, December 21, 2012.

85. Hacker and Pierson, *Winner-Take-All Politics*, 163–64.

86. David Maraniss, "First Lady Launches Counterattack," *Washington
Post*, January 28, 1998.

87. Elspeth Revere, "After 25 Years of Grant Making, I Worry We Have
Lost Sight of Nonprofit Struggles," Alliance for Media Arts + Culture,
www.thealliance.media/25-years-grant-making-worry-lost-sight-nonprofit
-struggles.

3: ELECTIONS HAVE CONSEQUENCES

1. Ari Berman, "Texas Republicans Intentionally Discriminated Against
Minority Voters, Court Rules," *Mother Jones*, August 16, 2017.

2. Ari Berman, *Give Us the Ballot* (New York: Farrar, Straus and Giroux,
2015), 17.

3. Jim Rutenberg, "A Dream Undone," *New York Times Magazine*, July 29,
2015.

4. Ari Berman, "John Lewis's Long Fight for Voting Rights," *The Nation*,
June 5, 2013.

5. Berman, *Give Us the Ballot*, 6.

6. Berman, 6.

7. Rutenberg, "A Dream Undone."

8. Rutenberg, "A Dream Undone."

9. Berman, *Give Us the Ballot*, 11.

10. Remarks to the Religious Roundtable (August 1980), quoted in Meteor Blades, "Paul Weyrich Wanted Fewer People to Vote for a Simple Reason: When More Do, Republicans Lose," *Daily Kos*, November 5, 2012.

11. Berman, *Give Us the Ballot*, 147.

12. Owen Fiss and Charles Krauthammer, "The Rehnquist Court," *New Republic*, March 10, 1982.

13. Antonin Scalia, "The Disease as Cure: 'In Order to Get Beyond Racism, We Must First Take Account of Race,'" *Washington University Law Review* 1 (1979), cited in Berman, *Give Us the Ballot*, 128.

14. Rutenberg, "A Dream Undone."

15. Berman, *Give Us the Ballot*, 151.

16. Rutenberg, "A Dream Undone."

17. Rutenberg, "A Dream Undone."

18. *Shelby County v. Holder*, 570 U.S. 529 at 2 (2013).

19. *Shelby County v. Holder*, 570 U.S. 529 at 27 (2013).

20. *Shelby County v. Holder*, 570 U.S. 529 at 33 (2013).

21. Berman, *Give Us the Ballot*, 262.

22. Justin Levitt, "A Comprehensive Investigation of Voter Impersonation Finds 31 Credible Incidents Out of One Billion Ballots Cast," *Washington Post*, August 6, 2014.

23. Joshua Green, "Karl Rove's Voter Fraud Fetish," *The Atlantic*, April 2007.

24. Green, "Karl Rove's Voter Fraud Fetish."

25. Al Franken, *Lies and the Lying Liars Who Tell Them* (New York: Dutton 2003), 150.

26. Andrew Rosenthal, "O'Connor Regrets Bush v. Gore," *New York Times*, April 29, 2013.

27. "Voting Integrity Symposium," C-Span, October 8, 2002, www.c-span .org/video/?173086-1/voting-integrity-symposium.

28. E.J. Dionne, "An Election Day Nightmare," *Washington Post*, November 5, 2002.

29. Franken, *Lies and the Lying Liars Who Tell Them*, 257.

30. Matthew Mosk and Avis Thomas-Lester, "GOP Fliers Apparently Were Part of Strategy, *Washington Post*, November 13, 2006.

31. Mosk and Thomas-Lester, "GOP Fliers."

32. Michael Waldman, "Voting Fraud Inquiry? The Investigators Got Burned Last Time," *New York Times*, January 26, 2017.

33. Richard L. Hasen, "Trump's Voter Fraud Endgame," *Slate*, June 30, 2017.

34. Mark Landler and Ashley Parker, "Obama Tells Trump: Stop 'Whining' and Trying to Discredit the Election," *New York Times*, October 18, 2016.

35. Ben Schreckinger, "White Nationalists Plot Election Day Show of Force," *Politico*, November 2, 2016.

36. Joel Kurth and Ted Roelofs, "Poor in Michigan with No ID. 'I Am Somebody. I Just Can't Prove It,'" *Bridge Magazine*, September 26, 2017.

37. Vanessa M Perez, "Americans with Photo ID: A Breakdown of Demographic Characteristics," Project Vote, February 2015, p. 1, www.projectvote.org /wp-content/uploads/2015/06/AMERICANS-WITH-PHOTO-ID-Research -Memo-February-2015.pdf.

38. Kurth and Roelofs, "Poor in Michigan with No ID."

39. John Nichols, "ALEC Exposed: Rigging Elections," *The Nation*, July 12, 2011.

40. Berman, *Give Us the Ballot*, 261.

41. Nichols, "ALEC Exposed: Rigging Elections."

42. Rutenberg, "A Dream Undone."

43. Wendy Underhill, "Voter Identification Requirements/Voter ID Laws," National Conference of State Legislatures, May 15, 2018, www.ncsl.org /research/elections-and-campaigns/voter-id.aspx.

44. Wisconsin Act 23 (2011), www.scribd.com/document/221004483 /WiscVoterID-195-Decision.

45. Kristen Mack, "In Trying to Win, Has Dewhurst Lost a Friend?" *Houston Chronicle*, May 18, 2007.

46. Kelly Cernetich, "Turzai: Voter ID Law Means Romney Can Win PA," *Politics PA*, June 25, 2012, www.politicspa.com/turzai-voter-id-law-means -romney-can-win-pa/37153.

47. Michael Wines, "Wisconsin Strict ID Law Discouraged Voters, Study Finds," *New York Times*, September 25, 2017.

48. Rutenberg, "A Dream Undone."

49. Rutenberg, "A Dream Undone."

50. Ari Berman, "Trump Election Commission Leader Sought a Radical Change to a Key Voting Law," *Mother Jones*, October 6, 2017.

51. Christopher Ingraham, "This Anti-Voter-Fraud Program Gets It Wrong over 99 Percent of the Time. The GOP Wants to Take It Nationwide," *Washington Post*, July 20, 2017.

52. Dan Froomkin, "Former Justice Department Lawyers Fire Back on Voting-Rights Reversal They Say Betrays Two Decades of Enforcement," American Constitution Society, September 25, 2017, www.acslaw.org/acsblog /former-justice-department-lawyers-fire-back-on-voting-rights-reversal-they -say-betrays-two.

53. Nina Totenberg, "Supreme Court Upholds Controversial Ohio Voter-Purge Law," NPR, June 11, 2018.

54. Remarks by Ben Jealous, Columbia, South Carolina, January 16, 2012, www.naacp.org/pages/martin-luther-king-day-speech-2012.

55. Darren Samuelsohn, "Clinton Likens GOP Effort to Jim Crow," *Politico*, July 6, 2011.

56. Berman, *Give Us the Ballot*, 263.

57. "What Is Same Day Registration? Where Is It Available?" Demos, www.demos.org/publication/what-same-day-registration-where-it-available.

58. "Automatic Voter Registration," National Conference of State Legislatures, August 10, 2018, www.ncsl.org/research/elections-and-campaigns /automatic-voter-registration.aspx.

59. *The Case for Automatic Voter Registration* (New York: Brennan Center for Justice, 2015), www.brennancenter.org/publication/case-automatic-voter -registration.

60. Will Drabold, "How Cities Are Bypassing States to Explore Registering Hundreds of Thousands to Vote," *Mic*, January 5, 2018.

61. Gilad Edelman and Paul Glastris, "Letting People Vote at Home Increases Voter Turnout. Here's the Proof," *Washington Post*, January 26, 2018.

62. Phil Keisling, "How to Bring Home Democratic Voters," *Washington Monthly*, January/February 2017.

63. Sari Horwitz, "More than 30 States Offer Online Voting, but Experts Warn It Isn't Secure," *Washington Post*, May 17, 2016.

64. Jonathan Elliot, *The Debates in the Several State Conventions on the Adoption of the Federal Constitution*, vol. 3, p. 257, available at memory.loc.gov /ammem/amlaw/lwed.html.

65. U.S. Const. article I, section 2, clause 3. A federal statute also requires that the apportionment take place every ten years. 2. U.S.C. Section 2a(a).

66. Justin Levitt, "Where Are the Lines Drawn?" All About Redistricting, redistricting.lls.edu/where.php.

67. Goodwin Liu, Pamela S. Karlan, and Christopher H. Schroeder, *Keeping Faith with the Constitution* (Washington, DC: American Constitution Society for Law and Policy, 2009), 83, www.acslaw.org/book/keeping-faith-with-the -constitution.

68. David Daley, *Ratf**ked: The True Story Behind the Secret Plan to Steal America's Democracy* (New York: W.W. Norton & Co. 2016), 71.

69. Louis Menand, "Been There: The Presidential Election of 1968," *New Yorker*, January 8, 2018.

70. Berman, *Give Us the Ballot*, 206.

71. "1988 Bush vs. Dukakis," Museum of the Moving Image, www.livingroomcandidate.org/commercials/1988/willie-horton.

72. Ari Berman, "How the GOP Is Resegregating the South," *The Nation*, January 31, 2012.

73. Daley, *Ratf**ked*, 35.

74. Daley, 36.

75. Remarks by Benjamin Ginsberg to Congressional Black Caucus Foundation, Washington, DC, September 28, 1990, cited in Richard L. Berke, "The Nation; GOP Tries a New Gambit with Voting Rights," *New York Times*, April 14, 1991.

76. Van Denton, "Party Loyalty, Black Gains Clash in Redistricting," *News & Observer* (Raleigh, NC), January 7, 1992.

77. Daley, *Ratf**ked*, xvi.

78. Daley, 76.

79. Quoted in Daley, 78.

80. Daley, 79.

81. Daley, xvii.

82. Daley, xvii.

83. REDMAP Summary Report, January 4, 2013, www.redistricting majorityproject.com. The + and – indicate the gain or loss of congressional seats in the state due to population changes.

84. Daley, *Ratf**ked*, xix–xx.

85. Daley, xxii.

86. REDMAP Summary Report

87. Daley, *Ratf**ked*, 206.

88. Berman, *Give Us the Ballot*, 247.

89. Daley, *Ratf**ked*, 55.

90. Sam Wang and Brian Remlinger, "Slaying the Partisan Gerrymander," *American Prospect*, Fall 2017, 43.

91. Gabriel Debenedetti, "Obama's Party-Building Legacy Splits Democrats," *Politico*, February 9, 2017.

92. Debenedetti, "Obama's Party-Building Legacy Splits Democrats."

93. Daley, *Ratf**ked*, 102.

94. Daley, 14.

95. Daley, 103.

96. Daley, 48.

97. Ari Berman, "How the GOP Rigs Elections," *Rolling Stone*, January 24, 2018, www.rollingstone.com/politics/politics-news/how-the-gop-rigs-elections-121907.

98. Daley, 23.

99. Daley, 242

100. Daley, 27.

101. Sam Wang, "The Great Gerrymander of 2012," *New York Times*, February 2, 2013.

102. Wang, "The Great Gerrymander of 2012."

103. David A. Lieb, "Analysis Indicates Partisan Gerrymandering Has Benefited GOP," Associated Press, June 25, 2017.

104. Alexander Burns, "Eric Holder's Group Targets All-G.O.P. States to Attack Gerrymandering," *New York Times*, February 6, 2018.

105. Robert Barnes, "Supreme Court Rules Race Improperly Dominated N.C. Redistricting Efforts," *Washington Post*, May 5, 2017.

106. Wang and Remlinger, "Slaying the Partisan Gerrymander," 45.

107. Nicholas Stephanopoulos, "The Research That Convinced SCOTUS to Take the Wisconsin Gerrymandering Case, Explained," *Vox*, July 11, 2017.

108. *Gill v. Whitford*, 585 U.S. __ (2018), www.scotusblog.com/case-files/cases/gill-v-whitford.

109. Burns, "Eric Holder's Group Targets All-G.O.P. States."

110. Joshua A. Douglas, "State Constitutions: The Next Frontier in Voting Rights Protection," American Constitution Society, August 6, 2015, www.acslaw.org/acsblog/state-constitutions-the-next-frontier-in-voting-rights-protection; Josh Douglas (@JoshuaADouglas), "Some thoughts on state constitutions . . . Twitter, January 22, 2018, 11:48 a.m., twitter.com/JoshuaADouglas/status/955527734125563905.

111. Allegra Kirkland, "Don't Expect Dems to Seek Redistricting Revenge Where They Get the Chance," *Talking Points Memo*, February 16, 2018, talkingpointsmemo.com/muckraker/why-democrats-probably-wont-gerrymander-much-2021.

112. Reid Wilson, "Ohio Voters Pass Redistricting Reform Initiative," *The Hill*, May 8, 2018.

113. Burns, "Eric Holder's Group Targets All-G.O.P. States."

114. Wang and Remlinger, "Slaying the Partisan Gerrymander," 45.

115. Kirkland, "Don't Expect Dems to Seek Redistricting Revenge."

116. Kirkland, "Don't Expect Dems to Seek Redistricting Revenge."

117. Michael Scherer, "Potential Citizenship Question in 2020 Census Could Shift Power to Rural America," *Washington Post*, January 24, 2018.

118. Editorial Board, "Save the Census," *New York Times*, July 17, 2017.

119. Kamala Kelkar, "Electoral College Is 'Vestige' of Slavery, Say Some Constitutional Scholars," PBS.org, November 6, 2016.

120. Kim Phillips-Fein, *Invisible Hands: The Making of the Conservative Movement from the New Deal to Reagan* (New York: W.W. Norton, 2009), 186.

121. Phillips-Fein, 190.

122. Phillips-Fein, 185.

123. John Spence, "Enlightened Self Interest in Business," *John Spence Blog*, April 15, 2010, blog.johnspence.com/2010/04/enlightened-self-interest-in -business.

124. Phillips-Fein, *Invisible Hands*, 187–88.

125. Phillips-Fein, 203.

126. Jacob S. Hacker and Paul Pierson, *Winner-Take-All Politics: How Washington Made the Rich Richer—and Turned Its Back on the Middle Class* (New York: Simon & Schuster, 2010), 121.

127. Hacker and Pierson, 122.

128. Hacker and Pierson, 121.

129. *Buckley v. Valeo*, 424 U.S. 1 (1976).

130. Haley Sweetland Edwards, "The Corporate 'Free Speech' Racket," *Washington Monthly*, January/February 2014.

131. *SpeechNow.org v. Federal Election Commission*, 599 F.3d 686 (DC Cir. 2010).

132. Daley, *Ratf**ked*, 12.

133. Michael J. Malbin and Brendan Glavin, *CFI's Guide to Money in Federal Elections: 2016 in Historical Context* (Washington, DC: Campaign Finance Institute, 2018), 21–22, www.cfinst.org/pdf/federal/2016Report/CFI Guide_MoneyinFederalElections.pdf.

134. "Social Welfare Organizations," Internal Revenue Service, www.irs.gov /charities-non-profits/other-non-profits/social-welfare-organizations.

135. "Political Nonprofits (Dark Money)," Center for Responsive Politics, www.opensecrets.org/outsidespending/nonprof_summ.php.

136. Josh Keefe, "How Republicans Protect Anonymous Donors and Their 'Dark Money' Groups," *International Business Times*, July 6, 2017, citing the Center for Responsive Politics.

137. Paul Blumenthal, "This Dark Money Group Is Spending Big on Judicial Races, and No One Knows Why," *Huffington Post*, November 3, 2016.

138. Blumenthal, "This Dark Money Group Is Spending Big on Judicial Races."

139. Robert O'Harrow Jr. and Shawn Boburg, "How a 'Shadow' Universe of Charities Joined with Political Warriors to Fuel Trump's Rise," *Washington Post*, June 3, 2017.

140. O'Harrow Jr. and Boburg, "How a 'Shadow' Universe of Charities."

141. Letter from Michael C. Dorf et al. to Speaker of the U.S. House of Representatives Paul Ryan and Minority Leader of the U.S. House of Representatives Nancy Pelosi, September 7, 2016, www.democracy21.org/wp-content /uploads/2016/09/Letter-from-Law-Professors-Opposing-Impeachment -9-7-2016.pdf.

142. Keefe, "How Republicans Protect Anonymous Donors."

143. Heather Long, "In Small Win for Democrats, the Final Tax Bill Will Not Include a Provision Allowing Churches to Endorse Political Candidates," *Washington Post*, December 14, 2017.

144. Editorial Board, "The House Tax Bill Unleashes a Dangerous Avalanche of Campaign Cash," *Washington Post*, November 18, 2017.

145. Hacker and Pierson, *Winner-Take-All Politics*, 180.

146. Lynn Adelman, "How Big Money Ruined Public Life in Wisconsin," *Cleveland State Law Review* 66, no. 1 (2017): 7–8.

147. Nicholas Lemann, "The Controller," *New Yorker*, May 12, 2003.

148. Daryl J. Levinson and Benjamin I. Sachs, "Political Entrenchment and Public Law," *Yale Law Journal* 125, no. 2 (November 2015): 403.

149. Noam Scheiber and Kenneth P. Vogel, "Behind a Key Anti-Labor Case, a Web of Conservative Donors," *New York Times*, February 25, 2018.

150. Benjamin Sachs, "*Janus* and Gerrymandering," *On Labor*, October 6, 2017, onlabor.org/janus-and-gerrymandering.

151. Rebecca Shimoni Stoil, "How the GOP Became a 'Pro-Israel' Party," *FiveThirtyEight*, December 8, 2017.

152. Jeremy Sharon, "US Jews Contribute Half of All Donations to the Democratic Party," *Jerusalem Post*, September 27, 2016.

153. Phillips-Fein, *Invisible Hands*, 230–31.

154. Phillips-Fein, 215–17.

155. Phillips-Fein, 221.

156. Phillips-Fein, 205.

157. Phillips-Fein, 253.

158. Phillips-Fein, 232–33.

159. Phillips-Fein, 234.

160. Hacker and Pierson, *Winner-Take-All Politics*, 203.

161. Hacker and Pierson, 204.

162. Hacker and Pierson, 211.

163. Thomas E. Mann and Norman J. Ornstein, *It's Even Worse Than It Looks: How the American Constitutional System Collided with the New Politics of Extremism* (New York: Basic Books, 2013), 152.

164. Richard L. Hasen, "Show Me the Donors," *Slate*, October 14, 2010.

165. "Why Our Democracy Needs Disclosure," Campaign Legal Center, August 13, 2018, www.campaignlegalcenter.org/news/blog/why-our-democracy-needs-disclosure.

166. Eric Lipton and Alexander Burns, "The True Source of the N.R.A.'s Clout: Mobilization, Not Donations," *New York Times*, February 24, 2018.

167. John Craig and David Madland, "How Campaign Contributions and Lobbying Can Lead to Inefficient Economic Policy," Center for American Progress, May 2, 2014, www.americanprogress.org/issues/economy/reports/2014/05/02/88917/how-campaign-contributions-and-lobbying-can-lead-to-inefficient-economic-policy.

168. Steven Strauss, "Actually, Corporations That Lobby and Make Campaign Contributions Get Special Benefits," *Huffington Post*, December 12, 2011.

169. Cristina Marcos, "GOP Lawmaker: Donors Are Pushing Me to Get Tax Reform Done," *The Hill*, November 7, 2017.

170. Jack Abramoff, *Capitol Punishment: The Hard Truth About Washington Corruption from America's Most Notorious Lobbyist* (Washington, DC: WND Books, 2011), 305.

171. Burt Neuborne, *Madison's Music* (New York: The New Press, 2015).

172. American Promise, "Building on Success: Americans Winning the 28th Amendment," higherlogicdownload.s3.amazonaws.com/AMERICAN PROMISE/1d433c9a-415a-48fd-b18a-48dc80e98c06/UploadedImages/18%20 State%20Map.pdf.

173. Daley, *Ratf**ked*, 210.

174. Ronald A. Klain, "The Democratic Party's Nomination Process Isn't Democratic Enough," *Washington Post*, September 25, 2017.

175. Alex Seitz-Wald, "Democrats Strip Super Delegates of Power and Reform Caucuses in 'Historic Move,'" NBC News, August 25, 2018, www.nbcnews.com/storyline/democrats-vs-trump/democrats-strip-super-delegates-power-reform-caucuses-historic-move-n903866.

4: THE LEAST DANGEROUS BRANCH

1. Hugh Hewitt, *The Fourth Way: The Conservative Playbook for a Lasting GOP Majority* (New York: Simon & Schuster, 2017), 107–108.

2. Ann Southworth, *Lawyers of the Right: Professionalizing the Conservative Coalition* (Chicago: University of Chicago Press, 2008), 13.

3. Southworth, 14–18.

4. "Factsheet: Pacific Legal Foundation, PLF," ExxonSecrets.org, exxonsecrets.org/html/orgfactsheet.php?id=60.

5. Southworth, *Lawyers of the Right*, 19.

6. Southworth, 19 (quoting Horowitz's report for the Scaife Foundation).

7. Jack M. Balkin, "From Off the Wall to On the Wall: How the Mandate Challenge Went Mainstream," *The Atlantic*, June 4, 2012.

8. Amanda Hollis-Brusky, *Ideas with Consequences: The Federalist Society and the Conservative Counterrevolution* (New York: Oxford University Press, 2015), 1–2.

9. Michael Avery and Danielle McLaughlin, *The Federalist Society: How Conservatives Took the Law Back from Liberals* (Nashville, TN: Vanderbilt University Press, 2013), 8.

10. Avery and McLaughlin, 8.

11. Zoe Tillman, "After Eight Years on the Sidelines, This Conservative Group Is Primed to Reshape the Courts Under Trump," *BuzzFeed News*, November 20, 2017.

12. Hollis-Brusky, *Ideas with Consequences*, 2–3.

13. Southworth, *Lawyers of the Right*, 134 (emphasis added).

14. Hollis-Brusky, *Ideas with Consequences*, 3.

15. Johnathan O'Neill, *Originalism in American Law and Politics: A Constitutional History* (Baltimore, MD: Johns Hopkins University Press, 2005), 1–2.

16. David Strauss, *The Living Constitution* (New York: Oxford University Press, 2010), 18.

17. Strauss, *The Living Constitution*, 12.

18. Molly McDonough, "Scalia: 'I Am Not a Nut,'" *ABA Journal*, April 8, 2008.

19. Avery and McLaughlin, *The Federalist Society*, 10.

20. Southworth, *Lawyers of the Right*, 133.

21. Jeffrey Toobin, "The Conservative Pipeline to the Supreme Court," *New Yorker*, April 17, 2017.

22. Geoffrey Stone, "The Behavior of Supreme Court Justices When Their Behavior Counts the Most," *Judicature* 97 (September/October 2013): 82.

23. Avery and McLaughlin, *The Federalist Society*, 10.

24. Avery and McLaughlin, 9.

25. Stephen Wermeil and Seth Stern, "Justice Brennan and Edwin Meese: A Constitutional Throwdown," *ACSblog*, September 30, 2010.

26. Hollis-Brusky, *Ideas with Consequences*, 162.

27. James B. Stewart, "How Broccoli Landed on Supreme Court Menu," *New York Times*, June 13, 2012.

28. Stewart, "How Broccoli Landed on Supreme Court Menu."

29. Stewart, "How Broccoli Landed on Supreme Court Menu."

30. "A Bad Day for ObamaCare at the Supreme Court," transcript from *The O'Reilly Factor*, March 27, 2012, www.foxnews.com/transcript/2012/03/28/bill-oreilly-bad-day-obamacare-supreme-court.html.

31. Hollis-Brusky, *Ideas with Consequences*, 155.

32. Sheldon Whitehouse, *Captured: The Corporate Infiltration of American Democracy* (New York: The New Press, 2017), 75.

33. Whitehouse, 73–74.

34. *Harris v. Quinn*, 573 U.S. __ 2014.

35. Southworth, *Lawyers of the Right*, 139.

36. Jill Lepore, "When Barbie Went to War with Bratz," *New Yorker*, January 22, 2018.

37. Hollis-Brusky, *Ideas with Consequences*, 164.

38. Hollis-Brusky, 155.

39. Toobin, "The Conservative Pipeline to the Supreme Court."

40. Joan Desmond, "Leonard Leo, the Pro-Life Catholic Behind Trump's Nomination of Gorsuch," *National Catholic Register*, April 17, 2017.

41. Toobin, "The Conservative Pipeline to the Supreme Court."

42. Henry Farrell, "Trump's Values Are Abhorrent to the Federalist Society of Conservative Lawyers. That Doesn't Stop Them from Helping Him," *Washington Post*, May 17, 2017.

43. David Dayen, "Trump's Judicial Picks Are Keeping Republicans Happy—and Quiet," *New Republic*, June 9, 2017.

44. Brady Dennis and Chris Mooney, "Neil Gorsuch's Mother Once Ran the EPA. It Didn't Go Well," *Washington Post*, February 1, 2017.

45. Dahlia Lithwick, "Polemicists in Robes," *Slate*, June 15, 2017.

46. Zoe Tillman, "Trump Is Winning on Judges," *BuzzFeed News*, July 31, 2017.

47. Right Wing Watch Staff, "The Obstruction Lobby: What the Outside Groups Working to Block a New Supreme Court Justice Really Want," Right Wing Watch, March 2016, www.rightwingwatch.org/report/the-obstruction -lobby-what-the-outside-groups-working-to-block-a-new-supreme-court-justice -really-want.

48. Viveca Novak and Peter Stone, "The JCN Story: Building a Secretive GOP Judicial Machine," *Daily Beast*, March 23, 2015; Land quote from Right Wing Watch Staff, "The Obstruction Lobby."

49. *Comcast v. Behrend*, 569 U.S. 27 (2013).

50. Adam Liptak, "Corporations Find a Friend in the Supreme Court," *New York Times*, May 4, 2013.

51. Novak and Stone, "The JCN Story."

52. Jay Michaelson, "Dark-Money Group Attacks Obama's Supreme Court Picks Before They're Even Nominated," *Daily Beast*, March 16, 2016.

53. Novak and Stone, "The JCN Story."

54. Right Wing Watch Staff, "The Obstruction Lobby."

55. Margaret Sessa-Hawkins and Andrew Perez, "Dark Money Group Received Massive Donation in Fight Against Obama's Supreme Court Nominee," MapLight, October 24, 2017, maplight.org/story/dark-money-group-recei ved-massive-donation-in-fight-against-obamas-supreme-court-nominee.

56. Robert Maguire, "Web of Secret Money Hides One Mega-donor Funding Conservative Court," McClatchy DC Bureau, November 21, 2017.

57. Novak and Stone, "The JCN Story."

58. Stephanie Mencimer, "These Right-Wing Groups Are Gearing Up for an Onslaught on Obama's Supreme Court Nominee," *Mother Jones*, March 19, 2016.

59. Alexis Simendinger and James Arkin, "Obama Picks Court Nominee Once Admired by GOP," RealClearPolitics, March 16, 2016, www .realclearpolitics.com/articles/2016/03/16/obama_picks_court_nominee_once _admired_by_gop__130012.html.

60. "Conservatives Have Been Praising Merrick Garland for Years," Media Matters for America, quoting *Wall Street Journal*, www.mediamatters.org/print /685846.

61. Mike DeBonis, "Why the Effort to Keep Merrick Garland off the Court Has Been Remarkably Successful," *Washington Post*, April 25, 2016.

62. Mike DeBonis, "Mitch McConnell's Senate Is Confirming Very, Very Few Nominees," May 5, 2016.

63. Jay Michaelson, "It's Not Just Merrick Garland: The Republicans Are Blocking So Many Nominees It's Caused a Judicial Emergency," *Daily Beast*, May 16, 2016.

64. Seung Min Kim, "Trump's Judge Picks: 'Not Qualified,' Prolific Bloggers," *Politico*, October 17, 2017.

65. Lawrence Baum and Neal Devins, "Ideological Imbalance: Why Democrats Usually Pick Moderate-Liberal Justices and Republicans Usually Pick Conservative Ones," *Slate*, March 17, 2016.

66. Michaelson, "Dark-Money Group Attacks Obama's Supreme Court Picks."

67. Right Wing Watch Staff, "The Obstruction Lobby."

68. Mencimer, "These Right-Wing Groups Are Gearing Up for an Onslaught."

69. Burgess Everett, "Conservatives Plan $10 Million High Court Ad Campaign," *Politico*, January 9, 2017.

70. Right Wing Watch Staff, "The Obstruction Lobby."

71. Everett, "Conservatives Plan $10 Million High Court Ad Campaign."

72. Fredreka Schouten, "Why the Koch Brothers Want to Kill an Obscure Senate Rule to Help Shape the Federal Courts," *USA Today*, July 4, 2017.

73. Katie Glueck, "Koch-Aligned Group Already Prepping for Next Supreme Court Fight," January 28, 2018, McClatchy DC Bureau.

74. Ronald A. Klain, "The One Area Where Trump Has Been Wildly Successful," *Washington Post*, July 19, 2017.

75. Sarah Binder, "The Senate Just Made It a Lot Easier for Trump to Appoint Federal Judges, over Democrats' Objections," *Washington Post*, November 20, 2017.

76. David Dayen, "Trump's Judicial Picks Are Keeping Republicans Happy—and Quiet," *New Republic*, June 9, 2017.

77. Schouten, "Why the Koch Brothers Want to Kill an Obscure Senate Rule."

78. Mark Holden, "The Democrats' Logic Is Upside-Down on Judicial Confirmations," *Time*, August 24, 2017.

79. Right Wing Watch Staff, "The Obstruction Lobby."

80. Peter Stone, "Seeding Campaigns to Remake State Supreme Courts," *Sacramento Bee*, May 16, 2015.

81. David Dayen, "Trump's Judicial Picks Are Keeping Republicans Happy—and Quiet."

82. Conversations between Brian Fallon and author, July 2018.

83. Mark Joseph Stern, "An Awful Ruling from One of Trump's Worst Judicial Appointees," *Slate*, January 18, 2018.

84. Sean McElwee, "Democrats Are in Denial About the Supreme Court," *Huffington Post*, May 4, 2018.

85. For more on this, visit Fix the Court's website: fixthecourt.com/the -fixes.

86. Alicia Bannon and Nathaniel Sobel, "Assaults on the Courts: A Legislative Round-Up," Brennan Center for Justice, May 8, 2017, p. 1, www.brennancenter.org/analysis/assaults-courts-legislative-round.

87. Email from Eric Lesh to author, November 13, 2017.

88. Stone, "Seeding Campaigns to Remake State Supreme Courts."

89. Novak and Stone, "The JCN Story."

90. Novak and Stone, "The JCN Story."

91. David Daley, Ratf**ked: The True Story Behind the Secret Plan to Steal America's Democracy (New York: W.W. Norton & Co. 2016), 10.

92. Novak and Stone, "The JCN Story."

93. Lincoln Caplan, "The Destruction of the Wisconsin Supreme Court," New Yorker, May 5, 2015.

94. Mary Bottari, "Undisclosed Dark Money Reigns Supreme in Wisconsin Campaigns and Elections," PRWatch, October 5, 2016. www.prwatch.org /news/2016/10/13154/dark-money-reigns-supreme-in-wisconsin.

95. Bottari, "Undisclosed Dark Money Reigns Supreme in Wisconsin."

96. Lynn Adelman, "How Big Money Ruined Public Life in Wisconsin," Cleveland State Law Review 66, no. 1 (2017): 16.

97. Christina A. Cassidy, "Control of State Courts Becomes a Top Political Battleground," Associated Press, April 3, 2016.

98. "Judicial Selection," Equal Justice Initiative, eji.org/judicial-selection.

99. Joanna Shepherd, Justice at Risk: An Empirical Analysis of Campaign Contributions and Judicial Decisions (Washington, DC: American Constitution Society for Law and Policy, 2013), www.acslaw.org/analysis/reports/justice -at-risk.

100. Joanna Shepherd and Michael S. Kang, Skewed Justice: Citizens United, Television Advertising and State Supreme Court Justices' Decisions in Criminal Cases (Washington, DC: American Constitution Society for Law and Policy, 2014), www.acslaw.org/analysis/reports/skewed-justice.

101. Joanna Shepherd and Michael S. Kang, Partisan Justice: How Campaign Money Politicizes Judicial Decisionmaking in Election Cases (Washington, DC: American Constitution Society for Law and Policy, 2016), www.acslaw.org /analysis/reports/partisan-justice.

102. Eric Lesh, Justice Out of Balance: How the Election of Judges and the Stunning Lack of Diversity on State Courts Threaten LGBT Rights (New York: Lambda Legal, 2016), www.lambdalegal.org/sites/default/files/justiceoutof balance_final_rev1_2.pdf.

5: THE RULES OF THE GAME

1. Regulatory Reform Act: Hearing on H.R. 2327 Before the Subcomm. on Admin. Law & Governmental Relations of the H. Comm. on the Judiciary, 98th Cong. 312 (1983) (statement of Rep. Dingell).

2. Erwin Chemerinsky, *Closing the Courthouse Door: How Your Constitutional Rights Became Unenforceable* (New Haven, CT: Yale University Press, 2017), 208.

3. Stephen B. Burbank and Sean Farhang, "Litigation Reform: An Institutional Approach," *University of Pennsylvania Law Review* 162, no. 7 (June 2014): 1583–84.

4. Burbank and Farhang, "Litigation Reform," 1547.

5. Burbank and Farhang, "Litigation Reform," 1547–48.

6. Burbank and Farhang, "Litigation Reform," 1613.

7. Paul Pierson, "The Rise and Reconfiguration of Activist Government," in *The Transformation of American Politics: Activist Government and the Rise of Conservatism*, ed. Paul Pierson and Theda Skocpol (Princeton, NJ: Princeton University Press, 2007), 33.

8. Burbank and Farhang, "Litigation Reform," 1582 (citing the work of Jacob S. Hacker and Paul Pierson).

9. Stephen B. Burbank and Sean Farhang, "Federal Court Rulemaking and Litigation Reform: An Institutional Approach," *Nevada ADA Law Journal* 15 (Summer 2015): 1560.

10. Burbank and Farhang, "Federal Court Rulemaking and Litigation Reform," 1561.

11. Chemerinsky, *Closing the Courthouse Door*, 98–99.

12. David H. Gans, "How Scalia Made It Difficult to Bring Cases to Court," *The Atlantic*, August 1, 2016.

13. *Lujan v. Defenders of Wildlife*, 504 U.S. 555 (1992).

14. Patrick Parenteau, "What Antonin Scalia's Death Means for Environment and Climate," *U.S. News & World Report*, February 18, 2016.

15. Chemerinsky, *Closing the Courthouse Door*, 173.

16. Leslie A. Gordon, "For Federal Plaintiffs, Twombly and Iqbal Still Present a Catch-22," *ABA Journal*, January 2011.

17. Chemerinsky, *Closing the Courthouse Door*, 178.

18. Burbank and Farhang, "Litigation Reform," 1599.

19. Caroline Fredrickson, *Under the Bus: How Working Women Are Being Run Over* (New York: The New Press, 2015), 54.

20. Jessica Silver-Greenberg and Robert Gebeloff, "Arbitration Everywhere, Stacking the Deck of Justice," *New York Times*, October 31, 2015.

21. Chemerinsky, *Closing the Courthouse Door*, 20–54.

22. Chemerinsky, 21–22.

23. Jonathan Elliot, *The Debates in the Several State Conventions on the Adoption of the Federal Constitution*, vol. 3, p. 554, available at memory.loc.gov/ammem/amlaw/lwed.html.

24. Rules Enabling Act, Pub. L. No. 73-415, 48 Stat. 1064 (1934).

25. "Powell Memorandum: Attack on American Free Enterprise System," p. 27, law2.wlu.edu/powellarchives/page.asp?pageid=1251.

26. Burbank and Farhang, "Federal Court Rulemaking and Litigation Reform," 1573.

27. *Rules Enabling Act: Hearings Before the Subcomm. on Courts, Civil Liberties & the Admin. of Justice of the House Comm. on the Judiciary*, 98th Cong. 191 (1983–84), at 29 (statement of Alan Morrison, director, Public Citizen Litigation Group).

28. Burbank and Farhang, "Federal Court Rulemaking and Litigation Reform," 1595.

29. Suja Thomas, "Via Duke, Companies Are Shaping Discovery," *Law360*, November 4, 2015, www.law360.com/articles/723092/opinion-via -duke-companies-are-shaping-discovery.

30. Email from Paul Bland to author, November 12, 2017.

31. Author conversations with Suja Thomas and Alan Morrison, November 10, 2017.

32. R. LaFountain, R. Schauffler, S. Strickland, S. Gibson, and A. Mason, *Examining the Work of State Courts: An Analysis of 2009 State Court Caseloads* (Williamsburg, VA: National Center for State Courts, 2011), p. 4, www.courtstatistics.org/flashmicrosites/csp/images/csp2009.pdf.

33. Bruce Henderson, "NC Hog Farm Neighbors Seek Court Help to Stop the Stink," *Charlotte Observer*, January 1, 2015.

34. John Murawski, "House Passes Limited Hog Farm Liability," *News & Observer* (Raleigh, NC), April 21, 2017.

35. Tom Philpott, "North Carolina Republicans Are Trying to Keep Residents from Suing Hog Farms," *Mother Jones*, April 21, 2017.

36. "Ag-Gag Laws Keep Animal Cruelty Behind Closed Doors," Humane Society fact sheet, www.humanesociety.org/issues/campaigns/factory_farming /fact-sheets/ag_gag.html.

37. American Association for Justice, "Reclaiming Justice: Battling Tort 'Reform,'" *Trial* 48, no. 12 (December 2012).

38. American Association for Justice, "Civil Justice Reform Group," http://www.takejusticeback.com/node/28.

39. American Association for Justice, "Reclaiming Justice: Battling Tort 'Reform.'"

40. Joshua Douglas, "State Judges and the Right to Vote," *Ohio State Law Journal* 77, no. 1, 2016.

41. Christina A. Cassidy, "Control of State Courts Becomes a Top Political Battleground," Associated Press, April 3, 2016.

42. Andrew DeMillo, "Outside Conservative Groups Overwhelm Arkansas Judge Races," Associated Press, February 26, 2016.

43. Andrew DeMillo, "With Vow to Represent 'Conservative Values' and the Backing of the National Rifle Association, Courtney Goodson Was Poised to Take Advantage of the Trend to the Political Right in Arkansas and Become the First Woman Elected to Lead the State Supreme Court," Associated Press, March 2, 2016.

44. "Arkansas Lawmakers Put Cap on Lawsuit Damages on '18 Ballot," Associated Press, March 1, 2017.

45. *Williams-Yulee v. the Florida Bar*, 135 S.Ct. 1656, 1675 (Ginsburg, concurring) (2015).

46. *Williams-Yulee v. Florida Bar*.

47. Alicia Bannon and Nathaniel Sobel, "Assaults on the Courts: A Legislative Round-Up," Brennan Center for Justice, May 8, 2017, www.brennancenter.org/analysis/assaults-courts-legislative-round.

48. Patrick Svitek, "Abbott Wants Broad-Based Law That Preempts Local Regulations," *Texas Tribune*, March 21, 2017.

49. David A. Graham, "Red State, Blue City," *The Atlantic*, March 2017.

50. Graham, "Red State, Blue City."

51. Lori Riverstone-Newell, "The Rise of State Preemption Laws in Response to Local Policy Innovation," *Publius: The Journal of Federalism* 47, no. 3 (July 1, 2017): 405.

52. "Preemption Watch" Grassroots Change, grassrootschange.net/preemption-watch.

53. Graham, "Red State, Blue City."

54. Graham, "Red State, Blue City."

55. Mitchell Hirsch, "Federal Court Suit in Alabama Seeks to Restore Birmingham's Minimum Wage Increase," National Employment Law Project blog, May 6, 2016, www.nelp.org/blog/federal-court-suit-in-alabama-seeks-to-restore-birminghams-minimum-wage-increase.

56. Nester M. Davidson, "A Legal Victory for Cities Working to Advance Equity," August 3, 2018, www.acslaw.org/acsblog/a-legal-victory-for-cities-working-to-advance-equity.

57. Karim Lakhani, "Birmingham and the Impact of Race on State Preemption Laws."

58. Madison Park, "Removal of Confederate Monuments Stirs Backlash in Statehouses," CNN.com, May 12, 2017.

59. Riverstone-Newell, "The Rise of State Preemption Laws," 417.

60. Max Bloom, "Let Liberal Cities Do What They Want," *National Review*, July 13, 2017.

61. Riverstone-Newell, "The Rise of State Preemption Laws," 418 (citing Elizabeth Daigneau, "Will States Stop Cities from Combating Climate Change?" *Governing*, January 2017).

62. Riverstone-Newell, "The Rise of State Preemption Laws," 419.

63. John Nichols, "ALEC Exposed: Rigging Elections," *The Nation*, July 12, 2011.

64. "Legal Strategies to Counter State Preemption and Protect Progressive Localism: A Summary of the Findings of the Legal Effort to Address Preemption (LEAP) Project," May 2017, Legal Effort to Address Preemption, docs.wixstatic.com/ugd/d91411_8f1689390f814dd6af709ba7ef412192.pdf.

65. Brendan O'Connor, "Koch Brothers' Former Right-Hand Man's New Gig: Helping Reactionaries Dismantle the Constitution," *Splinter News*, June 12, 2017, https://splinternews.com/koch-brothers-former-right-hand-mans-new-gig-helping-r-1796032402.

66. Convention on States petition to legislators, www.conventionofstates.com/sign_the_petition.

67. David Weigel, "Conservative State Legislators Plot Ways to Get Washington Under Control," *Washington Post*, July 21, 2017.

68. Jay Riestenberg and Dale Eisman, *The Dangerous Path: Big Money's Plan*

to Shred the Constitution (Washington, DC: Common Cause, May 2016), 11, www.commoncause.org/resource/the-dangerous-path-big-moneys-plan-to -shred-the-constitution.

69. Riestenberg and Eisman, 12.

70. Riestenberg and Eisman, 12.

71. Riestenberg and Eisman, 16.

72. Riestenberg and Eisman, 3.

73. Jay Riestenberg, "U.S. Constitution Threatened as Article V Convention Movement Nears Success," Common Cause, March 21, 2018, www.commoncause.org/resource/u-s-constitution-threatened-as-article -v-convention-movement-nears-success.

74. Jay Cost, "The Rules Matter," *Weekly Standard*, December 14, 2015.

6: THEY GO LOW

1. Kristine Phillips, "All the Times Trump Personally Attacked Judges—and Why His Tirades Are 'Worse than Wrong,'" *Washington Post*, April 26, 2017.

2. Gabriel Sherman, *The Loudest Voice in the Room: How the Brilliant, Bombastic Rogers Ailes Built Fox News—and Divided a Country* (New York: Random House, 2014), 209.

3. Russ Baker, "Murdoch's Mean Machine," *Columbia Journalism Review*, May/June 1998.

4. Lily Rothman, "How Rupert Murdoch First Got into the Media Business," *Time*, June 11, 2015.

5. Rothman, "How Rupert Murdoch First Got into the Media Business." (Quoting the 1977 story.)

6. Baker, "Murdoch's Mean Machine."

7. Baker, "Murdoch's Mean Machine."

8. Baker, "Murdoch's Mean Machine."

9. Al Franken, *Lies and the Lying Liars Who Tell Them* (New York: Dutton 2003), 61–62.

10. Franken, 135.

11. Franken, 139.

12. Michael Kelly, "Corporate Cronyism," Washington Post Writers Group, July 17, 2002, cited in Michael Lind, *Made in Texas: George W. Bush and the Southern Takeover of American Politics* (New York: Basic Books, 2004), 103.

13. Molly Ivins and Lou Dubose, *Shrub: The Short but Happy Political Life of George W. Bush* (New York: Random House: 2000), 33.

14. Nicole Hemmer, "The Conservative War on Liberal Media Has a Long History," *The Atlantic*, January 17, 2014.

15. Eric C. Miller, "Before Breitbart: How Right Wing Media Transformed American Politics," *Religion Dispatches*, October 31, 2016, interviewing Hemmer.

16. James Carville and Paul Begala, *Take It Back: Our Party, Our Country, Our Future* (New York: Simon & Schuster, 2006), 228.

17. Texas Jackson, "American Mainstream Media Continue Plunge into All-Time Low Trust and Confidence Ratings," *News Legit*, August 1, 2018, newslegit.com/2017/04/28/american-mainstream-media-continue-plunge -into-all-time-low-trust-and-confidence-ratings.

18. Aziz Huq, "When Government Defames," *New York Times*, August 10, 2017.

19. Hunt Allcott and Matthew Gentzkow, "Social Media and Fake News in the 2016 Election," *Journal of Economic Perspectives* 31, no. 2 (Spring 2017): 212.

20. Ashley Parker, Carol D. Leonnig, Philip Rucker, and Tom Hamburger, "Trump Dictated Son's Misleading Statement on Meeting with Russian Lawyer," *Washington Post*, July 31, 2017.

21. Editorial Board, "Who's Really to Blame for Fake News? It May Be President Trump," *Sacramento Bee*, August 1, 2017.

22. Farhad Manjoo, "How Twitter Is Being Gamed to Feed Misinformation," *New York Times*, May 31, 2017.

23. Alana Abramson, "How Donald Trump Perpetuated the 'Birther' Movement for Years," ABCNews.com, September 16, 2016.

24. Chris Megerian, "What Donald Trump Has Said Through the Years About Where President Obama Was Born," *Los Angeles Times*, September 16, 2016.

25. Abramson, "How Donald Trump Perpetuated the 'Birther' Movement for Years."

26. Sarah Burns, "Why Trump Doubled Down on the Central Park Five," *New York Times*, October 17, 2016.

27. Jim Rutenberg, "Trump Takes Aim at the Press, with a Flamethrower," *New York Times*, August 24, 2017.

28. Noah Bierman and Jim Puzzanghera, "President Trump Threatens NBC's Broadcast Licenses Following Critical Stories," *Los Angeles Times*, October 11, 2017.

29. Rutenberg, "Trump Takes Aim at the Press, with a Flamethrower."

30. Oliver Morrison, "Waiting for the Conservative Jon Stewart," *The Atlantic*, February 14, 2015.

31. Conversation between Liz Rose and author, January 23, 2018.

32. Nathan Harden, "The Death of Air America: Why Liberals Fail at Talk Radio," *Huffington Post*, May 25, 2011.

33. Conversation between Alison Dagnes and author, February 23, 2018.

34. Eric Zuesse, "Pew Finds: Conservatives Get Their News from Fox; Liberals Get Theirs Everywhere," *Huffington Post*, December 21, 2014.

35. Harden, "The Death of Air America."

36. Morrison, "Waiting for the Conservative Jon Stewart."

37. Author conversation with Katie Paris, February 26, 2018.

38. Kevin Roose and Sheera Frenkel, "4500 Tech Workers, 1 Mission: Getting Democrats Elected," *New York Times*, July 13, 2018.

39. Dana Priest and Michael Birnbaum, "Europe Has Been Working to Expose Russian Meddling for Years," *Washington Post*, June 25, 2017.

40. Brian Fung, "The FCC Just Ended a Decades-Old Rule Designed to Keep TV and Radio Under Local Control," *Washington Post*, October 24, 2017.

41. Callum Borchers, "How the Federal Trade Commission Could (Maybe) Crack Down on Fake News," *Washington Post*, January 30, 2017.

42. Barton Swain, "'Trust, but Verify': An Untrustworthy Political Phrase," *Washington Post*, March 11, 2016.

43. Nicholas Lemann, "Solving the Problem of Fake News," *New Yorker*, November 30, 2016.

44. Robert Farley, "Three Cabinet Appointees from Opposing Party Is Unmatched," PolitiFact, February 10, 2009, www.politifact.com/truth-o-meter /statements/2009/feb/10/barack-obama/Three-Republicans-Cabinet-Most.

45. Ewen MacAskill, "Democrats Condemn GOP's Plot to Obstruct Obama as 'Appalling and Sad,'" *The Guardian*, April 26, 2012.

46. Daniel Nexon, "Reflections on the Current Crisis," *Lawyers, Guns & Money*, July 21, 2017, www.lawyersgunsmoneyblog.com/2017/07/reflections -current-crisis.

47. Avik Roy, "How the Heritage Foundation, a Conservative Think Tank, Promoted the Individual Mandate," *Forbes*, October 20, 2011.

48. "Obama Holds Health Summit at White House," PBS.org, March 5, 2009.

49. Robert Pear, "Obamacare Took Months to Craft; Repeal May Be Much Swifter," *New York Times*, March 7, 2017.

50. Joshua Green, "Strict Obstructionist," *The Atlantic*, January/February 2011.

51. Pear, "Obamacare Took Months to Craft."

52. Jacob S. Hacker and Paul Pierson, *Winner-Take-All Politics: How Washington Made the Rich Richer—and Turned Its Back on the Middle Class* (New York: Simon & Schuster, 2010) 262.

53. Hacker and Pierson, 265.

54. Hacker and Pierson, 268.

7: HOW PROGRESSIVES CAN WIN BY REWRITING THE RULES OF THE GAME

1. Coral Davenport and Eric Lipton, "How G.O.P. Leaders Came to View Climate Change as Fake Science," *New York Times*, June 3, 2017.

2. Jonathan Kay, "How Climate Change Denial Set the Stage for Fake News," *The Walrus*, May 1, 2017.

3. Lee Fang, *The Machine: A Field Guide to the Resurgent Right* (New York: The New Press, 2013), 88.

8: PUBLIC MEMORANDUM

1. Democracy Alliance, "Rob Stein, Founder Emeritus," democracy alliance.org/people/rob-stein.

2. Author conversation with Gara LaMarche, March 22, 2018.

3. Noam Scheiber and Kenneth P. Vogel, "Behind a Key Anti-Labor Case, a Web of Conservative Donors," *New York Times*, February 25, 2018.

4. Rick Lyman, "Pennsylvania Voter ID Law Struck Down as Judge Cites Burden on Citizens," *New York Times*, January 17, 2014.

5. Roz Edward, "Voting Reform in Michigan Marches Forward," *Michigan Chronicle*, February 13, 2018.

6. Eric Bradner, "Democrats Put Hope in SCOTUS as They Race Against the 2020 Redistricting Clock," CNN.com, October 3, 2018.

7. Paul Booth, "Getting Serious About 2018," *American Prospect*, July 5, 2017.

8. Sean McElwee, Jesse H. Rhodes, Brian F. Schaffner, and Bernard L. Fraga, "The Missing Obama Millions," *New York Times*, March 10, 2018.

ABOUT THE AUTHOR

Caroline Fredrickson is the president of the American Constitution Society (ACS) and the author of *Under the Bus: How Working Women Are Being Run Over* (The New Press). She has been widely published on a range of legal and constitutional issues and is a frequent guest on television and radio shows. Before joining ACS, Fredrickson served as the director of the ACLU's Washington legislative office and as general counsel and legal director of NARAL Pro-Choice America. In addition, she was chief of staff to Senator Maria Cantwell and deputy chief of staff to then Senate Democratic leader Tom Daschle. During the Clinton administration, she served as special assistant to the president for legislative affairs. She lives in Silver Spring, Maryland.

PUBLISHING IN THE PUBLIC INTEREST